The Making of the 20th Century

This series of specially commissioned titles focuses attention on significant and often controversial events and themes of world history in the present century. Each book provides sufficient narrative and explanation for the newcomer to the subject while offering, for more advanced study, detailed source-references and bibliographies, together with interpretation and reassessment in the light of recent scholarship.

In the choice of subjects there is a balance between breadth in some spheres and detail in others; between the essentially political and matters economic or social. The series cannot be a comprehensive account of everything that has happened in the twentieth century, but it provides a guide to recent research and explains something of the times of extraordinary change and complexity in which we live. It is directed in the main to students of contemporary history and international relations, but includes titles which are of direct relevance to courses in economics, sociology, politics and geography.

The Making of the 20th Century

Series Editor: CHRISTOPHER THORNE

Titles in the Series include

Mussolini as Empire-Builder

Europe and Africa, 1932–36

Esmonde M. Robertson

St. Martin's Press   New York

Contents

Preface

I owe a great debt to scholars who have recently completed, or who are in the process of writing, monographs on topics related to my own. Dr D. Rotunda, Dr C. A. MacDonald, Dr M. Poulain, Mr M. Passmore, Dr Antoinette Iadarola and Dr Rosaria Quartararo.

I have greatly profited from detailed criticisms by Professor W. N. Medlicott and J. Petersen, of the German – Italian Institute in Rome, from P. Kent who has studied the Italian documents in Rome; from Drs A. Adamthwaite, R. Bullen and A. Polonsky. Mr Felix M. Pryor has helped me with stylistic improvements, and Mr Lalit Adolphus has been most generous in helping me with final revisions of the academic apparatus.

Miss Anne Ably, the Librarian of St Antony's College, Oxford; Fräulein Gertrud Fichtbauer of the *Staatsbibliotek* Munich; and the staff of the *Institut für Zeitgeschichte* Munich; Mrs Mary Dysch and the Secretaries of the Department of International History of the London School of Economics have gone out of their way to be helpful.

Above all, I owe a special debt to Frau Ilse von Hassell, widow of the late Herr Ulrich von Hassell, German Ambassador in Rome 1932 – 7 and hanged for the part he played in the conspiracy of 20 July 1944. Her perceptive memory of events and of the character of the leading personages concerned is unique.

E.M.R.

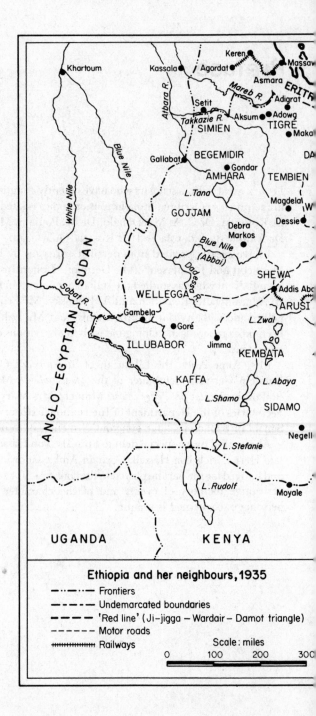

Ethiopia and her neighbours, 1935

---·--- Frontiers
---·-·-- Undemarcated boundaries
---- 'Red line' (Ji-jigga – Wardair – Damot triangle)
------ Motor roads
++++++++ Railways

Scale: miles

0   100   200   300

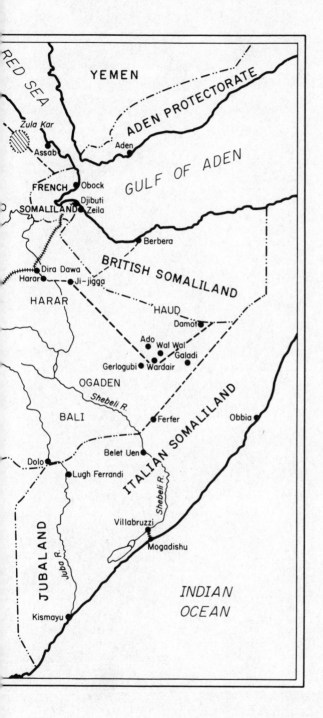

Introduction

MUSSOLINI's character and policy have given rise to almost as much controversy as Hitler's. Was he the supreme opportunist who played off Italy's opponents against each other and who waited for the occasion to drive a wedge between them and grab new territory for Italy (or to spread Italian influence) without having to fight a major war? Can Ranke's theory of the primacy of foreign over domestic policy be upheld with reference to Italy under Mussolini? If Mussolini adhered stead-fastly to the hotch-potch ideas proclaimed in the Fascist Manifesto of March 1919, Italy, having renounced imperialism, would have had to content herself with the acquisition of territory on the coast of Dalmatia and in Asia Minor.[1] But if Mussolini from the start considered himself the heir of his nationalist predecessors and looked to Africa, rather than to Europe, for the realisation of Italy's imperial glory, then the aim of expansion in Europe was merely to secure Italy's land frontiers in order to expand overseas. The number of options open to Italy can be attributed to her geographical position quite as much as to Mussolini's mercurial character. Italy, situated in the Mediterranean, stood on the circumference of a circle. Her position differed from that of Germany who stood on a point in a straight line facing East.

Although there were many differences of opinion within Italy over the direction which expansion should take, the Fascists (who looked to the Duce as leader) and most of the Nationalists (whose loyalty lay with either the King or the Pope) were at one in believing that Italy's so-called 'demographic problem' had to be solved. Italy's population in 1931 stood at 42 million. Within fifteen years this figure would have risen to 50 million by which time most Italians would be living well below the subsistence level.[2] Little, so it was mistakenly thought, could be done to raise agricultural production at home; and emigration to the United States, advocated by the liberals, had been regarded by an earlier generation of Italian imperialists as a 'perpetual haemorrhage thereby revealing the mentality of slaves'.[3] It was in any case, after the passage of the immigration laws in the United States in 1924, only possible on a limited scale. Instead of crossing the Atlantic those existing settlements of Italians outside Italy, in the Mediterranean, should, if possible, be brought under direct Italian rule, and new territory should be acquired, either by force or by bargaining, for future colonisation.

Mussolini was also confronted with a problem held in common by all states, even Italy, with totalitarian governments. Italian émigrés did not merely take refuge in other countries for fear of their lives; their avowed aim was to topple the Fascist regime. Conversely, certain groups of émigrés representing the Radical Right in other countries, settled in Italy or obtained funds from the Italian government. They planned the destruction of all vestiges of representative government at home and, at times, changes by force in the territorial status quo. The ideological aspect of Mussolini's policy, as Professor Jens Petersen points out, was not just window-dressing.[4] It meant that the struggle between the Revolutionary Left and the Revolutionary Right which took place in Italy before Mussolini came to power, was transferred to other countries, notably France, and to the international level. Seen in this light Mussolini's eventual intervention in the Spanish Civil War makes sense.[5]

It is scarcely surprising that our first accounts of Mussolini's foreign policy came from the pens of his opponents abroad. Of these émigrés the one who has exerted by far the greatest influence on later generations was Gaetano Salvemini, who since the late 1920s had been writing on Mussolini's statesmanship. Propaganda, Salvemini claimed, was an integral part of Mussolini's foreign policy, and his skill in manipulating the masses far surpassed that of Goebbels. But Salvemini thought that Mussolini was quite incapable of translating words into deeds; the appearance of success mattered more than success itself. Mussolini's fixed aim was the internal stabilisation of the regime and not territorial expansion for its own sake. Nevertheless Salvemini did not deny that the monopolisation of political power, the philosophy of violence, the glorification of war, the deification of the state, all lent to the regime a latent tendency towards aggression. But if Mussolini meant what he said, Salvemini continued, the very day he armed the Italian masses for a war of conquest, civil war would break out in Italy and the regime would collapse. Had Salvemini consistently held these views the outbreak of the Italian – Ethiopian war in October 1935 would for him have been an historical impossibility.[6] Instead of explaining the causes of this war Salvemini explains them away. Mussolini, he mistakenly claimed, only decided on war in August 1935 when he felt certain that

Britain and France would not oppose him. Yet Salvemini finds an ingenious way out of the impasse. Through their failure to stop Mussolini from conquering Ethiopia, and for not imposing effective sanctions, the rulers of Britain and France are as much, or more, to blame for the outbreak of the Second World War as Mussolini himself.[7] Salvemini's interpretation of Mussolini's policy has been adopted, not only in Italy by a scholar of the calibre of L. Salvatorelli, but by Anglo-Saxon historians such as D. Mack Smith and H. S. Hughes. That Italy failed to live up to the military performance expected of her under Fascism in the Second World War tended to lend weight to Salvemini's contention, that Mussolini was a buffoon or a 'sawdust Caesar'. Despite certain of Salvemini's shortcomings as a scholar, G. Carocci, the outstanding contemporary Italian authority on Mussolini's foreign policy in the 1920s, pays the highest tribute to his work. Lacking the documents now available, Salvemini had a remarkable historical insight, writes Carocci, and he stated his case with 'great lucidity'.[8]

Some of Salvemini's contemporaries in exile, who did not share his political assumptions, came to similar conclusions. Count Sforza, Italian Foreign Minister under Giolitti before Mussolini came to power, and active after his fall, described the Duce's foreign policy as a 'compound of sentiments and resentments'. Writing in 1932, Nenni, who before 1914 had been Mussolini's closest friend in the Socialist party, stated that the one thing Fascism in Italy lacked was 'coherence'. Even Salvemini's most bitter opponents in the Marxist camp, including Trotsky, did not dispute his claim that Mussolini's domestic policy governed his foreign policy which was one of hand-to-mouth improvisation.[9]

British and American scholars are less interested in interpreting Italian history within an ideological framework formed in conflicts in which they were not involved. Christopher Seton-Watson and Alan Cassels have with admirable clarity presented accounts of Mussolini's early policy from the recently published documents on Italian foreign policy in the 1920s. There was more continuity, these scholars maintain, than was once believed, and there was overlapping between domestic and foreign policy. More recently British and German unpublished documents have been used to reconstruct Italy's relations with other countries.[10] But until the Italian documents of the 1930s are fully accessible the story is still incomplete and it is better to talk about Italy's foreign relations under Mussolini than his foreign policy. Hence, the emphasis in the present study is on Italy between the powers.

A new generation of Italian historians have now come to the forefront who have had no personal memories of the Fascist regime. In the sixties serious doubts were cast on whether Mussolini totally lacked consistency. G. Rumi claims that Mussolini, even as far back as 1922, had a future programme in mind: 'The route is mapped – the Paris peace settlement had to be overturned and Italian rights recognised in the Adriatic. This was to be followed by Italian expansion in the Mediterranean and Africa.'[11] Rumi's thesis is supported by the impressions formed in 1920 by von Neurath, the German ambassador in Rome. Since France was bound to stand in Italy's way Mussolini's aim was, according to Neurath, to join forces with Germany for the inevitable conflict which lay ahead. At the end of a new war Italy would annex all of French North Africa.[12] That Italy's destiny lay in the Mediterranean and East Africa was thrown into high relief in subsequent years. Italy, Mussolini deluded himself into thinking, was an island, not a peninsula. The Mediterranean must thus be converted from an Anglo-Saxon Lake into a Latin Sea.[13] (See his speech of 18 March 1934, discussed in chapter 8.) But the acquisition of colonies on the southern shores of the Mediterranean and their protection was not enough. On 4 February 1939 Mussolini described Italy as a prisoner in the Mediterranean: 'The bars of this prison are Corsica, Tunisia, Malta and Cyprus – its sentinels are Gibraltar and Suez.' Italy had thus to fight her way to the ocean – either to the Atlantic from Libya through French-controlled territory (which now included the Cameroons), or to the Indian Ocean through the Sudan, controlled by Britain, and through Ethiopia. These grandiose ideas, entertained by Mussolini early in his career, came to the forefront only later.[14]

Expansion in the Mediterranean and in Ethiopia, which strengthened Italy's position in the Red Sea, was not the only object of Mussolini's policy, he also had to take the turbulent continent of Europe into account. Despite his thunderings about Italian military might, Italy can be described as the weakest of the great European powers or the strongest of the small powers. Mussolini dreaded nothing more than the prospect that Germany, France and Britain would decide between themselves the destiny of Europe to the exclusion of Italy. Instead of putting Italy at the head of the small powers, Mussolini tried to make Italy indispensable to the three remaining great powers and compel them to accept her as an equal. He could offer Germany Italian support for rearmament and for expansion in the Baltic; France, security on the Rhine or maintenance of the status quo in the Danubian area; Britain, unrestricted access across the Mediterranean or security for her imperial interests in East Africa. Mussolini, no less than his predecessors, took care, for instance, that a move towards France must not be made in such a way as to exclude an accommodation with either Germany or Britain. In two respects Italy was well placed for bargaining. First, her military strength was greatly exaggerated. Second, if war were to break out, Italy could keep all sides guessing on whether she would declare herself to be an ally, an enemy or a neutral. Unlike Britain three, not two, options were open to her. D'Amoja has described this manoeuvring between the powers as the policy of 'equidistance'.[15] It was already in evidence when Mussolini put his signature to the Treaty of Locarno in 1925. It found its fullest expression in the abortive Four Power Pact of 1933. So long as Italian expansion was restricted to certain safety limits the 'policy of equidistance' could be maintained. But it broke down, with disastrous results, at the end of the Ethiopian war when Mussolini agreed to the Rome – Berlin Axis. The fact he was planning for a war of aggression long in advance of the invasion of Ethiopia, and also constructing a modern fleet, renders necessary a reconsideration of the view that he was a mere opportunist.

Italian historians are not unanimous on whether a change at any specific date took place in Mussolini's policy and if so when it occurred. According to Carocci, Mussolini, despite his warlike effusions, was relatively peaceful until 1932 – 5 when the prospect of war gained a grip over his mind.[16] R. De Felice very recently maintains that a change took place earlier, with the appointment of Grandi as Foreign Minister in 1929.[17] For two years, with a Fascist in charge of the Foreign Ministry, Mussolini evidently did not personally interfere much in the day-to-day decisions in foreign policy. In 1929 there were, Carocci contends, four interested groups inside Italy who wanted to have their own way on future policy: the moderate and the extreme nationalists; the right and the left wings of the Fascist Party.[18] While the Nationalists as a body were most interested in colonial expansion, the moderates, who were anglophile, were anxious that Italy should only attempt overseas expansion by putting pressure on France to grant Italy a colony. In Europe their aim was to outbid France for an approchement with Yugoslavia. The extreme nationalists on the other hand were francophile and anglophobe. Italy, they contended, could only gain sufficient security in Europe for expansion overseas at Britain's expense if pressure could be brought to bear on Yugoslavia by supporting subversive movements in that kingdom. It will be seen how the extreme nationalists were to be supported by the Vatican in switching attention from Corsica to Malta. The left wing of the Fascist Party, led by Balbo, then Air Minister, was anti-clerical. He and like-minded men supported Germany over disarmament and hoped that Italy and Germany would work together against the League of Nations for the revision of the territorial status quo in Europe. The right wing of the Party, which stood nearest to Mussolini in 1929, and which was led by the Duce's brother, Arnaldo, editor of the *Popolo d'Italia*, was instrumental in bringing about the Concordat of 1929 with the Vatican. It favoured strengthening Italy's economic ties with Yugoslavia and attracting that country into Italy's orbit.

After 1932 it is less easy to draw such a clear-cut distinction between warring groups. There was much overlapping between them, and in the power struggle within Italy transfers of allegiance were so rapid that political aims and personal ambitions became blurred. Where, for instance, did Grandi stand: with the moderate nationalists or the right wing of the Party?

By 1932, moreover, Mussolini was becoming more restless, more inclined to reject the policy of peaceful penetration into Yugoslavia and to adopt terrorism; instead of bargaining for, he now favoured the conquest of, territory in Africa. Several explanations can be given for this change. Apart from the economic crisis, which made not only Italians, but discontented classes and subject nationalities all over the world, more listless, two important considerations personally affected Mussolini. On 21 December 1931 his brother Arlando died. He was the one person capable of restraining Mussolini.[19] On 11 February 1932 the Duce had his one and only interview with the Pope, who told him that the encroachments of Protestants, Jews and Communists must be resisted. The struggle with the Church over Catholic Action, which had reached its peak the previous summer and had rocked the country, had come to an end.[20] Also, by 1932 General Graziani, to the horror of the Arab world, had been successful in his terrorist campaign against the most dedicated defenders of Islam, the Senussi of Cyrenaica. Italy had tried to wrest this area from Turkey in the war of 1911–12, but only brought it under control after 1932. By the same year Italy had also consolidated her hold over northern Somaliland.[21] No longer on the defensive, she was now ready to revive the myth of Imperial Rome.

1 The Reshuffle of July–August 1932

THE Italians had never forgotten the 'shameful scar', as D'Annunzio had called it, of their defeat by the Ethiopians at Adowa in 1896. In 1906 they had concluded a treaty with Britain and France for the future division of Ethiopia into spheres of influence.[1] It was to take effect if political order in that country disintegrated after the death of the Emperor Menelik II. The fears of the three powers concerned seemed to be justified, for in the chaotic conditions in Ethiopia after the death of Menelik in 1913 and after the outbreak of the First World War, Emperor Lig Yasu tried to win support from the large Muslim population of the Empire and he turned to the Central Powers.[2]

In 1919 the Italians once again turned to East Africa. They claimed, in accordance with Article 13 of the Treaty of London, that in return for the occupation by Britain and France of former German colonies, Italy should be compensated in Africa: specific mention was later made of Djibuti in French Somaliland, and of British Somaliland. After the war Italian claims were exorbitant; in the subsequent bargaining they had hoped to obtain very great concessions from the British and the French.[3] The British Foreign Office, under Curzon, was prepared to cede Jubaland on the border between Kenya and Italian Somaliland, provided Italy evacuated the Dodecanese in favour of Greece, which she had promised to do in 1920.[4] In 1924 Austen Chamberlain, for several possible reasons, withdrew this condition and in June 1925 Jubaland with its port of Kismayu was handed over to Italy. (See map.) While Britain and Italy had already agreed – the former with great reluctance – to Ethiopia's admission to the League of Nations in 1923, they had not abandoned the policy of dividing Ethiopia into spheres of influence. The British cotton lobby was interested in erecting a dam on the Blue Nile near its source of Lake Tana for cultivation of cotton in the Sudan instead of in Egypt which was slipping from British control after 1922; the Italians were keen to increase trade in the fertile areas on the western highlands of Ethiopia. By an exchange of notes in 1925 Britain and Italy reaffirmed their respective spheres of influence. France was not even invited to accede to these agreements. Italy was to be allowed to construct a rail or motor road linking Eritrea and Somaliland, as well as to have economic privileges in the fertile area west of Addis Ababa; Britain to control the waters of the Blue Nile.[5] Since the terms of the agreements were ostensibly contrary to Article 20 of the Covenant, the Regent of Ethiopia, Ras Tafari (later Haile Selassie), protested to the Council of the League, as a result of which the British and Italians assured Tafari that they intended to uphold Ethiopian sovereignty.[6]

It is doubtful whether the Regent would have succeeded in mobilising the support of the League had it not been in the interest of at least one of the great powers that Ethiopia should remain a sovereign state. The French had completed their railway from Djibuti to Addis Ababa in 1917. They were thus able to tap much of the resources of the hinterland in return for the illicit (and lucrative) export of arms to Ethiopia. Although traffic on this line was frequently disturbed, because of political unrest, it brought in sufficient revenue to enable the French to keep Djibuti operating as a port of call in their long line of communications with Madagascar and the Far East. The French hoped to take the lead in developing Ethiopia's economic resources and promoting educational reform. They were prepared to adhere to this policy only on condition that Tafari made real progress towards the modernisation of his country; failure would mean a reversion to the policy of 1906 for the delimitation of spheres of influence.[7]

Both Mussolini and Tafari were later to labour under false assumptions. Mussolini assumed it would not be difficult to square the French if Italy were to resume her expansion in Ethiopia, and he gave insufficient thought to Britain. The Regent assumed that Ethiopia's admission to the League was tantamount to consecration of statehood, and that the League would rescue his country from falling a prey to the imperial ambitions of her neighbours.[8] In the late 1920s, however, there was still no immediate danger. The Italians were busy 'restoring order' both in northern Somaliland and in Cyrenaica. In these circumstances Mussolini wished to remain on good terms with Tafari, who also had trouble with his Muslim subjects and the Christian chieftains in Ethiopia. In 1928 a twenty-year Treaty of Arbitration and Friendship was concluded between Ethiopia and Italy. Italians were to be employed as Tafari's advisers. A motor road was to be built from Assab in Eritrea to Dessie in Wello province. That part of the road within Ethiopia was to be financed by the Ethiopian government.[9]

After Tafari's coronation as Haile Selassie in November 1930 (having been Negus, or Emperor, since 1928), he was confronted with the arduous task of modernising his country and of putting down revolts. But instead of choosing advisers from Italy, as he was obliged to do under the 1928 Treaty, he employed nationals from such countries as the United States, Sweden, Switzerland and Belgium; and Ethiopian army cadets were sent to train at St Cyr in France. In 1929 he did not disguise his fears from the German minister at Addis Ababa that Britain's and especially Italy's aims were hostile.[10]

The Italians pursued two apparently contradictory policies towards Ethiopia after the Treaty of Friendship of 1928. The Italian minister in Addis Ababa, Giuliano Cora, advocated that his country should seek to win a preponderant influence over the central government and assist Haile Selassie. But the aim of Corrado Zoli, governor of Eritrea, an impulsive Fascist, was to influence or bribe the local *rases* (chieftains) to switch their allegiance from Haile Selassie to the Italian government. This policy of disruption from within, known as the *politica periferica*, seemed to be proving successful.[11] In 1930 (a year of unrest in Ethiopia) many highly placed Italians, including Dino Grandi, then Foreign Minister, believed that the Emperor would soon die of malaria, with the subsequent disintegration of the Ethiopian state. With the appointment in 1929 of General Emilio De Bono as Minister of Colonies, in place of the more cautious Luigi Federzoni, Zoli's policy was continued with greater emphasis.

Hitherto Italian plans for expansion in East Africa had met with resistance from France. But by 1930 the French were a good deal less inclined to support Haile Selassie at the risk of a rupture with Italy. A partial explanation for this is that they did not expect Haile Selassie to succeed in establishing his authority fully over his rebellious chieftains. And indeed, if Ethiopia were to disintegrate, there was the possibility of its being partitioned in such a way that the Addis Ababa–Djibuti railway, together with the town of Harar, would fall within the French sphere of influence.[12] Far more significant to French attitudes, however, were events in Europe. In 1930 the French evacuated the Rhineland. In September of the same year Hitler won his first electoral successes. According to R. Guariglia, a prominent official in the Italian Foreign Ministry, an agreement between France and Italy was now practical politics.[13] He was proved right.

Having failed to reach an agreement with Germany early in 1931,[14] the French under Laval were anxious to settle their differences with Italy. In the middle of July 1931 Laval raised with Grandi the subject of an Italian occupation of Ethiopia. In a note to Mussolini Grandi welcomed the development. He found Laval the first Frenchman 'to whom I do not feel that instinctive dislike which always invades my spirit whenever I have contact with a Gaul'. Although Mussolini did no more than 'take note' of the French approach, his diplomats, as well as the officials of the Colonial Ministry, were now won over to the idea of the *politica periferica*.[15] It was the aim of the former to isolate Ethiopia, of the latter to draw up military plans.

After a tour of inspection in Eritrea early in 1932, De Bono came to the conclusion that Haile Selassie was now consolidating his authority, and that he intended to take up arms against Italy in the near future. (In fact, De Bono overestimated the Emperor's internal achievement.) De Bono therefore suggested to Mussolini on 22 March 1932 that, despite heavy expenditure, Italy should, with the consent of Britain and France, prepare for a preventive war.[16] The question of Ethiopia was evidently discussed at a meeting of the Fascist Grand Council held on 8 April 1932 as the persons interested in Ethiopia were present and negotiations between France and Ethiopia were at the time in progress. Also at the meeting Mussolini decided that Italy must now adopt a forward policy.[17] The next month, Lig Yasu, who had been deposed in 1916 because of his pro-Muslim policy, escaped from custody and was supported by a revolt in Gojjam. De Bono for a short time considered that the Empire would collapse and that an improvised invasion of Ethiopia might be launched even before agreement was reached with France.[18] But Haile Selassie was able to maintain his precarious authority.

Raffaele Guariglia, Political Director of Europe, the Near East and Africa in the Italian Foreign Ministry and a close friend of Grandi, was also a keen advocate of an expedition in a 'grand style' against Ethiopia. According to him, Ethiopia was the one area in the world where Italy could expand without colliding with the interests of other powers. This rich fertile country was not only capable of absorbing Italy's surplus population but could also provide her with black troops for deployment in other parts of Africa. Guariglia described the failure of the existing Italian policy in Ethiopia and outlined future aims in a long memorandum of 27 August 1932. This document was intended as his political testament.[19] Ethiopia's irredentism, he claimed, was directed principally against Eritrea, the defence of which would become all but impossible if Ethiopia were transformed from a feudal society into a centralised state. He held the 1906 agreement to be the Magna Carta of

Italy's rights and aspirations which had been given recognition by Britain and France. He acccused the government of Ethiopia of seeking after 1925 to play off one of its neighbouring powers against the others. In this analysis the question of rail routes was a crucial factor to Guariglia.

Ethiopia had invited Italy to cede a corridor of territory in Eritrea connecting the interior of Ethiopia with Assab on the Red Sea. (See map.) This would lessen Ethiopia's heavy economic dependence on France. Although the cession of this corridor could in no way endanger the position of Italy strategically, the Fascist government, for reasons of prestige alone, refused to alienate one single acre of territory. Instead, Ethiopia was offered the facilities of a free port at Assab in return for permission to construct the motor road connecting Assab with Dessie in the south. The Ethiopian government showed little enthusiasm for this project, on the grounds that it would have to finance construction of that part of the road which ran inside its own territory. An alternative route was then proposed. Baron Franchetti, an Italian explorer, was sent to Addis Ababa to win acceptance for a route, to be constructed by a private company, running from the town of Setit in Eritrea to Gondar, above Lake Tana in the north-west of Ethiopia. From the Italian point of view, this could prove of great strategic as well as economic value. Not surprisingly, the Emperor took no practical steps for its realisation.

In his memorandum of August 1932 Guariglia proposed that Italy should in future give the impression that the Setit – Gondar line was to be a public, not a private, enterprise. If the Emperor refused to fall in with Italy's wishes, her new minister, to be appointed to Addis Ababa, should be instructed to denounce the Treaty of Friendship of 1928. Recently Haile Selassie had again advanced the idea of an outlet to the sea at Assab, but this time he offered Italy compensation – a 'miserable' tract of territory in Ogaden, adjoining Italian Somaliland – as well as permission to construct the Setit – Gondar route. Guariglia strongly advised against negotiating on this proposal. Instead, he insisted that the ground for the conquest of Ethiopia should be prepared diplomatically in advance – as was done in the case of Tripolitania before Italy's war with Turkey in 1911.[20]

Ethiopia constituted one of the many outstanding causes of tension between Italy and France. In 1928 there were three outstanding issues in North Africa alone: the frontier of Libya, the status of Italians living in Tunisia and the future of Spanish Morocco. In 1919 the French had ceded to Italy a few oases on the frontier between Libya and Tunisia. In 1928 Italian claims were still modest, but by 1932 they were multiplied tenfold. Not only did Mussolini demand the Tibesti – Borku triangle north-east of Lake Chad, but also a large slice of the mandated French Cameroons, with a corridor linking it with Libya. This extravagant claim, if realised, would have provided Italy with access by land through Libya to the Atlantic. Since this cession of territory would have severed French communications in central Africa, it was roundly rejected.[21]

On one question Mussolini could apply leverage on France for concession elsewhere. Tunisia has been described as an Italian colony with a French government, for its 100,000 Italian inhabitants outnumbered the French and were concentrated in areas of major strategic importance: Tunis, Bizerta and Cape Bone. According to the Statute of 1896, which regulated Tunisia's relations with France, the Italians could claim Italian citizenship in Tunisia and French citizenship in Italy. During the First World War Italian irredentism caused such friction that even before the armistice the Statute was suspended, but remained provisionally in force pending a final settlement. Although the French were prepared to compromise and allow the Italians a relatively privileged status within a liberal constitution, Mussolini, moved by amour propre, demanded all or nothing. Either the 1896 Statute should come into full force for periods of at least ten years, or France should be allowed outright annexation of Tunisia and compensate Italy generously elsewhere.[22] Both alternatives were rejected by the French; the first, because it would deny France full sovereign rights in Tunisia; the second, because of the inevitable resentment which outright annexation would cause among the entire Muslim population of the French Empire, especially in Morocco.

The only success Mussolini scored in North Africa was in Morocco. In 1928, after many fruitless negotiations, and with British backing, Italy was at last allowed to participate in the international administration of Tangier, thereby limiting French, and later British, control of the western outlet of the Mediterranean.[23] Tangier was soon to become a vital centre for Italian propaganda. There was also, as in Tunisia, a considerable Italian colony in Spanish Morocco.[24] It was well organised locally and, like all Italian colonies oversea, subject to constant Fascist propaganda directed from Rome. Politically it proved a fertile seedbed for the extension of Italian interests in the western Mediterranean, an area which unexpectedly became a storm centre.[25]

After the fall of the monarchy in 1931 Spain, fearing an agreement between Fascist Italy and Germany, allowed herself to be used as a base for anti-Fascist propaganda organised principally by Italian free-masons. The following year Spanish counter-revolutionaries asked Italo Balbo, Italian Minister for Aviation, for arms. These were already on their way by sea when the revolt was crushed in July. There was evident fear in Rome that the Spanish Republic might allow the French to occupy the Balearic islands in return for support to maintain its authority on the mainland, and the aim of Italian naval manoeuvres held in the western Mediterranean in the summer of 1932 was to cut French communications with North Africa; the French held their manoeuvres in the eastern Mediterranean.[26] It was also mooted in left-wing newspapers in Madrid that Spain should withdraw altogether from her part of Morocco. If the Italians could not seize this colony themselves Mussolini was determined that the French should not cheat them, as they had done in Tunisia in 1882, and march in. The French were not finally to subjugate the Berbers in the interior until March 1934. They feared that, if Spanish authority broke down, Spanish Morocco might be annexed by Italy who might provide asylum for Berber nationalists.[27]

The French, however, were willing to pay their price for a free hand in North Africa, and certain pro-Italian newspapers in France thought they saw a way out. Why not let Italy realise her colonial aspirations in areas where they were not likely to come into serious conflict with French interests, for example in Turkey or Ethiopia? The Italians had been promised a large zone of Asia Minor by the agreement of St Jean de Maurienne of 1917. After the war they had to stand by and watch the British and French helping themselves to Palestine and Syria as mandates. In 1924 Mussolini still believed that the Turkish Republic would break up.[28] But he was soon to be disillusioned. Under the strong rule of Kemal Atatürk it became clear that any encroachments on Turkish territory would, with Russian support, be resisted. Hence in 1928 Italy concluded a Treaty of Friendship with Turkey. Mussolini later gave full publicity to unofficial hints, made in the French press, that France was favourable to Italian claims in Asia Minor, and this information was passed on to the government in Ankara. The upshot was a serious crisis in Franco-Turkish relations in 1932.[29]

Early in 1932, to meet the growing Italian threat, and suspicious of Britain, Haile Selassie proposed a treaty of alliance with France. The French, in no need of Ethiopian support in any case, turned down his offer with the disingenuous argument that they would contract alliances only within the framework of the League. Haile Selassie remained undaunted, and came back with a proposal for a treaty of friendship and commerce with France, the terms of which were highly favourable to France. The French gave no reply. Early in 1933 the Emperor sent Teckle Hawariat, one of his ablest henchmen, first as a private citizen, later as minister, to Paris to explore the ground for agreement. Although Hawariat took the view that French domination would be infinitely preferable to Italian, he was cold-shouldered.[30] To escape total isolation Haile Selassie in 1933 established valuable contacts with Japan. (For Japanese – Ethiopian relations in 1933 see chapter 8.)

Mussolini certainly knew that the French were reluctant to lend Ethiopia support and thereby antagonise Italy. Not surprisingly Grandi was prepared to follow up Laval's proposal made in July 1931. At the end of the year Marquis Alberto Theodoli, chairman of the Mandates Commission of the League, was sent unofficially to Paris to sound out the French government. The choice of Theodoli was exceptionally good. Although not a member of the Fascist party, he was persona grata with the French government. While working on the Mandates Commission he became friendly with Robert de Caix, the French representative, and he appreciated the extent to which the French needed Italian support in Syria, which was demanding independence and League membership.[31] On Theodoli's return Mussolini, who knew about Theodoli's visit, insisted to Grandi that Fascism needed an impressive diplomatic victory, such as the cession of a real French colony.[32] There was much discussion about which colony Italy should claim – and interest was not confined to East Africa. In June 1932 Grandi and a prominent Fascist, Federzoni, sounded out the French on the possibility of the cession of a mandated territory, evidently the Cameroons, to be connected by Tibesti and Borku with Tripolitania.[33] Augusto Rosso, Grandi's chef de cabinet, rejected the idea that Italy should realise her ambitions in Ethiopia, because of the stout resistance to be expected. Instead, the Italians should establish a colony in Angola, under a chartered company so as not to violate Portuguese sovereignty.[34] These alternatives, however, were not attractive to all political circles in Rome. In Guariglia's view, Italian expansion in the Cameroons (previously German) would encounter revived German claims no less than French resistance; and in Angola the interests of the government of South Africa would be threatened no

less than those of Portugal. He was also worried at the Fascist press's
clamour for the cession of Syria. Such an 'absurd' demand, he said, had
to be silenced by the Palazzo Chigi (the Italian Foreign Ministry) both
on the ground that the French were unlikely to make a gift of Syria to
Italy, and also because the acquisition of a country so riddled with
internal strife would prove nothing but a liability.[35] Guariglia's plan
was for Italy to win French as well as British acceptance of her aims in
Ethiopia. According to his account, the subject was raised for the first
time at the end of 1931 or early in 1932 by Philippe Berthelot, secretary-
general of the French Foreign Ministry, to Theodoli. News of the
proposal leaked out to Mussolini and surprisingly evoked from him
an outburst of 'gallophobia'. Mussolini wanted a gift of African
territory from France, not a bribe to deflect him from his main aim
which was a 'grand policy in Europe' and expansion at Yugoslavia's
expense.[36]

Despite Mussolini's hostile reaction, Guariglia succeeded in keeping
open future negotiations with France. In a long letter to Grandi of 9
February 1932 he systematically formulated his objections to the
passione adriatica which was likely to involve Italy in difficulties with
France and Yugoslavia.[37] In these circumstances Berthelot, on being
informed of Mussolini's attitude, had to tread with great caution in all
his subsequent dealings with Italian diplomats, above all because one of
the desiderata for discussion was the position of anti-Fascist refugees in
France, a subject on which Mussolini was exceptionally sensitive.[38]

Berthelot, and his successors, also had to take into account the
difficulties which a deal over Ethiopia (this came up again for discussion
between Theodoli and de Caix early in 1932) would encounter in his
own country. On the one hand, annexation by Italy of part of French
Somaliland, and the right to establish a motor road from the port of
Assab to Addis Ababa (connected by railway to Djibuti), would cause
an outcry from the very formidable French colonial lobby. The price for
this could be nothing more or less than a complete free hand for France
in North Africa.[39] On the other hand, if Italy were allowed to construct
the prospective route from Assab to Dessie, and thus threaten the
integrity of Ethiopia, there would be an uproar in the League on which
French security in Europe depended.[40] Even so, despite the sacrifices
entailed, for France a deal with Italy was attractive. It would put paid
once and for all to colonial disputes between the two countries.
However, when the subjects of Ethiopia and Turkey were again raised

in June or July 1932, Grandi maintained that discussion was only possible after, not before, all outstanding differences between Italy and France had been settled.[41]

Growing desire from the French side for agreement with Italy is understandable. On 11 December 1932 Germany was granted equality of status in armaments in a 'system providing security for all nations'. French military staffs dreaded the day when German rearmament would become a reality. In 1932 they made provision for two groups of potential enemies: Germany and Italy; Russia and Turkey. Of the two groups the former was considered to be incomparably the more dangerous.[42] Ever since the negotiations for the London Naval Agreement of 1930, Mussolini had been clamouring for equal status in naval armaments: a prospect which continued to cause dismay in the French admiralty.[43] With Britain showing little interest in the Mediterranean, it would mean virtual Italian control of this sea, as the French had to keep a part of their fleet in the Atlantic and North Sea waters. France had thus to maintain a margin of supremacy over the combined fleets of Italy and Germany. Moreover France possessed few ships with a speed and armament equal to the German pocket battleships of the *Deutschland* class or the fast Italian cruisers. There were also political difficulties. By the Treaty of Locarno Italy and Britain had guaranteed both France and Germany against an unprovoked attack. If France attacked Germany because the latter invaded the territory of one of France's allies in Eastern Europe, Italy might, the French service chiefs feared, go to the aid of Germany while Britain remained neutral.[44]

In other respects the French were more dependent on sea power than they had been before 1914. During the colonial disturbances in 1925 troops had to be sent from metropolitan France to North Africa. In the following year, after a provocative speech by Balbo to the Italian community in Tunis, the French held joint army and navy manoeuvres in Tunisia.[45] Since Franco-Italian relations did not improve, the French had to maintain the greater part of their fleet in the Mediterranean, and (as late as 1935) assign approximately one-fifth of their entire army – seven divisions in North Africa, ten near the Alps – for possible war against Italy. The fleet had to secure passage of troops and material across the Mediterranean, the eastern shore of which had assumed additional importance because Tripoli in the Lebanon was to be the terminal of the French oil pipeline from Mosul in Iraq.[46] France had to be ready also to dispatch troops to help her allies in Eastern Europe. According to General Maxime Weygand, in a memorandum for the Ministry of War dated 16 January 1933, the best port of disembarkation was considered to be Salonica.[47]

The weakest point of all in the French security position was Belgium, with whom France had concluded an alliance in 1920. Political opinion in Belgium was divided, and it was believed by the French that her neighbour would honour her obligations only if she were sure that France would be on the winning side and that Belgian territory would not be used as a mere shock-absorber in the event of a German attack on France. The question was frequently asked in interdepartmental meetings: where could France secure troops to reinforce the north-east frontier? She could maintain a preponderance over Germany only if Italy could be converted (as she had been in 1914) from a potential enemy to a neutral, or better still (as in 1915) to an ally. France's military leadership, moreover, was persuaded that the Italians had learned the value of military discipline under Fascism. It is no wonder that the service chiefs stressed the importance of conciliating Italy, which would also lead to better relations with Turkey.[48] In appraising their standpoint, it must be borne in mind that one of their main preoccupations was that, due to France's birth-rate decline, they could not call up the same number of reserves as Italy.

Rivalry between France and Italy throws light, not only on the Ethiopian war, but on the long-term causes of the Spanish Civil War. To all outward appearances Mussolini wanted action for its own sake and restlessly switched from one objective to another. Symptomatic of his attitude is a comment he made to Aloisi, chef de bureau of the Foreign Ministry on 14 January 1933: 'Possession of Corsica is better than that of Dalmatia. Ajaccio and Bastia would make two beautiful Italilan provinces. Whoever holds Corsica commands the western Mediterranean.'[49]

But Italian policy under Mussolini was not merely one of hand-to-mouth improvisation; there was, despite apparent contradictions, some system. If France and Britain refused to cede, or allow Italy to share in control over, important strategic points in the Mediterranean, an alternative was open to him: disruption of French or British rule in the territories they governed. Nowhere was this possibility more evident than in Malta, the most vital base of all in the central Mediterranean.[50]

Mussolini had not forgotten the Corfu incident of 1923 and the threat of British naval action in September of that year, the intention of which was to force the Italians into evacuating the island of Corfu. The incident, which also confirmed him in his contempt for the League of Nations, has been correctly described as a dress rehearsal for the Ethiopian crisis of the mid-1930s.[51] After 1930 the British had good reasons for wanting to avoid a second confrontation with Italy for which they were less well equipped than in 1923. Because of the economic crisis they had withdrawn two capital ships from the Mediterranean. A year later, as a result of the Manchurian crisis, they were more than ever dependent on unrestricted access across the inland sea.[52]

Events inside Italy caused Mussolini to take an interest in Malta and to create acute embarrassment in Whitehall. Immediately after the conclusion of the Lateran Agreements in February 1929 – Mussolini's most lasting achievement – the Holy See made an abortive effort to enlist the Italian dictator as 'defender of the faith'. The Church was the one institution which gave Malta a sense of social cohesion, and anti-clericalism (strongly entrenched in parts of central and southern Italy) had scarcely even a toe-hold in the island. Most of the inhabitants in the countryside spoke Maltese, basically a Phoenician language with many Arabic and Italian loan-words. As their second language the traders, the members of the independent professions and, above all, the clergy spoke Italian (which had been used by the Knights of Malta before 1815). Members of the administration, on the other hand, found it more convenient to use English. In 1921 the island was granted a constitution under which it enjoyed a measure of home rule within the British Empire. Many of the Roman Catholics felt that the distinctive culture of Malta could best be secured if Italian, instead of English, were to become the predominant second language. A small number of Maltese Nationalists were even drawn to Fascist dynamism before Mussolini came to power. The Nationalists, who were in office in 1921, encountered opposition led by a headstrong personage, Sir Gerald Strickland. He was half-Maltese, half-British, an aristocrat and a devout Roman Catholic. He had had a distinguished career and was elevated to the peerage in 1928. The previous year the Constitutional Party, which he led, was elected with a majority to the Maltese legislature. But he was tactless and, having taken office, he immediately banned the use of Italian in all government offices.[53]

There was at least one pressure group in Italy which was prepared to take up the cause of the pro-Italian Maltese. The extreme nationalists in Italy were pro-French and the expansion they advocated was intended to be at the expense of the British Empire, not of the French. They gave expression to their views in an ultra-Catholic newspaper,

La Tribuna. With Mussolini's approval, and despite protests from the Palazzo Chigi, it made personal attacks on Strickland.[54] After the Lateran Agreements were signed, the Vatican – which was most anxious to reconcile the two Latin sisters, Italy and France – sided with *La Tribuna,* and the protestations of the paper were taken up on a diplomatic level both by the Vatican and by Mussolini.[55] But the delicate honeymoon between the Duce and the Pope did not last long. Early in the summer of 1930 the hierarchy in Malta, backed by the Vatican, threatened to excommunicate Maltese citizens who voted for the Constitutional Party. Mussolini feared that the Vatican might behave in a similar fashion in Italy. Hence on 6 May 1930 Grandi told Graham, the British ambassador, that 'his experience in dealing with the Vatican since the Concordat had almost destroyed his Faith'. He went on to say: 'You do not realise how lucky you are to have had a Henry VIII.'[56] According to Peter Kent, divergent aims over Malta certainly contributed to the renewed quarrel between Mussolini and the Vatican over Catholic Action, which culminated in the summer of 1931. The Vatican, deprived of Italian support and aware of its weakness in Latin Europe after the fall of the monarchy in Spain and the establishment there of an anti-clerical republic, was also in need of British friendship. In mid-April 1931 the Pope agreed that the episcopal ban on Strickland's party should be lifted, provided that Strickland apologised to him in the House of Lords.[57]

The National Government in Britain, formed in August 1931, attributed the quarrel with the Vatican to Strickland's tactless anti-clerical policy, and it proposed that the 1921 constitution should once more come into force.[58] The real danger lay, the British now thought, in the extension of Italian culture; and this could only be stemmed by a ban, enforced in stages, on the use of Italian as an official language. Proposals to implement these ideas came into force early in 1932. Britain's new policy provoked in both Italy and Malta a wave of indignation. Mussolini was especially angry because he suspected that members of the Constitutional Party were supporting the French against Italy on the issue of Tunisia. But he had lost the Pope as his ally. Instead of using the Church, he introduced into the island a branch of the anti-clerical Dante Alighieri Society, under the cover of the Italian Naval League, together with an Italian Cultural Institute. These were established at great expense to promote Italian culture. At the elections held in June 1932 under the restored 1921 constitution, the pro-Italian Nationalist Party was re-elected. But Mussolini could not allow a quarrel with Britain to flare up at a time of crisis over Yugoslavia and when plans were being drawn up for the invasion of Ethiopia. On 14 October 1932 he assured the British that 'no sane Italian cast an eye on Malta or desired to encourage an irredentist movement in that island'.[59] By November 1933 the British government, evidently under pressure from the Admiralty, felt strong enough to dismiss the Nationalist Party and to suspend the constitution. The crisis over Malta created not only ill-feeling between Mussolini and the British government, but also resentment among many of the islanders themselves. Owing to Malta's supreme importance as a naval base, the British had in future to make provision for internal security against espionage and sabotage, as well as for defending the island and for feeding its population of approximately 300,000.[60] (See below, chapter 13.)

The immediate result of the quarrel with Britain was to undermine the position of the moderates in Rome. Grandi, while in office, was an Anglophile. Moreover, he sought not only to reach a compromise with France on the question of naval parity, but also to co-operate with both France and Yugoslavia against Germany, within the framework of the League. He was thus in full agreement with the ideas expressed in Guariglia's letter of 9 February 1932, against the *passione adriatica*, which apparently was never seen by Mussolini.[61] But Grandi's position was under attack. In the summer of 1932 the League of Nations came under constant criticism from Paolucci Baroni, the new Italian delegate; and General Balbo, one of Grandi's most bitter rivals, in an article published in the *Popolo d'Italia* early in July (which was approved personally by Mussolini) threatened Italy's withdrawal from the League.[62]

Moreover, both Balbo and De Bono, for different reasons, looked forward to the day the National Socialists would be in power in Germany: De Bono, in order that France could be put under pressure to reach an accommodation with Italy over Ethiopia; Balbo, to maintain the balance of strength in armaments by allowing Germany certain weapons prohibited to her under the Versailles settlement.[63] By the end of July 1932 it was quite clear that Grandi's policy of moderation had broken down. In a communiqué issued in Lausanne on 13 July the governments of France and Britain declared that, in accordance with the Covenant, they were in agreement on all matters decided at Lausanne, including provisions about reparations payments by Germany which practically amounted to their cancellation.[64] They invited other governments to co-operate with them on general matters. That the 'status quo powers' could come to such a self-interested arrangement in international affairs without even consulting Italy infuriated Mussolini. Bad news also came from other quarters. Towards the end of July the Germans refused to renew a commercial treaty whereby Italy could export foodstuffs to Germany in return for raw materials. More serious was the defection (albeit temporary, as it turned out) of Italy's two client states, Austria and Hungary. Earlier in the year they had been invited by the French to come to terms with Czechoslovakia and Yugoslavia. They angered Mussolini by making at Lausanne a deal with France for financial aid from the League. With Italy virtually isolated, Mussolini's policy of 'equidistance' was in jeopardy.[65]

He reacted by making radical changes in official appointments. In late July 1932 he became his own foreign minister. Grandi was sent reluctantly as ambassador to the Court of St James; Rosso to Washington; Guariglia to Madrid. These diplomats, too critical for Mussolini's liking at home, could yet be relied on to explain why Italy was in need of expansion to the governments of countries where there was an aversion to Fascist ideas or to Italian expansionist ambitions. Balbo was made Italian representative at the Disarmament Conference; he could be relied on to use strong language. Fulvio Suvich, a native of Trieste and anti-German, was appointed Deputy Under-Secretary of the Foreign Ministry; and Baron Pompeo Aloisi became chef de bureau of the Foreign Ministry and later Italy's representative at Geneva. Both these men, in key posts in the Palazzo Chigi, were experienced diplomats and were anxious to steer a middle course; but they were also experts on Eastern Europe and on Balkan affairs – areas in which Mussolini's main interest still lay.[66]

But Mussolini had not forgotten Ethiopia. After the reshuffle in Rome all questions pertaining to Africa were transferred from the Palazzo Chigi to the Colonial Ministry under De Bono.[67] By demarcating the tasks of both ministries, Mussolini could keep the one in the dark about his intentions in regard to the other. Lack of co-ordination in the conduct of policy between these ministries, and in that of the Italian service chiefs, makes it exceptionally difficult to establish the relationship between Mussolini's policies in Europe and in Africa. Whether he was pursuing separate policies in these areas, or whether they formed part of a grand design, remains to be considered.

2 Europe and Africa, 1932–33

THE reshuffle late in July 1932 certainly enabled Mussolini to exert a measure of centralised control over Italian foreign policy but there was more continuity than is sometimes assumed. Still smarting from the humiliation inflicted on Italy at Lausanne, he told Aloisi on 26 July that it was his aim 'straightaway to launch a great diplomatic movement': it was to be a 'veritable earthquake'.[1] But there were to be no immediate surprises, and the day-to-day decisions at the Palazzo Chigi were made without undue interference. Guariglia and Theodoli soon put Aloisi fully in the picture on Italy's aims in Ethiopia and on the possibility of a resumption of negotiations with France. Aloisi also learned early in October 1932 that the French might after all be willing to cede the Cameroons. He later told the Duce emphatically that, in view of the dangers of German rearmament, agreement should be reached with France. Mussolini rejected Aloisi's pleas on the grounds that greater pressure could be brought to bear on France if Germany were allowed to rearm in stages. Hence he did not favour the suggestion of starting negotiations with France over the cession of a mandate. He insisted that France must 'allow us complete liberty on the Danube where, united with Austria and Hungary, we will form a rampart which could prevent an *Anschluss*: on the Rhine we are against France; on the Danube, with France'.[2] Mussolini meant that Italy must hold the balance between France and Germany.

In one sense he shared with British statesmen an interest in maintaining the balance of power. But whereas the British wanted security in Europe and the appeasement of all those states which had a legitimate grievance, Mussolini wished to exacerbate conflicts in order to win some solid prize for Italy. The view that he followed the lead from the British in October 1932 to advocate a Four Power Directorate of Europe, or that he acted in co-operation with them towards these ends, has thus been correctly subjected to criticism.[3] In his speech of 22 October 1932 at Turin, Mussolini tentatively put forward a plan of his own. Although he championed the cause of the revisionist powers, he was far less bellicose than was his wont. Italy, France, Britain and Germany should, he claimed, co-operate within the framework of the League, an instrument which, he thought, might still prove effective for preserving the peace in Europe, but not in other parts of the world, namely the Far East and Latin America. He made no mention of Asia or Africa.[4] The speech, which was considered by Aloisi to be the 'apotheosis of Fascism', received a relatively favourable response in France.[5] The upshot was that Theodoli was allowed to continue negotiations with de Caix, provided that they were restricted to general topics; no mention was made of the Cameroons or of Ethiopia.[6] A pro-Italian speech made by Edouard Herriot at a conference of the Radical Socialists at Toulouse on 5 November created a better atmosphere. But Mussolini refused a request made by Aloisi to give the speech a favourable response, on the grounds that France was still not willing to allow Italy naval equality.[7]

New contacts with France were, however, made. Henri Jouvenel, a capable journalist, replaced Beaumarchais as ambassador; and Bérenger, president of the Committee of Foreign Affairs of the French Senate, visited Rome in November.[8] He was told by Mussolini that Britain and France should maintain their empires intact: Germany should be allowed to expand in the Baltic and at Russia's expense; Italy's aims were to be confined to economic expansion in the Danube area and in the Near and Middle East. Officials at the Quai d'Orsay laid great stress on the fact that Italian expansion in Ethiopia was not so much as mentioned by Mussolini. They drew the conclusion that, if Italy sought aggrandisement at the expense of that country, no agreement with France was necessary. France was 'expected to be a benevolent spectator in the attempts made by the Kingdom [Italy] to establish its economic and political preponderance in Abyssinia'. The French did, however, believe that Mussolini was sounding out Bérenger on the possibility of a deal by which France would no longer be molested in Tunisia, if, in return, she dropped Yugoslavia as an ally.[9] Mention of Yugoslavia was indeed ominous, for relations between her and Italy were heading precipitously towards a major crisis.

After King Alexander of Yugoslavia had consolidated his dictatorship in 1929, Croat terrorists, known as the *Ustaši*, had fled from the country. Having first established contact with the Macedonian Revolutionary Organisation in Bulgaria, which Mussolini had saved from bankruptcy, one group under Gustav Perčeć had organised armed camps, the most prominent being at Janka Pusta in south-west Hungary. Another group, under the notorious Ante Pavelić, had taken refuge in Italy, where it was protected by Ercole Conti and Arturo Bocchini, Italian chiefs of police. There was also a small group of *Ustaši* in Austria. Those in Italy were armed and concentrated in camps in the neighbourhood of Trieste, Fiume and Zara.[10] The *Ustaši* and other terrorist organisations were to play an important role in Mussolini's foreign policy. In 1929 a secret Italian – Hungarian military convention had been concluded to which the Croats acceded as consultative parties. Private arrangements were made later that year for the transit of arms through Austria to Hungary.[11] In 1927 Mussolini had concluded a military agreement with Albania, where Italian propaganda and military missions were active, and he had been able to keep King Zog under check by supporting the Catholic tribesmen against the Muslims. The actions of the Albanians, Montenegrins, Bulgars and Magyars within Yugoslavia itself were henceforward to be co-ordinated from Rome. Furthermore, Mussolini was now given some backing by the Vatican.[12] In short, by means of encirclement and promiscuous terrorism, he set himself to the task of dismembering Yugoslavia.

He failed to perceive the difficulties which this policy was likely to encounter. Admittedly Alexander's regime was far from popular, but most of the Croats were followers of Maček's Peasants Party, and, as such, they were autonomists, not separatists. They highly resented the privileged position enjoyed by the tiny minority of Italians in Dalmatia, who by the Treaty of Rapallo of 1920 were allowed to opt for Italian citizenship without changing their residence.[13] Propaganda from Italy by 'Dalmatian Societies of Actions', on behalf of these Italians, proclaimed noisily that Dalmatia was Italian. The treatment of minorities living in Italy itself was far from conducive to promoting Italian influence outside the country. In 1919 Italy was the only power with augmented territory which had not been required to sign treaties for the protection of minorities. Under Fascism, the 300,000 Slovenes in Istria and the 200,000 Germans in the Alto Adige (the South Tyrol) had been victimised and subjected to ruthless Italianisation.[14] No wonder that the Italians were hated in most areas of Austria and that the Slovenes in Yugoslavia were on the whole loyal to King Alexander. Alexander might have been more successful in meeting the threat to his country had he accepted a proposal, put forward by the French, for reorganising his kingdom on a federal basis. But there were too many areas of mixed population, and in July 1932 he preferred to maintain

Yugoslavia as a unitary state. Due to the economic crisis there was growing opposition, not only from minority groups, but also from the Serb Democratic Party. Early in 1932 Alexander attempted to give his country security by a direct agreement with Italy but the privileged position enjoyed by Italy in Albania – which was now challenged by pro-Serb Muslim chiefs there – proved to be a stumbling block. The Croats too were restive.[15] In the autumn there was a minor revolt in the Lika area in Dalmatia. Pavelić's men for a time entered Yugoslav territory from Zara in order to proclaim a Croat Republic. The action was supported by the presence of Italian troops, concentrated in Istria. Having crushed the revolt with little difficulty, Alexander protested vehemently that Italian collusion with the Croats was tantamount to a disguised attack on his country. He would oppose this with all means in his power and bring the matter before the League.[16]

Although Aloisi contributed to the crisis with Yugoslavia by sending Koch, one of his henchmen, as Italian minister to Tirana (where he made himself thoroughly detested), he had strong misgivings about the outcome of Mussolini's policy of attempting to dismember Yugoslavia. If Croatia were granted autonomy within Yugoslavia, the Serbs, thwarted in the north, would turn south and try to strengthen their position in the Balkans by attracting the Bulgars – with whom they had more in common through language and religion than with the Croats – into a Slav confederation. They would also try to come to terms with Albania.[17] Besides, the Italians traditionally feared the Croats more than any of the other Slav peoples, and Italian territorial claims on the northern coast of Dalmatia could only be at the expense of the Croats.

Instead of a policy of hostility there was much to be gained from an understanding with Yugoslavia. Italy absorbed 25 to 28 per cent of Yugoslavia's exports, and 8 to 10 per cent of Italian exports went to Yugoslavia. Late in October, after the Lika fiasco, Mussolini hoped to reach political and economic agreements, first with Austria and Hungary, and then with Yugoslavia, the aim of which was defence against Germany whose power, according to Italian diplomats, was growing dangerously and where all shades of opinion, before Hitler came to power, favoured an *Anschluss* (union) with Austria. As soon as the Germans learned that the dismemberment of Yugoslavia and the creation of a confederacy of Austria, Hungary and Croatia was Mussolini's aim, they became apprehensive. For if this new political structure were established – which was the aim of the Vatican also – it would stimulate the legitimists to seize power in Austria. This would put paid once and for all to an *Anschluss*.[18]

Mussolini's aims in Austria were two-fold. First, Italian control of Austrian territory was necessary in order to provide Italy with that vital link by land with Hungary, who needed Italian arms against Yugoslavia. With Austria and Hungary attracted into her orbit, Italy's economic expansion in the Danubian area was assured. Moreover, if Hungary menaced Yugoslavia from the rear, Italy could at the opportune moment seize that part of the coast of Dalmatia denied her in 1919. Second, a German entry into Austria had to be prevented. Mussolini, and above all Suvich, were only too aware that if the Germans were to breakfast at Innsbruck they would have lunch at the port of Trieste. Provided it is seen in the general context of Italian aspirations in the Mediterranean and as a means of preventing Germany from becoming a Mediterranean power, Mussolini's policy towards Austria was not in essence separate from that which he pursued towards Ethiopia. Seapower – to which he assigned very great importance – was a factor applicable to both of these land-locked territories. Austria was the hinterland of the Adriatic, Ethiopia of the Red Sea. Mussolini could thus switch his interest from the one country to the other without exposing himself to a serious charge of inconsistency.

Within the Republic of Austria he had, however, set himself the impossible task of fighting a political war on two fronts. He had rejected out of hand a proposal that Hitler had allegedly made in April 1930 to Prince Ernst von Starhemberg, the pan-German head of the *Heimwehr* (a para-military organisation of the Right), to the effect that Italy should allow Germany an *Anschluss* in return for German recognition of the Brenner frontier. In April 1932 the Nazis fared well, Starhemberg (who favoured the Habsburgs) badly, in the Austrian municipal elections. In financial difficulties and short of arms, Starhemberg again met Mussolini at the end of May 1932 and promised to use his influence to prevent the new Austrian Chancellor, Engelbert Dollfuss, from throwing in his lot either with the Social Democrats, who favoured co-operation with the Little Entente and France, or with the Nazis whose aim was an *Anschluss* with Germany.[19]

Having ruled out co-operation with either the Socialists or the Nazis, Mussolini could uphold Austria's independence only if he were supported by Hungary. Here internal events caused him once again to reverse his policy towards Yugoslavia. As a result of the economic crisis the Radical Right in Hungary attracted many supporters, especially among the German minority and, early in October 1932, Julius Gömbös was appointed Prime Minister. In a visit to Rome on 10-11 October he discussed with Mussolini plans for political and economic co-operation among Italy, Hungary and Austria. But Gömbös had more far-reaching ambitions. After his return he met Starhemberg and accepted a plan, evidently drawn up by Pavelić, for an uprising by the Ustaši. The inititiative was to be left to the Ustaši in Hungary but the arms were to be provided by Italy and dispatched through Austria. The exact circumstances in which Mussolini accepted the so-called 'Croat Plan' cannot be established. Aloisi, who evidently believed that the plan had been drawn up before he assumed office, became especially apprehensive. Late in November he warned both Mussolini and Paolo Cortese, the official in the Foreign Ministry responsible for Croat affairs, of its 'extremely dangerous repercussions'. It would cause a storm of indignation in the League of Nations and it would lose Italy support in the Balkans.[20]

Aloisi was correct in thinking that Yugoslavia was not diplomatically isolated. Czechoslovakia and Romania, her allies in the Little Entente, and France were already alarmed. On 28 October 1932 the Franco-Yugoslav Treaty of 1927 was renewed. Mussolini retaliated by proposing a customs union between Italy and Albania. It failed to materialise. Tension on the Italian – Yugoslav frontier and in Albania reached crisis proportions, and on 2 December the famous Lions of Trau, commemorating Venetian rule in Dalmatia, were mutilated by Serb activists.[21] The incident was discussed at a meeting of the Italian Senate held on 14 December. Mussolini let himself go against the Serbs, and he declared the Italian retaliation would not be confined to a diplomatic démarche.[22] The upshot was a violent campaign in the Italian press against Yugoslavia and, for a time, against France. The French received reports that Italian troops were concentrating near Trieste, that factories were stepping up war production, and that Italian officers in North Africa were learning Slovene and Croat dialects. The British minister in Belgrade, Nevile Henderson, advised the Foreign Office to make it known that the maintenance of Yugoslavia's independence was a British interest.[23] Whether the French General Staff were in fact giving serious thought to possible war with Italy in support of Yugoslavia is most problematic. But a report reached Mussolini on 25 December 1932 that General Weygand, who was said to be on good terms with Paul-Boncour, the new French Premier, was contemplating a preventive war. Mussolini's reaction was reported to be 'ferocious'. He declared that 'every invader of Italy had to pay dearly' for their action and 'the Italy of today is no different from what she had been at other times'. Aloisi expressed regret that such reports were allowed to reach the Duce.[24]

No sooner had the Yugoslav crisis reached its climax than attention was unexpectedly focused on Ethiopia. After a meeting on 15 December with Suvich and Buti (a Foreign Ministry official) Aloisi noted: 'As for Ethiopia, everything has remained in the state I left it in. It is necessary to start immediately the famous *politica periferica*.' A meeting to discuss this subject was to take place two days later. Aloisi had been kept, perhaps deliberately, in the dark on Mussolini's ambitions in East Africa, for also on 15 December Mussolini in fact sanctioned an operational plan, submitted to him by De Bono, for the invasion of Ethiopia. Since De Bono and the Italian High Command were as anxious as the diplomats to maintain the '*sicurezza adriatica*', which meant peace in Europe, Mussolini could not indefinitely pursue two policies of aggrandisement: one in the Adriatic, the other in East Africa.[25] By the end of 1932 he had to make a choice between them.

It is first necessary to consider the operational plans for war with Ethiopia. No sooner had De Bono of the Colonial Ministry been made responsible for matters pertaining to East Africa in August 1932 than he ordered Colonel Cubeddu, commander of Eritrea, to draw up plans for a defensive and an offensive war against Ethiopia. Before Cubeddu had completed his work King Victor Emmanuel III visited Eritrea and took a keen interest in the colony.[26] The royal visit was of more than symbolic significance. It heralded a long period of bitter rivalry between the King's men and Mussolini's: between Marshal Pietro Badoglio and General De Bono, and later both of them against General Rodolfo Graziani. Two questions stood out. How was the venture to be tackled? Who was to win the accolade?

Italian planners had to consider in practical terms how Italy's precarious foothold in East Africa was to be maintained. Given their exaggeration of Haile Selassie's capacity, their fear of an Ethiopian attack may well have been genuine. They also had to decide how an Italian advance could best be made into the heart of Ethiopia. Plans for an offensive and a defensive war were thus complementary. Eritrea, formally proclaimed an Italian colony in 1890, was divided for the purposes of defence into three zones. (The map will clarify the following description.)

1. The plain, of over 400 miles in length and between 10 and 50 miles wide, borders the Red Sea and is almost incapable of supporting settled communities. That part of it known as the Zula Kar in the Danakil desert falls to approximately 400 feet below sea level, and parts of it were still unexplored in the early 1930s. The main value of the plain was the port of Massawa (whose average mean temperature of over 30°C. was the highest recorded in the world). Thanks to its off-shore islands, Massawa was relatively secure from a naval attack and in 1933–4 was extended as a naval base. But Massawa lay 2000 miles from Naples and was capable of providing for only four or five ships carrying a monthly cargo of 2000 tons. From Massawa a narrow-gauge railway made the precipitous climb of 7500 feet to Asmara, capital of Eritrea, which lay fifty miles, as the crow flies, to the west. In 1928 the line had been extended to Keren and Agordat. The road, running parallel with the railway, could only be described as a camel track, and it was scarcely capable of carrying any traffic during the wet season from June to September.

2. The highland zone of Eritrea is considerably drier than that of Tigré in Ethiopia to the south, from which foodstuffs had to be imported. An Italian estimate of 1934 (there was no proper census until 1961) reckoned that Eritrea had about 600,000 inhabitants. Less than one-third of these were Coptic Christians speaking Tigrinya (also the language of most of Tigré province in Ethiopia), which resembles Ge'ez, the classical language of Ethiopia, more closely than does Amharic, spoken in Addis Ababa and in the north-west. The majority of Eritreans were Muslim. Since southern Eritrea had been wrested from Ethiopia in 1889, Italian colonial officials were fearful of Ethiopia's seizing an opportunity to win it back. From a defensive point of view it was thus vital to establish fortified positions covering Asmara as well as the exposed line of communication to Massawa.

3. In the western zone of Eritrea, adjoining the Sudan, the mountains sloped gradually towards the Nile.[27]

The Italian colony of Somaliland was prized less highly. Its principal port and capital, Mogadishu, lay 1600 miles beyond Massawa. Owing to the shallow waters, cargoes from ocean-going ships had to be unloaded and carried by tenders to the mainland. The only line of communications from Mogadishu was a railway 68 miles long to Villabruzzi, a small town, seldom marked on maps, situated on the

Shebeli river. Kismayu, which Italy had aquired from Britain in June 1925, offered better natural facilities as a port, but the Italians failed to make the fullest use of it by building a pier, evidently because of the cost. The inhabitants of Italian Somaliland were mainly south-eastern Cushites, living a nomadic life in the scrubland in search of grazing and water. Almost totally disregarding the governments concerned, they freely roamed across the largely undemarcated frontiers of Ogaden, which Italy had ceded to Ethiopia after the battle of Adowa, and across the borders of British and French Somaliland.[28] Ready to defend their Muslim faith in its pristine state against their infidel Ethiopian and British overlords, the Somalis early in this century had rallied to the banner of Islam under a leader, Mohammad Abdille Hassan, a man renowned for his piety and learning, whom the British mendaciously named the 'Mad Mullah'. The rising was finally put down with the use of aircraft after 1920.[29]

The Italians were not in control of northern Somaliland before Mussolini came to power, and the new government allocated a large sum for the pacification of this area under the command of a leading Fascist, Cesare De Vecchi. By July 1926 the subjugation, which cost 23 million lire, was well advanced but it was completed only in 1928. The Italians, however, had not made themselves popular among all the Somalis, and Omar Samantar, one of the local warriors whom they had entrusted to 'maintain order', revolted. He was pursued and took refuge in Ogaden in Ethiopia. Later, as will be seen (chapter 8), he was to enter the pay of Haile Selassie. The Italians were more successful in the south of the colony. Here the population, partly Bantu, was organised by private Italian companies into settled communities, cultivating fruit and cotton along the Juba and Shebelli rivers which were connected by an elaborate nexus of canals, 420 miles in length, for irrigation.

For several reasons the Italians attached little importance to Somaliland as a springboard for an attack on Ethiopia. An offensive from Eritrea could start only at the end of the wet season in October, and it had to be completed by June. In Somaliland, on the other hand, the first period of rain was from September to December; the second, from March to June. For reasons of climate alone it was virtually impossible to concert operations from the north and south. There were additional disadvantages. There was no mountain barrier in Somaliland which could be converted into a fortified line, capable of preventing an Ethiopian advance from the Bali plateau down the fertile Juba and Shebelli valleys towards Mogadishu. The most vulnerable area in Ethiopia, which the Italians could reach from the south, lay on the Harar mountains. Not only was the population in this area hostile to rule from Addis Ababa: it was regarded by the Italians as most suitable for European colonisation. However, because it lay hundreds of miles across open desert from the Italian supply base, it was not considered to be a feasible military objective.[30]

Although the total population of Somaliland amounted to about 1,400,000 (more than double that of Eritrea), the Italians reckoned that they could raise no more than 20,000 native troops named *dubats*, which was but one-third of the force of *askaris* expected from Eritrea. The *dubats* were willing to fight only in their own locality, whereas the *askari* were ready to fight in any part of Africa. It was later estimated by Italian service chiefs, who greatly overrated Ethiopian strength, that if Ethiopia went to war she would dispose of some 300-400,000 troops in the north and 80,000 in the south. The defence of the latter frontier could not be ignored. Since it was wrongly believed that the white man could not withstand the severity of the heat in the south, there was to be much controversy in Rome as to whether a division of the *askari* then serving in Libya should be deployed in Somaliland or in Eritrea. In either event Libya would be depleted of troops and exposed to a French attack.[31]

But Ethiopia presented Italy with a political, no less than a military, problem. The empire was not so much an organised territorial state as an archipelago of mountain chiefdoms which, during the wet season, were isolated both from each other and from the central government at Addis Ababa.[32] The degree of cohesion provided by the Coptic Church should not be exaggerated. In theory it was centralised and came under the Abuna, its head, who was appointed by the Coptic Patriarch of Alexandria. But, as an Egyptian foreigner, the Abuna was far from popular and was often challenged in the exercise of his office. Despite its hierarchic structure and the fact that it was so Erastian as to commemorate Pontius Pilate, the Ethiopian Church was divided on the complex theological question of the divinisation of Christ. It owned much of the land and resolutely stood out against any move towards social reform. Aksum, the ancient ecclesiastical capital, lay in Tigré; and the Tigreans, who regarded themselves as privileged, resented rule from Addis Ababa.[33]

South of Lake Tana, and bordering the Blue Nile, lay the province of Gojjam, where British interests were strong. Like Tigré, it had formed part of the ancient Solomonid kingdom, and its *rases* had resisted

Menelik II's attempts to shift the centre of gravity of the Empire from Gondar in Begemidir to Addis Ababa in Shewa, an upstart province. In the summer of 1932 there was a serious revolt in Gojjam, supported by the deposed Lig Yasu. Furthermore, Haile Selassie's rule was especially resented over most of the south, which had been conquered by Menelik II late in the nineteenth century.

Haile Selassie, no less than Menelik II, had not only his Christian subjects to contend with. The Afars and Issas of the Danakil desert spoke a different language from the Somalis but they were staunch upholders, like them, of Islam. Hence, if Ethiopia were to win a corridor through the desert to a port on the Red Sea – at Assab in Eriterea or at Zeila in British Somaliland or at Obock in French Somaliland – such a corridor would have to pass through territory inhabited by hostile tribesmen. The Emperor also had to take into account an assembly of peoples of Semitic origin called the Gallas, groups of whom had spread from the south over much of the empire. In part Christian or Muslim, in part pagan, they had to unite them only a common language. Those of them inhabiting the province of Wello between Shewa and Tigré were Muslims and their situation was such that they could prevent the Ethiopians from fighting a guerrilla war by disrupting their tenuous line of communications. The Gallas in Sidamo and Bali in the south were also waiting for the day when they could shake themselves free from their Ethiopian masters. To the west were the despised Negroes who made up the bulk of the slaves.[34]

Such, in brief, were the main factors to be taken into account in any plan for Italian action, defensive or offensive, against Ethiopia. When Colonel Cubeddu presented his report, De Bono adopted his ideas but, by manipulating the logistics, sought to infuse 'Fascist dynamism' into the proposals. Cubeddu estimated that 90 days would be needed for mobilising 60,000 askaris; De Bono reduced the period to 15 days. It was envisaged that 100 aircraft from Italy would start the attack, three weeks before the completion of mobilisation of land forces. The air force was to bomb strategic points in Ethiopia as well as the enemy's assembly areas. One month after mobilisation, and three months after the first air attacks, the army, reinforced by 35,000 Italian troops, would launch an offensive towards the communications centre of Adigrat. De Bono formulated this plan in letters dated 29 November 1932 to General Gazzara, Minister of War, Balbo of the Air Ministry and Ricardo Astuto, the newly appointed governor of Eritrea. Marshal Badoglio, chief of the General Staff and governor of Tripolitania and Cyrenaica (united to form Libya in January 1934), also received a copy of De Bono's letter but not of Cubeddu's original proposals.[35] He gave it a provisional approval but requested De Bono to make sure that the logistical problems were carefully studied. Badoglio was later to slash De Bono's plan.

On 15 December 1932 De Bono noted: 'I have submitted the project for an eventual action against Abyssinia to Mussolini. It pleases him. I am to be in command of it. It will be a beautiful swan song. We must be ready by 1935 but I fear that we have not calculated sufficiently the expense and consequences. We will see'. Certainly Italy's position in the Red Sea was ridiculous. He went on to say: 'We need money. That is the one thing which counts.' G. Rochat correctly draws the conclusion that Mussolini's acceptance of the plan was of greater political than military importance. He writes: 'The Ministry of Colonies planned and made its own decisions as if the entire air force was at its disposal . . . Without batting an eyelid and disregarding the international situation De Bono proposed that troops from Italy and from Libya should be sent to Eritrea.'[36] Badoglio's role was not that of a co-ordinator but of an adviser, and the military authorities were given De Bono's letter not in order to sanction it but to express an opinion on it. Rochat could have added that the Foreign Ministry was equally kept in the dark, for as late as 15 December 1932 Aloisi complained mistakenly that the *politica periferica* was neglected.[37]

Late in 1932 Mussolini was under pressure to reach a decision. Count Luigi Vinci, the new Italian minister at Addis Ababa, was in Rome awaiting instructions. On 3 January 1933, in the presence of Suvich and Aloisi, Vinci was told by Mussolini that Italy intended to pursue a policy of friendship with Ethiopia, 'the aim of which was to disguise in every way Italy's plans'. Mussolini went on to say that the *politica periferica* was to be pursued by Rome. Without altogether sharing the optimism of his military staff, Mussolini believed that a 'warlike operation in Ethiopia' would succeed, 'provided we have completely free hands in Europe'. The military committee, presided over by General De Bono, had already studied the plans. It was necessary that Vinci, during his mission, should remove all suspicion. 'If the Negus [i.e. the Emperor] made proposals for an exchange of territory, negotiations must simply be postponed.' Aloisi stated that it would be advantageous to Italy if she could secure a port, probably that of Djibuti. Mussolini also informed Vinci that the Italian government aimed at constructing a railway from Assab to Dessie.[38]

Certain general conclusions can be drawn from the meeting of 3 January 1933. It seems that the initiative for action in Ethiopia came from the conservative diplomats and soldiers such as Guariglia, De Bono, Theodoli, Aloisi and the Duke of Aosta, not to mention the Jesuits and the King. The late Professor Toscano's contention that Aloisi had been opposed to the Ethiopian venture, and G. Baer's that there was no central control, cannot be substantiated, at least for the period 1932–3.[39] It can be contended, but not proved, that the conservatives in Rome, alarmed by Mussolini's dangerous policy in Europe, tried to deflect their master's attention from Europe to a relatively 'safe' military operation in a more distant part of the world, in return for which Italy would agree to collaboration with France against Germany.

That the conservatives found it difficult to persuade Mussolini to turn from Europe to Africa, needs explanation. One consideration stands out. The *politica periferica* could yield no quick, spectacular returns. Two years of technical planning and political preparation lay ahead before a military expedition against Ethiopia could even start. Mussolini wanted some immediate dramatic success, which would win him the whole-hearted support of the rank and file of the Fascist Party. In March 1933 he told Starhemberg that if Italy could not get her own way in Europe she would be pushed into Africa.[40] This suggests that, in Mussolini's view, the *politica periferica* was of secondary importance. Security on the Adriatic, which the generals and diplomats stressed, was vital. But how was this to be achieved? By obsequiously following the lead of France in upholding the territorial status quo? Or by a political offensive against France with Italy at the head of the 'have-not' nations? Mussolini preferred the second course.

Early in January a slight change of emphasis in Italy's attitude towards Yugoslavia is evident. Previously Mussolini believed that Yugoslavia was on the point of collapse. But after the rumours that Weygand contemplated a preventive war reached his ears, he believed that Yugoslavia would join France and attack Italy. On 7 January 1933 he ordered the publication of facts relating to all public and clandestine measures directed against Italy by the government in Belgrade. This publication was evidently to be used to justify Italian action against Yugoslavia.[41] As a result of a serious security oversight a crisis came to a head prematurely. On 8 January a Viennese socialist newspaper, the *Arbeiter Zeitung*, published details of the import from Italy of captured

First World War weapons for repairs at the factory of their origin at Hirtenberg in Austria.[42] A part of these arms was to be used by pro-Nazi sections of the Austrian *Heimwehr* mainly in Styria, the rest was to be dispatched to Hungary for the *Ustaši*. The next day, at a meeting between Foreign Ministry officials and members of the Italian High Command, the plan, submitted by Pavelić, was discussed. All present had the impression that it would 'lead inevitably to war', and that Italy should extricate herself immediately from a situation which exposed her to arraignment before the League. Aloisi also dismissed Mussolini's contention that Yugoslavia was on the point of breaking up.[43] In fact Yugoslavia had won the full backing of the Little Entente which was now greatly strengthened. The reason for this is not surprising. If Mussolini were allowed to have his way and a political organisation, comprising Slovenia, Croatia, Austria and Hungary, was established, the Habsburg Empire could later be restored approximately within its old framework. Beneš, the Czech Foreign Minister, was no less determined than the Germans to prevent this at all costs. Hence both he and Titulescu, the Romanian Foreign Minister, supported Yugoslavia in pressing to have the Hirtenberg affair brought before the Council of the League. But Britain and France, not for the first or last time, were prepared to allow Italy a remarkable degree of immunity from international censure. On 11 February they insisted to the Austrian government alone that the arms should be either destroyed or returned to Italy.[44] German documents indicate that approximately half the arms were in fact sent by lorry to Hungary, and the rest intended for the *Heimwehr*. It is improbable, as D'Amoja contends, that the arms were earmarked for the Austrian army. For the Italians later complained that, because two rail truck-loads of arms for the *Heimwehr* were returned to Italy, Starhemberg was not in a position to carry out a coup against Dollfuss in Vienna and rule Austria through the *Heimwehr*.[45]

The strengthening of the Little Entente as a result of the Hirtenberg affair[46] made it all the more important for Mussolini to win the support of Germany. On 14 January 1933, in the presence of Aloisi, he discussed with Cerruti Germany's internal problems and her foreign policy. Hitler, according to Cerruti, had lost two of the three cards he could play. He had not taken advantage of an opportunity for a *Putsch* and had spoilt his own chances (presumably by failing to co-operate with other German parties of the Right) of forming a government by legal means. The one opportunity now open to him, according to Cerruti, was to win an election by a majority vote. To Mussolini's question as to whether Germany was prepared to co-operate with Italy, Cerruti answered that she would only do so after Germany was rearmed and strong. Mussolini was so favourably disposed towards Germany that he dismissed Cerruti's argument out of hand, but Aloisi considered it to be correct. The Duce also posed two questions on which he had always been extremely sensitive. First, whether Germany might reach an agreement with France. On being told by Cerruti that this possibility could not be ruled out, Mussolini said, 'In this case we must anticipate her' – by which he meant that Italy should reach an agreement with Germany as soon as possible. Second, he asked whether the Germans considered Italy to be powerful. Cerruti replied, perhaps to please the Duce, that 'a profound change was taking place' among Germans, some of whom were beginning to believe that Italy was strong. Having discussed the proposal, broached to Bérenger, of allowing Germany to expand at Poland's expense (which Cerruti considered was Germany's real aim), Mussolini himself put forward a plan for the economic division of South-East Europe: Germany should be allowed to build factories for heavy industry and chemicals; Italy, for textiles, medium and light industry. Later it will be seen that Ulrich von Hassell, the German ambassador, sponsored this idea.[47] In this conversation Mussolini reaffirmed one of his basic principles: 'We are able to march together with Germany on the Rhine but not the Danube.' On the question of the Brenner he was adamant. The watershed of the Alps must remain the frontier between Germany and Austria. Of great importance for future German – Italian relations was a comment which had been made some years before by von Schleicher, Hitler's immediate predecessor as Chancellor, and which later was made known to Cerruti. The Germans would rather import their arms from Italy than from Russia, for if war were to break out with Poland communications with Russia would be cut. For similar reasons Göring later turned to Italy to train pilots of the future *Luftwaffe*.[48]

But Mussolini did not depend solely on his diplomats for information and interpretation of events. Major Giuseppe Renzetti, a member of the Italian team appointed to supervise the plebiscite in Upper Silesia, became Italy's consul-general in Leipzig in 1925; he was later president of the Italian Chamber of Commerce in Berlin and head of the Fascist Party Office for Foreign Affairs. Early in 1933 he was by-passing the Italian embassy in Berlin and communicating directly with Mussolini. In a perceptive report of 23 January, on the eve of Hitler's so-called seizure of power, Renzetti claimed that a theatrical takeover, comparable with that of the 'March on Rome', was not to be expected. Later he claimed that if Hitler attempted to lead a coalition he could be persuaded to accept Mussolini's fraternal advice and shake himself free from the Nationalists in the coalition government by using the S.A.[49]

Mussolini's congratulations to Hitler on 31 January were conveyed personally by Renzetti, not by Cerruti. Hitler took advantage of the occasion and said: 'That I have reached this point can certainly be attributed to Fascism.' Hitler could not subdue his enthusiasm: 'This new revolutionary idea', he said, 'must spread over the whole of Europe and inaugurate a new era.'[50] On 3 February, elaborating on this theme to the Italian consul-general in Munich, the Fuehrer said that, whereas the need for the friendship of Britain was dictated by reason, 'for Italy my heart speaks in favour of it'.[51] Fascism was part of that covenant ordained by Providence to link the two countries. In his talk with Renzetti Hitler did not restrict himself to pious utterances. He expressed the wish to have a conversation with the Duce and he was prepared to fly to Rome, if necessary in his capacity as a private citizen. For a short time after Hitler came to power Renzetti continued to steal the limelight from the professional diplomats. He told Mussolini that objectionable party bosses such as Rosenberg should not be allowed to carry out important missions abroad,[52] and he established good relations with Göring, who had crushed the Communists in Germany and who had made it his personal aim to establish German – Italian relations on a special footing.[53]

While Mussolini might have felt flattered that Hitler wished to pay him a visit, he had to think in terms of power politics. On 6 February, in the middle of the quarrel between Italy and the Little Entente, he received the German ambassador, von Hassell, for the first time since Hitler came to power. In conveying Hitler's personal greetings Hassell quoted the words of Laetizia Bonaparte, Napoleon's mother: 'provided it lasts' – a phrase which Mussolini considered most inappropriate on the lips of an ambassador. Hassell had been sent by Chancellor Brüning in 1930 to Belgrade, in order that he should acquaint himself with the problems of Eastern Europe before taking up the more important post of ambassador to Rome which fell vacant in November 1932. He had been on friendly terms with King Alexander, and there is no evidence to suggest that he supported Hungary in her revisionist claims on Yugoslavia. The promotion of economic co-operation between Germany and Italy was his main object, and it will be seen how the German Foreign Ministry was to pour scorn on the initiatives he took.[54]

But Mussolini wanted active political, and not just economic, co-operation with Germany and he found a better ally than Hassell in Julius Gömbös of Hungary, who believed that Germany as a revisionist state could under Hitler be won over to their side in their fight against the Little Entente. In fact it was Gömbös who coined the expression 'the Axis'.[55] Early in February 1933 he sounded Hitler out on the possibility of German support for the Dollfuss regime in Austria, and he felt assured that Germany would collaborate in an economic plan for the Danubian area. News that Gömbös had made some proposal reached Paris, where it was mistakenly believed that an alliance among the revisionist powers – Italy, Germany, Austria and Hungary – had been concluded.[56] When questioned on the subject Herriot, president of the Foreign Affairs Committee of the French Chamber, did not deny the existence of such an alliance. The upshot was an indignant protest lodged in Berlin and a 'violent anti-Italian' campaign in France and Yugoslavia. It was even believed in Rome that Yugoslavia was mobilising and that there was a real threat of war.[57]

Dollfuss was also anxious, because of the threat from the Little Entente which favoured the Left, to strengthen Austria's conservative regime. On 15 February Starhemberg again visited Rome. He told Mussolini that the position of Dollfuss was precarious and that immediate action was necessary to prevent the Socialists, who were supported by the Czechs, from seizing power. Mussolini, who at this stage held Dollfuss in contempt, was prepared to support him only on condition that Austria gave a written undertaking confirming Italian sovereignty in the South Tyrol.[58] After the visit Mussolini chose his favourite weapon for discrediting his opponents. On 18 February he ordered press publication of the recent Anglo-French note to Vienna. As a result there was a widespread feeling of humiliation in Austria. The French came under heavy fire. Their offer of a loan, made earlier in the year in order to put pressure on the Austrian government, was rejected. After the Hirtenberg affair the Austrian Socialists also began to lose ground.[59]

At this stage Mussolini did not feel unduly alarmed by German policy in Austria. He fully realised that Hitler was willing to renounce German claims on the South Tyrol, and eagerly awaited the German Chancellor's reply to his démarche of 6 February. But Hitler did not show the slightest interest in the Gömbös – Mussolini plan.[60] Indeed he had strong reasons to oppose it. Before and after taking office he had told German generals that the 'psychological' and 'spiritual' rearmament of the German people should precede technical rearmament. On no account should Germany provide France with a pretext for a preventive war before her rearmament was complete.[61] Close association with Italy and Hungary had in fact given rise to the rumour that an alliance had been concluded among the trouble-makers.[62] But Hitler had not given up the idea of a personal visit to Rome. What, it must be asked, did he hope to achieve by the meeting? According to François-Poncet, Hitler wanted to receive his 'consecration' by the laying on of hands directly from his brother dictator in Rome. The visit was to take place after the Reichstag elections of 5 March. This suggests that the meeting was intended to enhance Hitler's personal prestige in Germany. Mussolini was invited to pay a return visit.[63]

Hitler most certainly intended to use the occasion to reassure Mussolini that Germany had no interest in the South Tyrol. In order to create a favourable atmosphere he did not personally show his hand on German policy in Austria but still allowed the Wilhelmstrasse (the German Foreign Ministry) a free hand. Alternative proposals were put forward by two officials, Heeren and Köpke. The former suggested that the National Socialists in Austria should receive direct financial support from the Reich; the latter, that the aim should be the formation of a Black – Brown (clerical and radical right) coalition under Dollfuss. All the senior diplomats – including Bülow, the State Secretary – were agreed that the final aim of German policy should be an *Anschluss*, achieved strictly by constitutional means so as not to precipitate a crisis with France or Italy.[64]

Events in Austria itself and in the Reich were to force the pace. On 4 March 1933, amidst a tumult, a motion was carried by a majority of one vote in the Austrian *Bundesrat* for measures against transport strikers. On the 7th, Dollfuss suspended parliamentary government.[65] The Socialists and the National Socialists, who were less hostile to one another in Austria than they were in the Reich, now joined forces and demanded a restoration of constitutional government. For a time there was speculation on whether Dollfuss would be removed and his government replaced by a Red – Brown Coalition. Meanwhile, on 5 March,after a terrorist campaign had been launched against the German Communists and Socialists, the two avowed enemies of the Nazis in Germany, the Reichstag elections were held. Hitler and his allies, the Nationalists, won a working majority. These events in Austria and Germany coincided precisely at a time when Mussolini was highly alarmed by events elsewhere.

Rumours reached Rome from Paris early in March that France, allied with Yugoslavia, intended to launch a preventive war against Italy early in April.[66] Although Mussolini certainly felt flattered by the triumph of a regime in Germany which had borrowed so much of its trappings from Fascist Italy, he realised, because of the French threat, that close fraternisation with Hitler was fraught with danger.

He was therefore forced to revise his order of priorities. He still wanted to co-ordinate his policy with Germany, but now believed that an agreement with that country should only be concluded after, not before, the establishment of a Concert of Europe, represented by the four leading powers. He also dismissed the alternative of an Italian agreement with France, on the grounds that this would rule out all prospects of accommodating German (and possibly Italian) demands for a revision of the territorial status quo. Pondering these questions, Mussolini early in March took refuge in his country retreat of Rocco del Caminate. Here he decided to give up, at least for the time being, all thought of changing the status quo in Italy's favour by forceful means. Once more Italy had to pursue the policy of 'equidistance', and co-operate with, and not choose a partner from, the three remaining European powers. The means by which he hoped to achieve this was a Four Power Pact, the terms of which will be discussed later.[67]

Italian diplomats were thoroughly alarmed by the pro-German course which they thought that Mussolini was still pursuing.[68] At a meeting with Sir John Simon, the British Foreign Secretary, on 8 March, Grandi courageously said that he was 'much discouraged by what he had learned of Mussolini's present attitude'. The Duce had used indications of Anglo-French collaboration as an argument 'for the decision to promote closer contact between the Fascist and Nazi regimes'. Grandi had done his 'utmost to disabuse Signor Mussolini's mind of these suspicions' and had warned him that there had recently been an adverse change of British opinion towards Germany. In Grandi's personal view, 'the pursuit of Italian – German co-operation would in the long run have results highly unfavourable to Italy. It would involve the acceptance of the *Anschluss*, which hitherto had not been regarded as favourable to Italian interests.' Grandi said that Mussolini had 'no qualms' about the new orientation of Italian policy. After the meeting Grandi telegraphed Rome, stating that Simon had warned him that the British government, in agreement with the United States, had no alternative but to oppose revisionist plans achieved through violence. He added that, even if the aim of close Italian – German co-operation were confined to political revisionism, collaboration between Italy and Britain would become very difficult. Simon is reported to have said: 'We have the impression that Italy has gone over to the other side of the barricades.' These words might have been put into Simon's mouth deliberately by Grandi himself, who did all in his power to deter Mussolini from dangerous acts.[69]

Receipt of Grandi's telegram had repercussions in Rome. According to the French, it was read to a meeting of the Fascist Grand Council held on 9–10 March, where all present agreed that the pro-German trend in Mussolini's policy should be abandoned. Mussolini's plan for a Four Power Pact was discussed. By chance, it corresponded approximately with the ideas of Ramsay MacDonald, who later in the month put forward a plan of his own for general disarmament. Mussolini argued that if Britain could be persuaded to restrain France, Italy would restrain Germany. Both powers would act within a Four Power Directorate of Europe.[70]

Mussolini first sounded out the German government on its reactions to the plan. On 14 March, on instructions from the Duce, Cerruti, the Italian ambassador in Berlin, met Neurath. He first described the double threat of a preventive war, launched by France and Poland against Germany, and France and Yugoslavia against Italy. He also said that the prospective visit by Hitler to Rome could take place only after agreement to the Four Power Pact had been reached, because of the probable excitement it would cause in France and Britain. The independence of Austria, which was still supposed to be threatened by the Little Entente, could best be maintained by keeping the Dollfuss government at the helm with the help of the *Heimwehr*. Dollfuss's fall would probably bring a Black – Red government to power. Although the question of an *Anschluss* was not yet acute, Italy could in no circumstances tolerate it. Cerruti also submitted the draft of the Four Power Pact to the German government.[71]

The tedious negotiations and amendments to the text of the Four Power Pact have been fully discussed by K. H. Jarausch.[72] Stated briefly, the French objected that in article 1 no reference had been made to the League or the Treaty of Locarno but merely to the Kellogg Pact. The Germans proposed that treaty revision should be considered in consultation between the Four Powers themselves and not, as stated in article II, 'in accordance with' the Covenant of the League. The British proposed that, instead of making provision for failure of the Disarmament Conference (article III), the signatories should regard the MacDonald Plan as a satisfactory basis for future negotiations. They also succeeded in deleting article IV by which the signatories would pursue a concerted policy, not only in Europe, but on the future of colonies overseas.

The most serious objections of all came from Poland and the Little Entente states, who contended that the operation of the Pact would put the small powers at the mercy of the great; the latter, posing as champions of the League, and in their capacity of permanent members of the Council, could fend for themselves. On 13 April Mussolini published a scathing counter-attack against what he regarded as parvenu states who, having climbed on top of a billiard table to increase their stature, posed as the Fifth Power of Europe. But he told Aloisi a few days later: 'I realise that I was wrong to write this article against the Little Entente but I composed it in March . . .'. Reversing his earlier policy, he now wished to reconcile Hungary and Yugoslavia and not take advantage of the quarrel between them. This change in policy was all the more important in that, should an *Anschluss* prove impossible to prevent, it would be necessary for Italy to organise a second line of defence based on Italy, Yugoslavia and Hungary.[73] Mussolini, far from thinking of revisionism in central Europe, was now allowing Italy to drift towards the status quo powers. His reasons for continuing to do so were due to initiatives Hitler himself had taken.

After the Reichstag elections of 5 March 1933 Hitler could switch his attention from his opponents on the Left to those on the Right. His attack on the government of Dollfuss, as will be seen, affected Italy directly. But the conflicts in which Hitler had involved the Nazi regime (the attacks on the Roman Catholic Church, as well as the economic boycott proclaimed against the Jews on 28 March) went down extremely badly in Italy. On 31 March, Cerruti, whose wife was Jewish, met Hitler, who politely informed him that, although he held the Duce as a statesman in the highest esteem, Mussolini 'understood nothing about the Jewish problem'.[74] Hitler failed to realise that Mussolini would champion the cause of the Jews. After the German boycott against the Jews came into force on 1 April, Mussolini told Dr C. Weizmann, president of the World Jewish Congress, that he had every sympathy for a plan for settling German Jews in Palestine. As a result many Jewish emigrants either settled in Italy or passed through Italian territory on their way to other countries including Palestine. R. De Felice maintains that, both for humanitarian reasons and for those of political expediency, the Duce deliberately chose to act as the protector of the Jews in retaliation against Germany after Hitler personally decided to take up the cause of the Austrian Nazis.[75]

In March 1933 a marked change in Mussolini's policy is perceptible. Early in the month he feared that noisy revisionism might provoke France into launching a preventive war: later he perceived that the danger came from Germany. Italy could achieve optimum security in Europe and also leave the way open to revisionism only if she could organise an instrument for crisis management: the Four Power Pact.

3 Strained Relations with Germany over Austria, 1933

It has been seen that in February 1933 the Wilhelmstrasse had (somewhat confusedly) defined future Germany policy in Austria without undue interference from Hitler; there was as yet no radical divergence of views between the attitudes of the party and those of state officials. Hitler hoped that events in Austria would follow a parallel course with those in Germany, with the Austrian Nazis in time coming to power on their own resources. Dollfuss was especially worried by the electoral successes scored by the Nazis in Bavaria, which had cleared the way for the *Gleichschaltung* (fusion) of Bavaria with the Reich. He had reason to be worried. There were strong similarities in culture and dialect between the Bavarians and the Austrians.

After the Four Power Pact had been submitted to the German government on 14 March there was a change of emphasis in its policy towards Austria. Whereas the Wilhelmstrasse had hitherto merely demanded that new elections should be held in Austria, giving the Nazis the place they deserved in the Austrian government, Hitler went a stage further. He now openly demanded that Dollfuss himself should be removed.[1] To Aloisi, this meant that Austria 'would find herself directly under German influence'; after a short lapse of time the *Anschluss* would be accomplished. Suvich correctly commented that this would be 'worse than defeat'.[2] Hitler, in undermining Dollfuss's position, found his popular spokesman in Hans Frank, the Bavarian commissioner of justice and his private solicitor. In a broadcast from Munich Radio on 18 March, Frank accused the Austrian authorities of depriving the Nazis of their civic liberties. The upshot was a protest delivered by the Austrian chargé d'affaires, in support of which Cerruti met Köpke, the diplomat responsible for Austrian affairs, on 23 March. Cerruti said that the overthrow of Dollfuss would mean 'falling from the gutter into the rain'. He also described, in some detail, an earlier conversation with Hitler, in which the Fuehrer had told him that he did not at present want an *Anschluss* as this would mean the strengthening of the Catholic Centre Party in Germany which had not yet been dissolved. On Mussolini's instructions Cerruti truculently replied that it was 'not wise to quarrel with the Church' and that, if Hitler came to Rome, he would also have 'to pay his respects to the Pope'.[3]

Shortly after the meeting Paolo Cortese, head of the Croat Department in the Palazzo Chigi, returned from Austria. He described to Suvich and Aloisi the 'vigorous campaign' launched by the Nazis. Although Dollfuss was putting up stout resistance, he was not co-operating adequately on a political level with the *Heimwehr* which would have to be strengthened and engage in more active propaganda. 'For us', noted Aloisi, 'the capital problem is the *Anschluss*'; it would prove 'fatal for Italy in central Europe'. Mussolini himself now took a firmer line and even instructed Preziosi, the Italian minister in Vienna, that if the worst came to the worst Italy herself would favour new elections in Austria and adopt a waiting attitude to see what was to be gained from a Red – Black coalition which he so thoroughly disliked.[4]

While Hitler himself had to give up the proposal for a visit to Rome, he still cherished the idea of establishing personal links with the Duce. On 11 April, at a most inopportune time, Papen (the German Vice-Chancellor, who was negotiating a Concordat with the Vatican) and Göring (who regarded himself as Hitler's spokesman for Italy) arrived in Rome to discuss the numerous proposals and counter-proposals for a Four Power Pact. Göring, 'by his violent manner', created the immediate impression of being much less malleable than his suave colleague Papen, to whom he spoke 'brusquely and appeared to give orders'. Also present were Prince Philip of Hesse and his wife. Altogether the visit was an abysmal failure. Aloisi was disappointed to learn that Mussolini 'gave way' to Göring who, against the advice of Hassell, raised the delicate question of an *Anschluss*. According to a contemporary observer, Göring tactlessly lectured his host, but Mussolini did not understand what was being said because the table between them was six metres broad and bedecked with roses.[5]

It is not known for certain what Mussolini told Dollfuss, who was also in Rome that Easter. He no longer toyed with the idea of a Red – Black coalition, but insisted that Dollfuss must fight against the Socialists, 'otherwise he is lost'. Later Mussolini told Aloisi that if Dollfuss 'declares openly that he will adopt the Fascist regime we would more readily give him aid. For it is natural that not only the Italian government, but our regime itself, should assist him.' However, a change of emphasis in Mussolini's thinking is already evident. Previously he had stressed that Dollfuss might have to be propped up in order to prevent Austria from drifting into the camp of the Little Entente. Now he feared that she would be swallowed up by Germany. But in the changed circumstances he still clung obdurately to the view that Dollfuss must strike first at the Socialists, so as to cut the ground from under the feet of the National Socialists.[6]

Nothing was more galling to Austrian national pride than Mussolini's tutelage. Dollfuss looked for alternatives, and was under strong pressure from his associates and friends to do so. In a letter of 4 May 1933, Ernst Winter – a devout Catholic and both a friend and critic of Dollfuss – implored Mussolini to change his Austrian policy. The government of Vienna could, according to Winter, base its policy on two social groups: the peasants in the Alps, whose gaze was fixed on Hungary; and the urban and industrial masses of Vienna, who looked towards France and the Little Entente. After the dissolution of parliament in March 1933 internal affairs in Austria had got out of control. The future direction of Austrian policy now depended on the stand Italy would take. She could not, Winter stressed, simultaneously establish a Fascist regime in Austria and also prevent an *Anschluss*, for the line of demarcation between the country's National Socialists and Fascists was dangerously thin. Austria's salvation depended on federalism, democracy and socialism. 'You must thus decide, Your Excellency,' Winter concluded, 'whether you want to see the Swastika hoisted over the Brenner or Democracy established in Austria.'[7] Winter could not have written more courageously, and his analysis of the political groupings was penetrating and lucid. One possible future development, however, he overlooked: a switch of allegiance on the part of the urban population in Vienna from the Social Democrats to the National Socialists.

Neither Mussolini nor Dollfuss heeded Winter's advice. Dollfuss was also under pressure from the Vatican, for by March 1933 the Pope had come to the conclusion that Hitler's Germany would act as a bulwark against Communism, and hence he now sought a direct deal with the Reich.[8] While in Rome, Dollfuss sounded out Papen on the feasibility of his visiting Hitler and of a direct agreement with the Reich. Hitler, on learning of the proposal, made no bones about it: in no circumstances would he receive Dollfuss. The Austrian leader instead negotiated with Habicht, Inspector of the Austrian Nazi Party, who had no objection to a provisional coalition between the Christian Socialists and Nazis pending new elections. But Habicht made one condition which Dollfuss was bound to reject: the *Heimwehr* and the *Landschutz* (a more liberal para-military group) had both to be excluded from the government.[9]

After the breakdown in these negotiations Habicht concluded a formal alliance with Pfrimer (head of the *Heimwehr* in Styria and an opponent of Starhemberg) who recognised Hitler as 'head of the German nation'. He also attracted most dissident groups in the 'National opposition'. But the Austrian Nazis were still too weak to achieve, on their own, the downfall of Dollfuss. They needed help from the Reich. In his capacity as leader of the Nazi Party and not as Reich Chancellor, and without consulting the Wilhelmstrasse, Hitler sent Frank and Kerl (the Prussian Minister of Justice) on a propaganda mission to Austria. At a meeting in Graz on 14 May, at which he claimed to be acting as the official representative of Hitler, Frank ridiculed Dollfuss as a '*Millimetternich*' (mini-Metternich). The next day, after a protest lodged by Tauschitz, Austrian minister in Berlin, against this 'vile insult' and after an acrimonious passage of words between Cerruti and Hitler, Frank and Kerl were expelled from the country. The Austrian protest was regarded as justified by officials in the Wilhelmstrasse.[10]

Later in May Hitler took up a new line of attack. First, in order to secure Nazi leaders in Austria against arrest or expulsion, he proposed appointing Habicht and Cors (chief of the Nazis in Vienna) as press attachés at the German legation; in this capacity they would enjoy diplomatic immunity. Second, he aimed a blow at the Austrian economy, which was largely dependent on tourism. At a cabinet meeting of 26 May, Hitler declared that visas would be issued to German citizens, intending to visit Austria, only on payment of 1000 Reichmarks. 'This measure', he said, 'will presumably lead to the collapse of the Dollfuss government' and to new elections. The result would, in effect, be Austria's *Gleichschaltung* (fusion) with Germany, which would obviate the need for an actual *Anschluss* (Union). Italy's position over the *Anschluss* question was described as 'perfectly understandable'. Her consent would have to be 'paid for with concessions in other areas'. Hitler did not indicate where these areas lay.[11]

There was much wishful thinking here on Hitler's part. Economic sanctions did not lead to the fall of Dollfuss but, if anything, rendered it easier for him to rally patriotic opinion behind him to combat acts of terrorism. On 12 May Dollfuss, who had refused to accept Habicht as a member of the German legation, now arrested him along with about eighty other prominent Nazis.[12] Hitler in retaliation expelled Wasserback, the Austrian press attaché in Berlin, whereupon Habicht and his

associates were released and took refuge in Munich. On 19 June
Dollfuss banned the Nazi Party and its affiliated organisations. The
same day Hitler informed the Wilhelmstrasse that Habicht alone was to
be his spokesman for all questions concerning Austria. With the
Austrian Nazi leaders now on German soil, Hitler could, admittedly,
exert greater control over them; but he could no longer pretend that
they were acting legally. The attacks made on Dollfuss from Munich
radio constituted a violation of recent international agreements.[13]
Propaganda leaflets were also dropped by German aircraft flying over
Austrian territory. The most serious threat of all was constituted by the
Austrian Legion, made up of Nazi refugees from Austria, which, under
the leadership of Reschny, a senior S.A. officer, was concentrated in
camps, the foremost of which was established at Lechfeld near the
Austrian frontier, from which incursions could be made into Austrian
territory.[14]

By the second half of June 1933 the crisis over Austria could no longer be
regarded as a domestic quarrel between political parties in two
countries which were united by language and culture. It was now an
issue which was bound to attract the notice and even the intervention of
the great powers. Dollfuss attended in person the World Economic
Conference which opened in London on 12 June 1933. Here he found a
ready-made platform from which to voice his country's grievances. His
quotation from Schiller: 'The best man cannot live in peace if an evil
neighbour will not let him', was greeted with 'tumultuous applause'.
Neurath, who also attended the conference and who was booed by the
crowd, complained bitterly to Hitler and Hindenburg about German
policy in Austria. The French, he wrote, were following the crisis closely
and might find in it a pretext for intervention even of a military kind.[15]
Mussolini certainly was thinking in terms of a military solution, and
early in June tried to persuade Dollfuss to conclude a military
convention with Italy. But Dollfuss realised that Mussolini still
regarded the Socialists, rather than the Nazis, as the real threat to
Austria and thus rejected the offer. The attitude of the two Western
powers had also to be considered. The British disliked the role Mussolini
assumed as 'honest broker', entailing use of his direct influence over
Hitler instead of acting collectively under the League. There was a
greater danger. On 11 June Suvich, in a private capacity, told Graham,
British ambassador in Rome, that his government would regard a
violent incursion by Nazi formations very seriously and would be likely

to send Italian troops to the Austrian frontier as a deterrent. The Yugoslav and Czech governments would probably take separate action. The Italian government, which could not openly co-operate with the states of the Little Entente, with whom it had quarrelled, was therefore unwilling to tie its hands by agreeing to bring the matter before the League. Suvich certainly did not misrepresent the Duce's intentions.[16] On 19 June Mussolini asked Aloisi to enquire from the Italian consulates whether armed encounters had actually taken place between groups of Nazis and those supporting the Austrian government. If this were so, 'we also will despatch forces to the frontier' and 'hurl ourselves against the Nazis with whom it is difficult to co-operate even if one is allied to them'. Hitler's actions were, according to Mussolini, 'none other than those of an elephant in a china shop'.[17]

The last thing that the British government wanted was, in Simon's view, the countering of a *Putsch* by a *Putsch*. It was precisely in order to prevent such a situation from arising that the League was constituted. But Simon, and more especially Vansittart, the permanent head of the Foreign Office, was no great lover of the League, an institution which was regarded as the sick man of Europe. There was another more recent international instrument for crisis management which could be used to constrain Germany: the Four Power Pact.[18]

When Mussolini first submitted his draft of the Four Power Pact to Britain, France and Germany, he laid great stress to the Germans on the absolute necessity of getting through the ensuing three months without a conflict, and of preventing France from launching a preventive war. The kinship between the two regimes and their leaders was such as to place Italian–German relations on a special footing; by April 1933 Germany had somehow to be rescued from her isolation or else she would become more dangerous as a friend than as an enemy. On 20 April Mussolini told Hassell that 'the conclusion of the Four Power Pact would be for Germany the best counterblow that could be dealt to anti-German propaganda throughout the world'. But he warned him that the integrity of Austria must remain untouched. The deletion from the draft, on the insistence of the British, of article IV of the Four Power Pact, which provided for consultation between the signatories on non-European and colonial problems, caused misgivings in Berlin.[19] Hence Mussolini agreed to a 'gentlemen's agreement' with Germany by which neither party would negotiate with Britain or France on the future of colonies without mutual consultation. This was to prove important later because of Ethiopia.[20] French amendments to the original draft were more radical than those of the British. Mussolini wanted the League to be made dependent on the Pact; the French wanted the Pact to be dependent on the League. On most points the French got their way.[21] Hitler was most reluctant to sign the revised agreement submitted to him: it meant relying too much on Italian goodwill which, because of the quarrel over Austria, was far from dependable. Still, the Pact was better than complete ostracism. In his famous peace speech of 17 May 1933, he 'welcomed' on behalf of the German government the 'far-sighted and reasonable plan' of the head of the Italian government.[22]

On 7 June, after much quibbling over the meaning of article III, pertaining to the principle of equality of rights, and after a direct appeal from Mussolini to Hitler, the Four Power Pact was initialled.[23] Subsequently there was an exchange of notes between France and the governments of the Little Entente and Poland, to the effect that the provision for treaty-revision would in no way violate the rights of the smaller powers. Mussolini also assured the Little Entente powers that he had no intention of restoring the Habsburgs in Austria. More important was an Italian proposal for bringing Austria and Hungary under Italy's patronage for political and economic co-operation. The main purpose of this was to prevent Hungary from reaching a separate agreement with Germany.[24] Mussolini was anxious that the Pact should be formally signed as soon as possible and that it should come immediately into force. The problems which the World Economic and Disarmament Conferences had failed to solve could, he claimed, be subsequently dealt with at meetings, held regularly, of representatives of the Four Powers. He also did all in his power to persuade Hitler that Germany would 'win an immense moral victory' if she concluded a Concordat with the Vatican. After some delay from the German side, the Four Power Pact was signed in Rome on 15 July 1933; and Germany's Concordat was signed a few days later. Hitler evidently believed that the Concordat would serve as proof to the Vatican that the Reich was not anti-Christian (and thus make things easier for him in Austria), and that he could go ahead with anti-Jewish propaganda.[25]

On 15 July 1933 Mussolini had at last achieved a major diplomatic victory. Italy had placed herself at the head of a new Concert of Europe, the aim of which was the revision of the 1919 peace settlement in accordance with the principles of the League. But the Pact had been signed at a time of crisis, and only the future could tell whether it would prove workable before its ratification. Its actual application soon came up for consideration.

On 29 June Dollfuss, through Rost van Tönningen (a Dutch financial expert), made to London the request that, in the event of a sudden threat to the independence of Austria, the matter should be submitted to the League. Simon welcomed the idea and made an approach to Paris and Rome. The Italian reply was negative.[26] Mussolini evidently did not wish to see a dangerous precedent established, for if the Covenant could be invoked against Germany over Austria, could it not also be invoked by Yugoslavia or Ethiopia against Italy? Besides, Dollfuss did not want to be too dependent on Italy; and on 25 July, against Mussolini's advice, he requested the British government to use its direct influence in Berlin to restrain Germany. With Simon on sick-leave, Vansittart was in charge of the Foreign Office. In instructions to the British embassies in Paris and Rome he suggested that resort to article XI of the League might not after all be necessary. As an alternative, the governments of France, Italy and the United Kingdom could, in accordance with the Four Power Pact, call the attention of the German government to its violations of Austrian integrity and urge it 'to put an end without further delay to all further activities against the Austrian government'.[27]

A few days later Cerruti, on instructions from Mussolini, discussed this British note with Bülow. He said that 'Mussolini wished to avoid putting into effect the English proposal and asked us urgently to consider whether and how the ground could be cut from under the Austrian protest'. Mussolini indicated politely that Hitler should call a halt to further subversion, otherwise Italy would have no choice but to assent to the British proposal. Although Bülow pretended that there was no substance to the Austrian complaints, he undertook to contact Neurath, and if possible Hitler, on the matter. Already both Neurath and Papen had tried to persuade Hitler to modify his Austrian policy. But on 5 August he 'categorically rejected any interference by Mussolini'. Bülow persisted in thinking that something should be done. With difficulty he persuaded Hitler that greater moderation should be shown in German propaganda and that terroristic acts should be forbidden; 'the economic struggle', however, should be continued in all severity. Hitler also refused to give a written undertaking to abstain from an *Anschluss*. On 5 August the gist of Hitler's orders to party agencies was passed on to Cerruti.[28]

Mussolini's success in persuading Hitler to restrain his party extremists was only temporary. On 9 August Habicht again made a hostile broadcast against the Austrian government. The next day Cerruti told Heeren at the German Foreign Ministry that the Duce, on learning the news, was 'quite unusually excited'. Germany had broken her promises, and if Britain and France were now to make a joint démarche, Italy would find it extremely difficult to dissociate herself from it. Hitler's policy in Austria was a threat to the peace of Europe. But Mussolini had no wish at this stage to apply the principles of the Four Power Pact against Germany: it would thereby defeat its own ends and become a Three Power Pact. Besides, it had not yet been ratified, and if it were to be used against Germany, Hitler could simply declare it to be null and void. On 14 August Neurath and Hitler discussed the situation created by Habicht's broadcast. Hitler was most 'indignant over the manner of Mussolini's intervention and declared that he would not stand for that sort of tutelage'. Cerruti was informed that the speech in no way violated the promises given and that the Reich Chancellor rejected the idea of a compromise with the Dollfuss government.[29]

Later in the month it was rumoured in Vienna that the Austrian Legion, which now numbered approximately 6000, was preparing for a *Putsch* early in September – but, if the worst came to the worst, Austria could count on military aid from Italy. This rumour caused more consternation in London than in Berlin. Mussolini still believed that Italy could pour oil on the troubled waters. At all costs he wished to prevent Dollfuss from turning to Italy's opponents in the Little Entente by bringing the question of Austria before the Assembly of the League at its regular meeting in September. As an alternative to Austrian co-operation with the Little Entente, an Italian–Hungarian agreement was concluded late in July.[30] While the two countries agreed to co-operate to prevent an *Anschluss*, they would also try to improve their relations with Germany. Mussolini could now exert greater leverage over Dollfuss, whose country could no longer stand up to the German threat on its own resources. On 19–20 August Dollfuss met Mussolini at Riccione. He had no choice but to agree to appoint Fascists to cabinet posts and to dismiss the remaining liberal members. In return Mussolini agreed to a military convention. Subsequently, he denied to the British that there was any substance to rumours that armed aid had been promised to Dollfuss.[31]

After Dollfuss's visit to Riccione, Habicht informed Bülow that he had learnt from a 'reliable source' that a military convention was about to be concluded between Austria and Italy. In these circumstances

Hitler and Habicht were under great pressure from the Wilhelmstrasse to allay Mussolini's fears.[32] After a cabinet meeting on 12 September, at a time when propaganda attacks had died down, Hitler on his own initiative told Neurath that the Austrian Legion must be moved from its camp at Lechfeld and quartered elsewhere. The immediate danger of rupture between Germany and Italy over Austria had thus passed. But there was still much bitterness in Italy. According to Hassell, National Socialism was no longer regarded as the 'legitimate daughter or sister' revolution of Fascism but 'something different and Germanic'. For several months tension over Austria posed no major international problem. The way was open for Mussolini to promote the Four Power Pact to solve an even more dangerous issue, that of disarmament.[33]

4 Mussolini and Disarmament, 1933

THE crisis over Austria in 1933 was sufficiently serious to persuade Mussolini that the kinship between Italian Fascism and German National Socialism was not strong enough to enable the two countries to regard each other as bound by destiny to pursue a parallel foreign policy. It was only later that this proved possible. Against her will, Italy had no choice in a last analysis but to co-operate with Britain and France over Austria. But there was a simultaneous issue on which Italy could mediate between Germany and France and thus act as a leading European power in her own right.

German action over Austria had made the French and British more intransigent in regard to the practical realisation of the principle of equality of rights which had, within limits, been accorded to Germany by the MacDonald Plan of 16 March 1933. Hitler had accepted the plan as a basis for negotiation after his famous peace speech of 17 May.[1] At the end of the first session of the Disarmament Conference, on 9 June 1933, the French started bilateral negotiations in preparation of the second session, due to meet in the second half of September. On 19 June they submitted an amended draft convention to Arthur Henderson, chairman of the conference. The new convention was to cover two periods of four years, instead of one period of five as envisaged in the MacDonald Plan. In the first period no rearmament of Germany was to be allowed, and provision was made for stricter supervision of the German military establishment. Disarmament of other nations would only start in the second period provided that Germany had first fulfilled her obligations.

While the British, alarmed by internal developments in Germany, sympathised with the French, Mussolini still thought he could restrain Germany in Austria by taking an intermediary position. Moreover, Italy herself was still, in 1933, considered to be a relatively well-armed power, partly because of her stock of First World War weapons, partly because she possessed modern aircraft. It was not in her interests, despite French attempts to win her over to their side, to conclude a convention that would prohibit the kinds of weaponry her own economy was capable of producing. Also, Mussolini had demanded, and continued to seek, parity with the French at sea.[2] He still overestimated the strength of France and underestimated that of Germany. Early in September 1933 he told Aloisi: 'I do not understand why France, with 84 milliards of gold, with formidable defences in the East and colonies . . . trembles before Germany. There are only two ways of solving the problem of German rearmament: a preventive war, or control.' He went on to say: 'France must remember that at this moment I alone am pursuing an anti-German policy.'[3] In the negotiations on the French plan, Mussolini told Arthur Henderson that he was taking a realistic view in believing that it would be rejected by Germany—as in fact it was.

On 19 July Germany put forward new proposals of her own, demanding 'defensive' weapons. The *Reichswehr* was to be transformed from a force of 100,000 men, serving for a long period, to 200,000 men on short-period service. At the end of July Aloisi considered the German proposals to be sufficiently moderate to be used as a basis, first for negotiations between Italy and France, and later between the Four European great powers.[4] Because of the crisis over Austria, Mussolini told Hassell on 8 August that he did not believe that the time had come for a conference of the Four Powers, which in any case needed much preparation. Nevertheless he promised 'to use quite plain language' with France in commending the German proposals.[5] Although Hitler had just quarrelled with Mussolini over Austria, he yet dreaded nothing more than a united anti-German front.

On 4 September the German embassy in Rome was asked again to take up the idea of Italian mediation. 'We are exceedingly appreciative', wrote Bülow, 'of the Italian efforts to bring about a German—French agreement and would like to be informed about the present state of the matter' before the Disarmament Conference reconvened at Geneva. There were already indications of what Hitler would do if there was a complete collapse of the disarmament negotiation.[6] At a cabinet meeting on 12 September, Neurath declared that in such an event Germany would leave the League of Nations. Neurath, who frequently spoke bitterly about Italy, added that the Italian government was also 'antagonistic' to the League but used it to promote 'its own goals', by which he most certainly meant the Four Power Pact. Whatever else was to be said in its favour, the Pact would have had the effect of binding Germany to the League.[7]

Mussolini realised that strong opposition was also to be expected from the French to the German proposals. He therefore put forward a plan of his own. Germany was to be allowed 'sample' weapons and very restricted rearmament in stages. The Italian plan was submitted to the other three powers on 16 September on the eve of a meeting to be held in Paris between British and French ministers, who were to be joined by Norman Davis, representing the United States.[8] During a meeting between British and French ministers on 22 September there was much discussion on what Mussolini meant by 'defensive weapons'. Paul-Boncour understood that they were to be those allowed to Germany under the Treaty of Versailles, plus perhaps light tanks. There thus seemed to be 'an approximation of views' held by the Italians and French, and a good prospect of the Four Power Pact's bearing fruit. Still, Mussolini was required to define his position more explicitly before the French would negotiate on his plan. At a further meeting on 22 September Mussolini's reply was discussed at length. It was considered 'extremely cautious' and 'somewhat obscure'. The Italians also inconspicuously raised the matter of naval parity with France and invited the representatives of the Four Power Pact to a meeting at Stresa. The French were anxious that future meetings on disarmament should be held at Geneva.

During this further meeting Daladier, the French Premier, dramatically produced a dossier of details, evidently obtained from the Soviet Union, of actual German rearmament in violation of the Treaty of Versailles, and he invited the British to state whether they would be prepared to support France and impose sanctions on Germany. Simon, backed by Baldwin (at this time Lord President of the Council), replied that Britain would assume no new commitments on the continent and that public opinion at home would not tolerate sanctions. But France had to be given some satisfaction. The British declared that they would back France in making it clear that the second period, as provided for in the French plan, should come into force only if the first trial period were observed.[9]

During these negotiations Mussolini had an exceptionally strong hand, for his support was keenly sought by France and Germany alike. On 23 September the French went a long way towards accepting the Italian compromise. They were now willing to allow Germany, in the second period, prototypes of arms possessed by other powers. When approached on this concession, the Italians did not envisage such a clear-cut division between the two periods as the French, and they were even prepared to allow Germany aircraft during the first probational period.[10] (Italy was, indeed, soon to export aircraft to Germany.) Mussolini had thus failed to win French acceptance of his compromise plan.

Nor was he to make much headway with Germany. Hitler had not replied to the Italian proposal of 16 September; both he and Blomberg, the Defence Minister, considered that it fell short of Germany's needs. Neurath also suspected that Italy was 'acting as a go-between' and therefore refusing to commit herself. Bülow, on the other hand, correctly sensed that the French (and probably the British) would refuse to negotiate at Stresa, and he favoured acceptance of Mussolini's invitation: failure to negotiate could thus be blamed on the French and the British. Hitler at the end of September still believed that Germany would have to conclude a convention 'even if it did not fulfil all German wishes'.[11] On 4 October he had every reason to change his attitude. He learned that the British would probably put forward their own plan, one essentially dictated by the French. Both he and Blomberg agreed that 'we must not run the risk of negotiating at all on a new draft that was unacceptable to us. Otherwise we would find that the others would agree on this plan and force it on us to accept it. As in the case of the Rome [Four Power] Pact the Italians would play the part of "biased mediator . . .". A breakdown on the conference as a result of our rejection of supervision must be avoided.' It was thus time to demand by ultimatum the disarmament of others and to declare that Germany would leave the conference as well as the League of Nations.[12]

Mussolini was having a difficult time in playing the role of 'honest broker'. Before any reply had been received from Berlin, he made a further fruitless attempt at mediation. On 11 October he told Sir Ronald Graham, the British ambassador, that German policy was at the moment 'in the hands of two men, Hitler and Göring', one a 'dreamer', the other an 'ex-inmate of a lunatic asylum, neither of them conspicuous for reason or logic'. Germany would rearm in any case, and at a given time France would apply sanctions. Germany could be kept in the Disarmament Conference only if she were allowed samples of weapons, possibly a few anti-aircraft guns and observation planes. Graham 'emphasised the very strong opposition in England and France to this idea'. The next day Cerruti presented the new Italian plan to Hitler.[13]

Hitler saw in Mussolini's new plan a chance of detaching Italy from France and Britain. On 13 October he instructed Hassell to inform

Mussolini at once that Germany was on the point of leaving the Disarmament Conference. The Duce showed neither surprise nor annoyance on receiving this news, and he strongly recommended that Hitler in his speech, which was to be made in the evening of 14 October, should 'indicate the possibility of negotiating on the basis of the Four Power Pact'. Reference to the Pact was, in Hassell's opinion, 'absolutely necessary for further co-operation with Italy'. Cerruti, after a meeting with Hitler, reported that he was enraged with France, claiming that the huge defences established by the French served to immobilise Germany and enable them to prepare for war against Italy and Britain. Aloisi regarded Hitler's remarks as so wildly untrue that he put three exclamation marks at the end of the sentence. The interview, he claimed, did not mark a single step forward in the question.[14]

Hitler had already taken his decision. At a cabinet meeting on 13 October he admitted that the 'immediate future would bring with it increased political activity by Italy. Italy would want to mediate, since she had no interest in Germany's destruction. . . .' If Germany 'were condemned to complete impotence, that would be the end of Italy's role in Europe'. While Mussolini's proposal was acceptable to Germany, it could not be discussed at Geneva, where Italy would use it to promote the Four Power Pact. Although receiving Hassell's telegram from Rome early on the 14th, Hitler made no reference to the Four Power Pact in his speech later that day, announcing Germany's intention of leaving the Disarmament Conference. He most certainly reasoned that, if the Pact were adopted, Italy would be jockeyed into supporting France and Britain.[15]

By mid-October 1933, Mussolini still regarded Italy as the mediator between Germany and the Western powers, and thus the leading partner of an emerging Four Power Directorate of Europe. He had achieved relative success in restraining Hitler in Austria; and, while he had won the favour of Germany for his compromise stand on disarmament, he remained on speaking terms with the French. If Hitler were in future to follow his advice, Mussolini's prestige would be enhanced both inside Italy and abroad. If, on the other hand, Hitler were to ignore him, Italy's status as a power factor in Europe would be reduced to such an insignificant level that he would have no option but to seek glory for the Fascist regime in Africa – a continent which he had never neglected.

5 Disenchantment in Europe, October 1933–March 1934

IMMEDIATELY after Mussolini had learned from Hassell on 14 October 1933 that Germany had left the Disarmament Conference and would in all probability act in future within the framework of the Four Power Pact, he was elated and took a swim. One hour later it was announced in Berlin that Hitler had also decided that Germany would leave the League of Nations. This announcement was of capital importance. Mussolini had been given only a partial pre-notification of his brother dictator's intentions, and that only at the very last moment. This was to be a constant cause of complaint in future years. According to Hassell, Mussolini must have gained the impression of deliberate disloyalty on the part of Berlin. For days on end he sulked.[1] On 16 October he exclaimed to Graham, who was about to leave Rome: 'These dirty Germans, by a single stroke, have broken all the panes of glass, those of the Disarmament Conference, the League of Nations and the Four Power Pact. I am no longer in the humour to demean myself and pick up the bits and pieces. Should France, England, the United States and Germany again wish to discuss the matter of disarmament, Italy will join them. But for my part I will take no initiative. It can be seen that the lines between Germany and Italy, far from meeting, are diverging.'[2]

For a time Aloisi hoped that, in spite of Germany's departure from the League, the Four Power Pact would remain an instrument by which Italy could mediate among the other great powers.[3] He was soon to be disillusioned. The French, with promptings from the Little Entente and Poland, had in any case not ratified the Pact. With those clauses which made it dependent on the League emptied of meaning, the basis for further negotiations had been destroyed. Hitler, who in any case disliked the Pact, could now lay the blame squarely on the French for its failure to come into force.

No one was more aware of the deterioration in German–Italian relations than Ulrich von Hassell, German ambassador in Rome.[4] Hassell had his own ideas on how good relations with Italy should be established. He realised correctly that Mussolini could only be won over to the idea of an ultimate *Anschluss*, achieved by peaceful means, if Italy felt immune from the threat either of a German drive towards the Mediterranean or of economic control over the states of South-East Europe. Germany should thus not monopolise, but share with Italy, the markets of these states; the field could be divided, as suggested by Mussolini, in accordance with different branches of industry. Although Hassell's economic proposal was considered feasible by Ritter, head of the Economic section of the Wilhelmstrasse, it was never officially taken up. On 13 June 1933 Hassell had also proposed a 'gentlemen's agreement' between Germany and Italy. Its terms were to be broader than the agreement of 19 April, which obliged the two parties to keep each other informed if negotiations took place on the redistribution of colonial territory. It was now proposed that there should be no negotiations on any subject with a third party, meaning France or Britain, without prior consultation between Italy and Germany. Hassell correctly surmised that such an agreement would greatly strengthen Germany's hand; for, though the French were constantly making overtures to Italy, they saw little hope of permanent agreement with Germany. Hassell certainly enjoyed the full confidence of Mussolini, with whom he was on good terms personally. According to members of the French embassy, Mussolini tried to use him to make the authorities of the Reich 'see reason'.[5] But he carried little influence in Berlin. Even Bülow, the hardheaded Prussian State Secretary, who on so many issues – above all over Austria – tried to act as a moderating influence on Hitler, ignored Hassell's rather long dispatches, and Neurath dismissed one of them as a 'needless sermon'.[6] Moreover, Göring's frequent surprise-visits to Rome showed little regard for Hassell's position there, and aroused his objections.

Hitler failed to realise in October 1933 that Italy's position had greatly changed since he had come to power. Come what may, Hitler thought, Italy and France would remain potential enemies. Germany could thus hold out the olive branch to France or Britain without taking Italy into account. Shortly after Germany left the League he declared that, once the matter of the Saarland had been solved, there was absolutely nothing to stand in the way of good relations with France; Germany had no designs on Alsace and Lorraine, and regarded the Treaty of Locarno as binding. He made no mention of Austria or the Brenner frontier. Although Britain had taken a far more intransigent stance on future German rearmament than had Italy, Hitler late in October submitted first to the British, and not to the Italian, government new proposals for an army of 300,000 men. No wonder that

Aloisi indignantly noted that Italy was being treated as an inferior, a matter on which Mussolini was extremely sensitive.[7]

Totally oblivious of Mussolini's sensitivity, Hitler had persuaded himself that the relations between Nazi Germany and Fascist Italy transcended national interests. For ideological reasons alone they stood on a special footing. Causes of friction could, he thought, be ironed out by personal visits and by a direct exchange of ideas. On 26 October it was learned in Rome, through interception of the telephone line to Berlin, that Hitler intended sending a personal letter to the Duce. Hassell urged the Wilhelmstrasse to send it as soon as possible, and suggested that he himself should present it personally to Mussolini. Although the letter was drawn up on 1 November, Hitler delayed sending it until a few days before the plebiscite, held in Germany on 12 November, in the knowledge that his policy would win the unanimous applause of his own people.[8]

It was open to Mussolini to use the delay in order to improve Italy's relations with France and the Little Entente. On 11 October, at a time when the Treaty of Locarno was subject to much criticism in London, he told Chambrun, the French ambassador, that Italy would honour her obligations under that treaty. 'German aggression against Calais or the Brenner would', he said, 'imperil equally the security of Italy. If you are attacked we are on your side.'[9] Mussolini had also won over the French to a plan which he announced at a meeting of the Danubian states held at Stresa on 24 September, by which the industrial products of Austria and the agricultural products of her neighbours would be given preferential treatment. The plan, if put into effect, might have bolted the door on German economic penetration in South-East Europe. There was, however, an unforeseen impediment to Italy's scheme: towards the end of 1933 a revival of sentiment in favour of a restoration of the Habsburgs manifested itself in Austria. There were fears, especially in Belgrade, that close association between Austria and Hungary might open the way to the restoration of the Dual Monarchy.[10] Moreover the *Ustaši* were still active both in Italy and, especially, in Hungary.

In other respects, however, there had been an improvement in Italian – Yugoslav relations. After Germany had left the League of Nations, the Yugoslavs feared a *Drang nach Südosten* almost as much as the Italian threat. There was now less talk in Yugoslav military circles of mobilisation to resist the entry of Italian troops into Austria, and more of collaboration with France and Italy.[11] For several months, however, Austria ceased to be a problem of acute international importance. On 10 September, at the behest of Mussolini, Dollfuss had jettisoned those members of the Austrian cabinet with liberal leanings (one of whom, Winkler, was later to join the Nazis). Yet Dollfuss resented abject dependence on Mussolini. As an alternative he put out feelers to the Austrian Nazis, inviting them to join his government in some limited capacity. The time was well chosen for such negotiations, for there had been a considerable decline in Nazi violence. Concrete results depended on whether the internal differences in both camps could be settled.[12]

On 6 November, when there were promising signs of a German – Austrian détente, and when Mussolini had recovered from the initial shock of Germany's departure from the League, Göring – again accompanied by Prince Philip of Hesse – arrived in Rome bearing Hitler's 'personal letter', awaited since 26 October. It proved to be nothing more or less than a dreary, repetitive 'pièce justificative'. On reading it Hassell noticed that no explanation was given for Hitler's failure to inform Italy in advance that Germany intended to leave the League. Göring's lame excuse – that Hitler was under the impression that Mussolini had in fact received full details – cut no ice with Hassell, who persuaded him to tell the Duce that the decision was taken at the very last moment, allowing Hitler no time to communicate with the Italian government. Göring insisted that he should meet Mussolini unaccompanied by Suvich who, as a native of Trieste, mistrusted the Germans and did not conceal his pro-League, pro-French sentiments. With some tact and skill on Hassell's part, this request was granted. Göring told Mussolini that Cerruti, who had often spoken his mind too plainly about Hitler, should be recalled from Berlin. He also suggested that, because so many prominent Germans had come to Rome, the impression had been created that the Reich stood under the tutelage of Italy. The balance could be redressed only by the visit to Berlin of a high-ranking Italian, such as Suvich (regardless of his unpopularity there). The main subject of discussion was the future of Austria. Göring said that the government of the Reich was willing to give a 'written' undertaking that it had 'no desire to annex Austria'. An *Anschluss*, still the ultimate goal of German policy, could wait until some future date.[13]

Mussolini regarded this development concerning Austria as a personal triumph, not as a change of heart in the Nazi leaders.

Immediately after the meeting of 7 November he boasted to Pierre Dupuy, editor of the *Petit Parisien*: 'If the *Anschluss*, which is as dangerous to Italy as to France, has not been accomplished it is to a large extent because I have opposed it with my veto. The Germans know that I have sent more troops to the frontier and that if they enter Austria I will intervene by force of arms.' Dupuy was struck by Mussolini's more favourable attitude to the Little Entente.[14]

Finally Göring discussed from notes Hitler's proposals on the future level of German armaments and, much to Mussolini's pleasure, said that Germany had no objections to the revival of the idea of the Four Power Pact. After the visit Mussolini certainly gained the impression that German – Italian relations were on a special footing. But he did not allow Hitler to act outside the official diplomatic channels. In future, communications between the dictators were to pass through their respective ambassadors. For a time Cerruti's dismissal was under consideration in Rome, but this wily diplomat complained to Mussolini that his bad press in Berlin was due to the fact that his dispatches fell into Hassell's hands. He was thus allowed to stay.[15] It was also arranged that Suvich should visit Berlin. Early December, on the eve of his departure, Mussolini won a minor diplomatic victory. Hassell was informed by Hitler that no German – French or Italian – French agreement should be reached without pre-notification.[16]

But if Mussolini took Hitler's declaration to mean that Germany would henceforward concert her general policy in consultation with Italy, he was soon to be disillusioned.

At the end of 1933 Hitler launched out, at first secretly, on a new policy in Eastern Europe that was completely at variance with Mussolini's wishes and expectations. Before he made known his plan for a Four Power Pact, Mussolini (as noted in chapter 2) had encouraged Germany to realise her revisionist aims in the Polish corridor.[17] The most significant result of the subsequent developments was to be the precise opposite of that desired by Mussolini. The Four Power Pact aroused resentment in Poland against France and indirectly paved the way for a German – Polish rapprochement, which Papen had told Mussolini was on the cards.[18] The Soviet government, suspecting a deal between the Reich and Poland, did all in its power to retain the close relations with Germany established by the Treaty of Rapallo of 1922. But it had to make provision for failure and thus sought to secure Russia's frontiers by non-aggression pacts all round. On 2 September 1933, at a time when Russia was on the worst possible terms with the

Vatican, she concluded a non-aggression pact with Italy. Each party agreed not to join a political or economic combination directed against the other. The Soviet government was keen to take further advantage of its new relationship with Italy. Early in December Litvinov, People's Commissar for Foreign Affairs, arrived in Rome. He plainly exposed his government's fear that Germany, Poland and Japan harboured hostile intentions against Russia, and asked Mussolini to use his good offices with Hitler to assuage Soviet anxiety. Now that the Four Power Pact was for all practical purposes dead, the threat of a rapprochement with Russia seemed a convenient tool whereby Mussolini could bring pressure to bear on either Germany or France.[19] Hence, during his visit to Berlin on 13–14 December, Suvich drew the German government's attention to Litvinov's apprehensions. But he elicited no response.[20]

Nevertheless, the Italian government continued in the endeavour of coaxing Germany back to its Rapallo relationship with Russia. On 26 January 1934 Hassell reported from Rome that, if Germany succeeded in allaying the persistent nervousness of Russia over alleged German expansionist aspirations, 'it would still be possible even today to mend the broken wire between Berlin and Moscow'. If nothing were done to achieve this, it was more than likely that France would draw Russia into her security system and take a firmer stand on the issue of disarmament. The same day the German–Polish Declaration was concluded. Thereafter German and Italian policy in Eastern Europe diverged. On 8 February 1934 amidst great pomp and ceremony a Commercial Treaty was concluded between Russia and Italy.[21]

Connected with the Italian–Soviet rapprochement, a more general plan was canvassed by Mussolini with the aim of maintaining Germany's friendship. He decided that the time had come for the 'reform' of the League of Nations. He never showed much respect for the ancestry and the 'sterile parliamentary' procedure of this institution. On 26 October 1933 he told Hassell that Germany must remain firm and show no weakness towards British proposals for her return to the League. He described both the League and the Disarmament Conference as 'Anglo-French enterprises for the mutual assurance and the protection of vassals'. Italy herself was just 'a guest' of the League.[22] On several previous occasions he had undermined the League's authority, and he played the weak man performing great deeds. Mussolini had no desire to invoke the Covenant in order to prevent an *Anschluss*; and after Germany had left the League it seemed to serve no useful purpose for Italy.

Why, it must be asked, did Italy not follow Germany's example and also withdraw from the League? There are certain general reasons to explain Mussolini's continuing his country's membership. Fascist Italy had no desire at this stage to be left in the cold or to associate herself too closely with the troublemakers, Germany and Japan, especially at a time when the Soviet Union was drawing closer to the League. In Mussolini's view the League should be reconstituted in such a way that it would cease to act as a forum through which the small powers of Europe could effectively express their grievances. At the same time he wished the League to remain strong enough to prevent the three other great powers in Western Europe from acting without reference to the fourth, Italy.

Having attacked the League publicly on 14 November, Mussolini discussed his plans for 'reform' at a meeting of the Fascist Grand Council on 5 December 1933. Treaty revision was no longer to fall within the competence of the League but should be dealt with by a council of ambassadors. The principle of 'one state, one vote' should no longer apply. He summed up his attitude to the League with the remark that it was 'excellent when sparrows quarrelled, but would not avail if eagles fell out'.[23]

His proposals provoked an immediate outcry of indignation from the smaller states, led by the Netherlands. Yet once the idea of 'reform' had been raised it was, according to F. P. Walters, to be kept alive in a number of ways.[24] While the British were most anxious to attract Germany back into the League, Mussolini was thinking on rather different lines. He wanted first to coax Germany back to the League as it stood, so that Italy and Germany could later work jointly for its reform. Needless to say, Hitler – who wanted other powers but not Germany to act according to the rules of the League – easily found excuses to wriggle out of accepting Mussolini's proposals.[25]

No sooner had the Duce raised the matter of 'reform' than the League was once again put to the test. Negotiations were secretly arranged to take place between Dollfuss and Habicht early in January 1934. This news was leaked to Starhemberg, who sabotaged the plan. As a result Habicht was forbidden on direct orders from Hitler to land by plane in Vienna. The upshot was renewed Nazi violence in Austria, supported by German propaganda. Dollfuss again, as in June 1933, proposed bringing his quarrel with Germany to the attention of the League.[26]

This time there was to be a reversal of positions. While the French, under their new Foreign Minister, Barthou, were willing to support Dollfuss, the British, anxious to win Germany back to the League, were not. Mussolini certainly did not wish to invoke the Covenant. Instead, he tried to tie Austria directly to Italy. With this end in view he sent Suvich to Vienna in the middle of January. It can be contended that the aim behind Italian pressure on Dollfuss to eradicate the Socialists by force, was to alienate Austria from the League.[27] However, the outcome of the short civil war in Austria from 12 to 16 February 1934 (which has been described by L. Jedlicka)[28] was, in fact, a weakening of the Italian hold over the country.

The Austrian S.A. leadership, which resented attempts made by its party rivals to reach a settlement with Dollfuss, had evidently been planning a rising of their own before Dollfuss struck. The S.A. refused to take part in the fighting on either side, and were thus in the eyes of the Austrian Socialists guiltless of shedding German blood.[29] After 16 February National Socialism, which in Austria stood more to the Left and had a stronger anti-clerical bias than in the Reich, proved more popular than Fascism and won many adherents in Vienna. Moreover, both Mussolini and Dollfuss were now branded by European social democrats and liberals as blood-stained executioners, acting jointly in the name of Fascism – which was now regarded, along with National Socialism, as an international force. The hostility between the two regimes was not fully appreciated. In fact, three days after the suppression of the Viennese Socialists, the Italian police for the first time turned against the Nazis inside Italy.[30] Fascism and National Socialism could still, in certain important circumstances, be described as mutually exclusive.

Nor were the ties between Dollfuss and Mussolini so close as is usually supposed. In Mussolini's own words, 'the mentality of Dollfuss was in keeping with the old Austria – Hungary regime'; and the Duce did not share the view of certain Italian diplomats, notably Cerruti, that if Austria were lost all was lost. He had for long reconciled himself to the idea that ultimately an *Anschluss* was inevitable. The only option open to Italy was to delay it and to build up that second line of defence on the Brenner to which Mussolini attached such importance.[31]

Security on the Brenner was imperative for an additional reason. Early in 1934, as will be seen, Mussolini felt frustrated in Europe and again took an interest in a military operation against Ethiopia.[32]

On 17 February Italy, Britain and France issued a joint declaration supporting the independence and integrity of Austria.[33] Mussolini was also willing to explore the possibility of co-operation with France's allies in South-East Europe. A commercial treaty between Italy and Yugoslavia was concluded on 4 January, followed two days later by a similar agreement with Romania. There was subsequently to be much discussion in Rome of the idea, suggested by Aloisi, of a customs union among Austria, Hungary and Yugoslavia to which Italy could later accede. Success depended on whether Italy could reconcile Hungary and Yugoslavia.[34] Rome was soon disappointed. The government at Budapest, with strong public support, was not prepared to waive its revisionist claims against its old antagonist. Although King Alexander desired a settlement with Italy, he did not wish to join an alignment which might jeopardise Yugoslavia's relations with the two remaining members of the Little Entente, Czechoslovakia and Romania, who were now more closely associated with Turkey under the recently established Balkan League. As an alternative to falling within the Italian orbit, both Hungary and Yugoslavia competed with each other to win the support of Germany and anxiously waited to learn what Hitler's policy would be towards the most burning issue of all, that of Croatia.[35]

In the autumn of 1933 *Ustaši* groups in Hungary, under their leader Perčec, had hatched a plot to assassinate King Alexander together with the Queen on the occasion of a royal visit to Zagreb. Perčec indiscreetly revealed his secrets to his lover who passed the information to the Yugoslav secret police. He was thereupon ordered by Pavelić to Italy. With the help of the Italian police he was arrested and put to death as a renegade at Pavelić's own hands.[36] Revelation of the plot resulted in renewed acts of terrorism on the frontiers of Yugoslavia and Hungary. In contrast to the previous year, however, the Yugoslav government was much better organised, and with equal brutality it launched a counter-terrorist campaign which included amongst its victims Hungarians living in Yugoslavia. The outcome of the quarrel early in 1934 depended on the attitude of Germany, where *Ustaši* groups, under a certain Jelić, were also active.[37]

In 1933 both the Army High Command and Rosenberg (head of the Foreign Organisation of the Nazi Party) were anxious to afford the *Ustaši* protection. There were strong remonstrances from the Wilhelmstrasse.[38] Hitler himself had to decide the issue. He had no desire to fight other people's battles, particularly at a time when his hands were tied in Austria. After the attempt on Alexander's life, Jelić was expelled from the Reich and two Croat newspapers, edited in Germany, were ordered to discontinue publication. But it was still open to Hitler to change his policy towards Croat extremists, many of whom preferred liberation by the Reich than by Italy. He could thus hold both Hungary and Yugoslavia to ransom. Moreover, Germany was economically once again in a position to resume the *Drang nach Südosten*. By 1934 German agriculture had largely recovered from the depression: imports from South-East Europe were not likely to hit the German farmer, provided they were controlled. On 21 February 1934, Germany and Hungary concluded a supplementary commercial treaty. In the course of the negotiations the Hungarians tried to win German backing for their revisionist policy; but Hitler only promised them 'moral' support. He was no less successful in establishing better relations with Yugoslavia. On 9 March the Yugoslav envoy in Berlin, Balugdžić, allegedly on his own initiative, made the first move. He told Hitler that his country had no desire to be tied too closely to France: 'A love affair which lasts too long grows wearisome'. After a brief visit to Belgrade he succeeded in opening negotiations for a trade agreement with Germany, but he failed to elicit political promises. On 1 May a German – Yugoslav trade agreement was concluded.[39]

By March 1934 Mussolini still hoped to establish a second line of defence through agreements with the Danubian states.[40] But it was too late for him to squeeze Germany out of South-East Europe, and he had to satisfy himself with a far less grandiose agreement than that contemplated earlier in the year. After hard bargaining, especially with Gömbös, the Rome Protocols were concluded on 17 March[41] by Italy, Austria and Hungary. The signatories agreed to discuss not only questions affecting their own specific interests but also those of general importance. Austria and Hungary also agreed to lower their tariffs in each other's favour. Italy later offered Austria and Hungary port facilities, at Trieste and Fiume respectively. Although the Rome Protocols provided for no binding political commitments, they came as a surprise to Berlin, where they were regarded as a formidable setback. Mussolini, according to Hassell, was 'elated'. On learning that the agreement was about to be concluded, Hitler on 16 March gave strict orders to the Nazi Party, prohibiting further attacks against the Dollfuss regime – with the result that some of the Austrian Nazis became so embittered that they turned their backs on the Reich and looked to Yugoslavia for support.[42]

Anxious as ever to enhance Italy's standing as a naval power,

Mussolini also needed security in the western Mediterranean. At the end of March 1934, in the presence of Balbo, he concluded agreements with Spanish monarchists and army officers. Italy was to support them in an insurrection if they, having formed a government, agreed in the event of war to adopt a policy of benevolent neutrality towards Italy, perhaps allowing her to use the Balearic islands as bases.[43]

In the belief that Italy was secure on the continental mainland and in the western Mediterranean, Mussolini could now turn his thoughts to other parts of the world. On 18 March, the day after the conclusion of the Rome Protocols, he addressed the Second Quinquennial Assembly of the regime. The greater part of the speech, which is discussed later (chapter 8), was taken up with Italian policy in Asia and Africa. In regard to Europe he declared that, if the Disarmament Conference broke down, Germany should be immediately granted equality of status. He recognised that the future of the League might thus be jeopardised; This was taken by Aloisi as a hint that Italy would withdraw from the League. Mussolini expressed doubts on the possibility of improving Italy's relations with France and with Yugoslavia, and he spoke in favour of Hungarian claims on Yugoslavia.[44]

It was a fighting speech. The first reaction came, not from Ethiopia, but from Yugoslavia and Turkey. According to Balugdžić, it was a 'terrible speech', provoking 'a storm of anger and fear which was not going to die down soon'. The Turkish ambassador in Rome immediately lodged a protest. He was told that Italy regarded Turkey as a European, not an Asian, power: an explanation which, in view of Italy's record in such a country as Albania, cut little ice. In the light of the Italian menace, Turkey stepped up her armaments and firmly supported Italy's opponents in the political upheavals of 1934 and 1935.[45] However, Mussolini was not unduly concerned about the potential threat from Yugoslavia and Turkey. He had achieved, at least temporarily, that security on the Brenner which his generals considered vital for the prosecution of war in East Africa.

From April 1934 preparations in Eritrea were no longer paid for from the proceeds of taxation from the colony but from official funds in Italy.[46] The success or failure of future planning depended on whether Mussolini could use his charismatic gifts to tame Hitler and persuade him to keep the Austrian Nazis on a short leash and thereby maintain that peace in Europe which Italy needed if she were to become an imperial power.

6 The Assassination of Dollfuss

It has been seen how Nazi terrorism in Austria had, on direct orders from Hitler, died down just before the conclusion of the Rome Protocols. Mussolini hoped that he could now come to a direct agreement with Germany over Austria. The idea of a meeting between the two dictators was still popular among certain members of Hitler's entourage, and it was strongly supported by the Hungarian premier, Gömbös.[1] During an interval at the opera in Rome on 29 March 1934 Mussolini, in conversation with Papen, the German Vice-Chancellor, 'very vigorously took up the idea' of an early meeting with Hitler – preferably in Venice, a city which Mussolini had not visited for eleven years.[2] At a cabinet meeting in Berlin on 10 April (from which Bülow hoped there would be a change in German policy) the matter was discussed at length. Hitler agreed 'to write off Austria for some years to come and hand her over to economic fertilisation by Italy'. But his diplomats insisted that he should not go to Canossa and use 'such precise language' to Mussolini, which would give Dollfuss the impression of having won a diplomatic victory. Neurath came round in favour of the meeting, and Blomberg made the obsequious comment that it was 'abnormal and unhealthy' for two such leaders not to get to know each other.[3] No final decision was reached on whether the meeting should take place. A successful result depended on whether Hitler wished, or could be persuaded, to restrain his restless party followers from resorting to violence, at least until the outcome of the disarmament negotiations was known. By the time, in mid-May, that Hitler came to accept the proposal for a meeting with Mussolini, very significant developments were in train within the Nazi movement in Germany and Austria alike.

Oblivious to the policy advocated by the Wilhelmstrasse, party organisations both in Bavaria and within Austria itself were pressing for direct action. Assuming at first that Hitler's order of 16 March prohibiting terrorism and propaganda against the Dollfuss regime was a temporary expedient only, they grew restless at its continuance.

Habicht began to encounter increasing difficulties in maintaining authority over his followers. Inactivity bred either resignation or an urgent demand for action for its own sake, regardless of the consequences. The underground party in Austria felt left in the lurch, not only by Berlin, but by their own headquarters in Munich. There was also growing tension between the Nazi Party and the leaders of the S.A., who controlled the Austrian Legion. Both tried to undermine each other's position in a power-struggle behind the scenes in Vienna. Wächter, head of the party in Vienna, negotiated with Fey, head of the Vienna contingent of the *Heimwehr*; while S.A. Obergruppenführer Reschny negotiated with Starhemberg, head of the *Heimwehr* as a whole. News that a meeting between Hitler and Mussolini was under discussion came as a further shock. The Austrian Nazis were convinced that an Italo-German agreement would strengthen Dollfuss's hand, for he was believed to be acting on the assumption that Mussolini would support Hitler on the issue of disarmament in return for the promise of good behaviour by the Nazis in Austria.[4]

In the middle of April 1934 Habicht discussed internal affairs in Austria with Winkler (head of the *Landbund* who had been dismissed from the Austrian cabinet by Dollfuss in September) and Foppa (a prominent Pan-German). All three agreed that something must be done to boost the morale of those Austrians 'who wanted to drive the priest-ridden bureaucrats to the devil' (*die schwarzen Bonzen zum Teufel jagen*). They decided that this aim could best be achieved if economic warfare against Austria were intensified by the reduction of German exports to that country. On 18 April Hitler agreed to meet Habicht half-way: some restrictions of exports were imposed.[5]

Meanwhile Dollfuss had strengthened his position internally. On 1 May 1934 Austria was declared to be a corporative state, organised in theory by the trade unions and business interests in accordance with the papal encyclical *Quadragesimo Anno* of 1931. The change took place at a time when anti-clericalism was accorded a degree of official recognition in Germany – to which the Vatican reacted by anathematising the works of Alfred Rosenberg. The Pope was supported by the Fascist pundits who regarded Rosenberg's racial doctrines as an insult to Italian cultural pride. Habicht, at one time associated with Rosenberg, also took over many of the anti-clerical slogans of the Social Democrats and launched a vigorous propaganda campaign against the new Austrian constitution. Towards the end of May he could no longer restrain his own supporters. Armed clashes occurred between the

Austrian Legion and the *Heimwehr* on the frontier, as well as acts of violence within Austria itself. But there was no central control over the Nazi movement. Instead of 'marching separately and fighting together', different units were fighting separately and at times against each other.[6]

Hitler's generals and diplomats did all in their power to bring under control a situation which could lead to international complications. On 23 May General Muff, German military attaché in Vienna, told General Fritsch, the commander-in-chief of the German army, that it was not known in Austria whether the Reich's policy was formulated by the Wilhelmstrasse or by the Party. Nazi plans, Muff maintained, had miscarried because of Italian influence in Austria, and added that 'we must come to an understanding with Italy' – which, in his view, was the only salvation of German policy in Austria. He remarked that it was expected abroad that Hitler was about to sever ties with certain of his subordinates at home; abroad, this would be taken as a sign of strength.[7] Habicht is clearly referred to here – though the remark has an ominous tinge to it in view of what was to befall Röhm and his associates at the end of June. Renzetti, who had been instructed by Mussolini to advise Hitler to drop Rosenberg (and most probably Habicht also), reported on 14 June that conservative circles in Berlin were expecting Mussolini, in the projected meeting with Hitler, to urge the latter to make the more fanatical elements in the Nazi movement come to their senses.[8] There is, however, no evidence of Mussolini's asking Hitler to get rid of the S.A. High Command. The Duce was mainly concerned with the Austrian extremists; these were, in fact, to be relatively immune from the purge of 30 June.

Mussolini's anxiety was shared by the Wilhelmstrasse. In a letter of 24 May to Frick, Minister of the Interior, Neurath explained how border incidents might endanger Germany's foreign policy. He therefore urged the necessity of counter-measures. One of Röhm's subordinates, Langer, promised to withdraw paramilitary organisations from the frontier. Neurath's protests led to no significant change. The party leader, Wächter, also protested loudly that the S.A. were allowed to do 'just as they pleased'. The absence of a centralised policy was most certainly discussed by Hitler and Habicht in June, but no record of the meeting has survived and it apparently led to no result. On 12 June Rieth reported from Vienna that 'events were assuming threatening forms which might soon bring about an extremely serious situation'. It was too late for him to report personally to Berlin before

Hitler's departure for Italy. However, Frick, at the instigation of the Wilhelmstrasse, succeeded for a time in persuading the S.A. and the authorities in Bavaria to take speedy and effective action against terrorism. The letter was circulated to all ministries concerned; in particular, the S.A. High Command (who controlled the police)were remainded that the 'intolerable state of affairs may jeopardise their reputation'. This order was put into force in the nick of time, just before Hitler's arrival in Italy.[9]

The seed sown at the end of March, 1934 had finally germinated. On 15 May Hitler had agreed to meet Mussolini, but not in Rome; 'somewhere in northern Italy' was proposed. Venice was eventually fixed on. A profound change had come about in the international atmosphere since the idea of a meeting was first mooted.[10] On 17 April the French had categorically refused to sanction future German rearmament. They had rejected both British and German plans for a compromise, and they still opposed Italy's demands for maritime equality.[11] There was no doubt in Mussolini's mind where the blame lay for the failure of the disarmament negotiations. On 28 May, when it was agreed that the meeting should take place in Venice, he told Hassell that France by 'her hysterical screaming for security' wanted to prevent legal recognition for German rearmament.

In the same interview he made a vital concession regarding Austria. While still insisting that Austria remain 'independent', he averred that 'Austria was absolutely a German state which in the long run could never conduct a policy against Germany but only always with Germany'; Italy strongly desired a settlement of Austria's differences with the Reich. To Hassell's objection that Dollfuss was still intent on suppressing the National Socialists, Mussolini replied that the Austrian leader would 'seize the initiative' for better relations if the National Socialists 'really kept the peace'.[12]

There is an obvious explanation for the Duce's conciliatory remarks about the 'German character of Austria'. An essential condition for a successful military operation in Africa – on which subject the Germans at this time were totally ignorant – was the security of the Brenner frontier. For German policy the implications of Mussolini's attitude were very interesting. If Hitler could be persuaded by the Duce to put a firm end to terrorism, might not the latter in exchange be willing to drop Dollfuss and agree to his replacement by someone with better 'German' qualifications?[13]

There have been many differences of opinion over Hitler's policy towards Austria: whether he deliberately encouraged terrorism there and planned the attempted *Putsch* of 25 July 1934; or whether he allowed matters to drift, thereby enabling the Austrian leaders to take the law into their own hands.[14] Two factors should be borne in mind. First: however much Mussolini feared a *Drang nach Südosten*, he had frequently admitted that Italy could only delay, not indefinitely prevent, an *Anschluss*. Had he known that Hitler on 10 April had declared that, for the time being, Austria could be left to 'economic fertilisation' by Italy, Mussolini might have felt a good deal easier in his mind about the prospects for his European policy. Second: Hitler had stated on 26 May 1933 that Mussolini would reconcile himself to an *Anschluss* provided Italy was adequately compensated in other areas. But where? Early in 1934 Hitler had no inkling that Mussolini had abandoned all hope of Italian expansion in Europe and instead was pursuing two parallel policies: that of converting Italy into a first-class naval power in the Mediterranean, and that of establishing Eritrea as a base for operations against Ethiopia.

At Venice neither dictator was to trust the other sufficiently to divulge his plans for the future. Mutual mistrust, bombastic talk and the confusion caused by overlapping party and state organisations in each country prevented their addressing themselves to each other directly and unambiguously. Besides, neither knew fully his own mind. On the grounds of expediency alone Hitler had no alternative but to pursue a policy towards Austria in keeping with his definition of Germany's vital interests. Circumstances demanded that rearmament should precede an *Anschluss*.[15] But Hitler's disposition was such that he often allowed his lust for revenge to override lucid considerations of power politics. He told Rosenberg that Dollfuss was a 'traitor' to his people and that the Nazis would 'use bombs' in retaliation for any attempt by Dollfuss to rule by coercion.[16] Perhaps Hitler hoped that Dollfuss would be assassinated without this necessitating a *Putsch* or a violent uprising by the Nazis in Austria.

Just before the meeting took place there was much discussion in Berlin of a plan which would, it was hoped, fulfil Mussolini's wishes. According to Muff, Fabbri (the Italian military attaché in Vienna) had suggested to Mussolini before the conclusion of the Rome Protocols that a solution to the Austrian question could be found with 'completely new men'. The heir presumptive whom Fabbri had in mind was not Habicht but Rintelen.[17] The latter had been the Christian Socialist Minister of

Education in Dollfuss's cabinet, as well as head of the *Heimwehr* in Styria: a province where the Austrian Nazis were more sympathetically inclined towards Italy than elsewhere. In May 1933 he was appointed Austrian minister to Rome. To all outward appearances he had the best qualifications for leading a new Austrian government. But early in 1934, apparently unknown to Mussolini, Rintelen had thrown in his lot wholeheartedly with the Austrian Nazis, and in fact was now taking an even more intransigent view than Habicht on the 'absolute necessity' of removing Dollfuss. He even hinted that, if the worst came to the worst, force should be used. On 13 June Fabbri informed Rieth that Mussolini recognised 'the weakness of the present Austrian government' and in certain circumstances might be prepared to drop Dollfuss. He suggested that Rintelen's name should be put forward at Venice. But Rintelen was far too astute a tactician to fall in with this proposal. It was therefore agreed in Berlin that some neutral person should be proposed to Mussolini as Dollfuss's successor, but that no name was to be specified. In fact Hitler had been misled about Mussolini's intentions. The Duce had not reacted at all to Fabbri's reports, and was prepared to give Dollfuss even more support after the fresh wave of Nazi violence than before. Besides, he rightly considered Rintelen to be a thoroughly 'slippery' character. If, for some reason or other, a successor to Dollfuss were needed, Mussolini would have preferred the 'more outspoken' Fey (who, we should note, was thoroughly unpopular in Austria because of his conspicuous part in the civil war in February 1934).[18]

Hitler, accompanied by a small detachment of S.S. men, duly arrived in Venice on 14 June, dressed shabbily in a raincoat.[19] Physically, Aloisi noted, 'il a l'aspect très boche'; but 'there was something in his eyes which expressed profundity of thought'. After a lavish lunch the first tête-à-tête took place. Mussolini himself described it as 'a turbulent debate' about Austria. According to Rosenberg, 'Hitler spoke with brutal openness'.[20] At this first meeting Hitler was invited to put his ideas in writing for further discussion next day. He drew up a five-point programme: 1. An *Anschluss* was of no immediate interest to Germany: 2. An independent person should be appointed to succeed Dollfuss. (To this proposal Mussolini merely asked Hitler whether he had any specific person in mind, to which Hitler replied that he had not. Since Mussolini had raised no objection on this point Hitler mistakenly drew the conclusion that he had accepted the programme as a whole.) 3. Elections should be proclaimed by the new head of government. 4. After these elections the National Socialists should be included in the newly constituted Austrian government. 5. The German and Italian governments should have joint consultation over Austrian questions. (The precise bearing of point 5 is unclear. According to the Italian, but not the German, text, 'all' – and not merely 'economic' – questions pertaining to Austria should be subject to joint consultation.) The meeting at the Alberoni golf club was, in Aloisi's judgement, indecisive because the Germans, no less than the Italians, refused to budge over Austria.[21]

This first personal encounter between the dictators was of psychological rather than of practical significance. Throughout the entire performance of a concert, given in Hitler's honour, the audience applauded Mussolini. The resulting discord was frightful. Later, during a speech delivered by the Duce from the balcony overlooking St Mark's Square, which was packed to capacity, the enthusiasm of the crowd effervesced into delirium. 'Hitler was visibly under the spell of the Duce.' Immediately after the speech there were 'wild scenes of disorder', provoked by 'excited Fascists' who broke open the gates in order to embrace the Duce. The fastidious Aloisi was disgusted by this 'terrifying spectacle'. Mussolini (he wrote), 'prisoner of the enthusiasm' engendered by his speech, turned 'pale' and 'trembled with nervous energy'.[22] Rosenberg described Hitler, after his return to Germany, as 'inebriated' by the experience. The 'fanaticism' he had witnessed 'was not artificial'. The Italians 'bowed in veneration' before their leader 'as if they were in the presence of a pope'. Mussolini, Hitler found, had adopted in Italy 'the necessary caesarlike pose'. In private conversation, however, all this changed; then 'Mussolini was human and likeable' (*menschlich und liebenswürdig*).[23] The meeting in Venice, according to Hassell, had made a profound impression over the whole of Italy. At last an 'association of trust' had been established between the two leaders.[24]

But almost immediately there was to be a serious disagreement on the nature of Hitler's five-point programme. Mussolini insisted that peace should first be established inside Austria in order to make possible joint German – Italian consultation (point 5).[25] Hitler, on the other hand, still demanded that first Dollfuss should be removed and new elections held (points 2 and 3) as a condition for peace.[26] Mussolini never intended to drop Dollfuss, whom he invited to a second meeting (also at Riccione, as in August 1933) to be held at the end of July.[27] This was to cause a dangerous misunderstanding.

The immediate impact of the Venice meeting on the Nazi party-organisation in both Germany and Austria was electric. Mussolini, so the party publicly proclaimed, had agreed that Dollfuss's cabinet must resign and that, pending new elections, Rintelen would take over. Hitler had in fact told Rosenberg that Mussolini had agreed to such a programme.[28] As soon as the Wilhelmstrasse discovered that the German and Italian texts of the communiqué were at variance, and it emerged that nothing concrete had come out of the meeting, the attitude of party-members changed. They once more took the law into their own hands and resorted to violence. This took two forms: first, sporadic uncoordinated terrorist acts, committed mainly by the S.A. on the frontier and within Austria; and second, making plans for a coup. Late in June Rieth strongly urged the government of the Reich to intervene and prevent the export of high explosives. Neurath failed to heed his pleas. The upshot was a major incident on 28 June.[29] The party leadership took almost as serious a view of these incidents as did the Wilhelmstrasse, but it saw a completely different outcome. Terrorist incidents were goading the Austrian government into counter-terrorism which would enable it to consolidate its hold permanently over Austria. If violence were to be used, it must be directed swiftly and 'hygienically' towards a defined object. On 25 June Habicht and others decided at a meeting in Zürich that the time had come to strike. Sturmbannführer Glass, who also attended the meeting, was to use S.S. Standart 89 to surprise the Austrian cabinet while it was in session, and take over the government by force. For security reasons the S.A. leaders were not to be informed. It was believed that the S.A. would 'march separately but fight together' with the S.S. when the latter took action.[30]

On 30 June, a few days after the meeting at Zürich, Röhm and the S.A. leaders in the Reich and scores of others were slaughtered by firing squads of the S.S. Surprisingly, the party and S.A. leaders of the Austrian Legion were left virtually untouched. On 4 July Neurath instructed Hassell that 'nothing had happened in Germany [meaning the Röhm purge] to alter the view that Dollfuss must go before terrorism would cease'. Mussolini was extremely indignant at this. In Hassell's words, the purge had 'cast a shadow over the days of Venice'. It had proved the instability of the Nazi regime and the unpredictability of Hitler's policy.[31] Renzetti reported that Germany (unlike Italy) lacked an island for undesirable persons, hence the shootings.[32] A deep impression was made in Austria when a Nazi spokesman declared over

Munich radio that Dollfuss deserved Röhm's fate. Dollfuss's reaction was resolute. On 10 July he set up a emergency cabinet in which Fey, who had Nazi sympathies, was replaced by Dollfuss himself as Minister of Security. On 14 July the death penalty was prescribed for the unlawful possession of arms and for acts of terrorism.[33] The Nazi leadership in Austria, more conscious now of its weakness than of its strength, became more determined than ever on action. Executions could only lead to intensified terrorism and perhaps civil war, from which Dollfuss was bound to emerge victorious. The same leaders again met on 16 July in Habicht's home in Munich. This time they were joined by Reschny, the S.A. leader. Rintelen (envisaged as head of the new Nazi government) on learning of the plan was determined that it should be implemented before the meeting at Riccione between Mussolini and Dollfuss, fixed for late July; for Dollfuss was bound to get practical help from Italy as a result of the meeting.[34]

The final problem facing the conspirators was to win Hitler's approval; and for this the moment was most inopportune. In the second week of July 1934 Hitler had at last woken up to the fact that Mussolini would not drop Dollfuss. He therefore informed Hassell that he was 'in no hurry' to solve the Austrian problem, which could be put on ice. With some satisfaction, Hassell maintained that Hitler's attitude now corresponded, albeit for different reasons, with that of Mussolini, who was pressing the Germans to 'let passions die down'.[35] Hitler had many reasons for desiring peace in Austria. He had not yet fully imposed his authority over party and state at home, and Hindenburg was still head of state. His major preoccupation was the expansion of the armed forces, which would be seriously jeopardised by a premature international crisis. Habicht (Dieter Ross claims), knowing that the idea of a *Putsch* might be turned down, tricked Hitler into rendering him support by a subtle stratagem. He falsely told him that the Austrian army was planning a *Putsch* of its own and asked Hitler what action the Austrian Nazis should take. Hitler allegedly replied that they should, of course, support the army.[36]

The details of the *Putsch* of 25 July, which have been adequately described elsewhere,[37] need not concern us here. Although Dollfuss was killed, it failed, partly because the S.A. leaders in Vienna refused to join in it (and even warned the Austrian government that a *Putsch* was imminent), and partly because the Austrian army – for all that Fey had told the Nazis leaders that it would join in the *Putsch* – by and large remained loyal to the government. Hitler was attending a Wagnerian festival at Bayreuth when the *Putsch* occurred. On receiving the first reports, with the news of Dollfuss's murder, he showed considerable satisfaction. One event seemed to suggest active complicity on the part of the German government. Rieth, in a private capacity, injudiciously witnessed an agreement between Fey and the insurgents by which the latter were offered a free passage across the frontier to Germany. Hitler immediately decided to wash his hands of the whole business. Rieth was sacked and Papen, who had narrowly escaped the Röhm purge of 30 June, reluctantly agreed to take Rieth's place with the grandiose title of 'Minister on Special Mission to Vienna'. Habicht was also dismissed and the Austrian Legion ordered to take up so-called welfare duties.[38] In the event, the Austrian Legion remained in Bavaria and its existence continued to be a cause of grave friction in German – Italian relations.[39] Hitler needed an excuse which would carry sufficient weight to assuage Mussolini's wild anger. Röhm was made the scapegoat. According to Renzetti, the *Putsch* was the legacy of Röhm and his followers. Their action was all the more treasonable in that Röhm's Austrian followers had switched their loyalty, after 30 June, from Berlin to Belgrade where the Yugoslav government had for long pursued a policy that was decidedly anti-Italian.[40]

Long before the abortive *Putsch*, Mussolini had seen the danger signals north of the Brenner. Yet he failed abysmally to take the one course of action that would strengthen Italy's hands against Germany: a rapprochement with Yugoslavia. Admittedly, he told Aloisi on 27 April 1934 that it was time to have no more truck with the *Ustaŝi* whom he described as 'useless and dangerous'. He later told a British diplomat that he would dispatch them to the United States, and if necessary have them drowned on the way.[41] But he failed to translate his words into deeds, probably because the influence of the pro-Yugoslav Albanians was gaining ground. King Zog, who in any case resented Italian tutelage, started in 1934 to cut down the number of Italian instructors training his army. On 23 June an Italian squadron of warships sailed menacingly into Durazzo harbour and remained there for a few days to overawe the Albanian government. There was talk in the world press of a new 'Agadir crisis'. After a protest lodged by Britain and France, a statement from Rome explained that the failure of the commanders of the Italian ships to announce their friendly approach to the Albanian authorities was due simply to an administrative oversight. The incident led not only to an exchange of abuse between the Italian and Yugoslav press but even to the threat of hostilities.[42]

Yugoslavia now had little or nothing to fear from encirclement. Not only was Albania comparatively friendly but a new government had come into power in Bulgaria in May 1934 which renounced the idea, so unpopular with the Balkan League, of a great South Slav state constituted by a union of Bulgaria and Yugoslavia. It also clamped down on the IMRO, the erstwhile allies of the Ustaši, the Croat terrorist organisation.[43]

In her new quarrel with Italy, Yugoslavia looked to Germany. A visit by Göring on 16 May smoothed the way for negotiations for a commercial treaty with Germany which came into force on 1 June. On 22 June King Alexander let the Germans know that he regarded a Habsburg restoration with even more profound misgivings than an Anschluss.[44] In these circumstances the Austrian military attaché in Rome even suspected that a secret military convention had been concluded between the two countries. What can be said is that certain Yugoslav agencies had since April been plotting with the Nazis in Carinthia. After the murder of Dollfuss a baffling situation thus emerged. Whereas the S.A. in Vienna did not raise a finger in support of the Putsch, their comrades in Carinthia and Styria, bordering Yugoslavia, acted on their own initiative. Moreover, the Yugoslav government itself did not follow the example of the German government and ruthlessly close the frontier, but even provided shelter for the insurgents, thereby causing actute difficulties for the Austrian army and police. Nazi refugees were organised in a camp at Vazasdin on a similar basis to that of the Austrian Legion, and the inmates did not leave for Germany until 1935.[45]

On 25 July Mussolini was faced with a hostile Germany and a hostile Yugoslavia. He had first the unenviable task of breaking the news of Dollfuss's murder to his widow, who was already in Riccione. If Mussolini was 'incapable of being shocked, he was nevertheless infuriated'.[46] He launched a press campaign against Germany whose inhabitants, he later claimed, were illiterate barbarians at a time when Rome could boast of 'Caesar, Virgil and Augustus'.[47] More significantly, he took practical measures and dispatched most of the Italian four divisions then available in northern Italy to the town of Tarvis in north-east Istria, from which they could invade Carinthia; only a few reinforcements were sent to the Brenner.[48] Yet the news from Austria came in some ways as a relief. Aloisi reported Mussolini as saying, on his return from Riccione, that he regarded the outcome of the

Putsch as an escape-route for the Germans to bring to an end Nazi terrorism. The Germans, Mussolini said, had in one way or another to extricate themselves from this venture. Concerning international measures, he preferred to wait for further news before taking action.[49]

The next day (1 August) the Yugoslavs announced that an Italian invasion of Austria would be a casus belli.[50] The Yugoslavs enjoyed an advantage in that they would operate on a favourable system of communications running over the frontier to Klagenfurt and in an area where there were many Slovenes to welcome them. 'The greatest danger', noted Aloisi, is the possibility of a German – Yugoslav alliance. It represents an enormous and lasting peril for Italy.' He much regretted that Mussolini had failed to put into force his own idea, advanced earlier in the year, for a rapprochement with Yugoslavia.[51]

Hitler was thrown into a state of 'considerable excitement' on receiving reports of large-scale slaughter of National Socialists in Styria and Carinthia. He was anxious to know whether other powers might be persuaded to intervene on their behalf. Neurath suggested 'that it might be possible to interest Yugoslavia'. Bülow in reply mentioned rumours of an Italian invasion of Carinthia. This was dismissed by Neurath as it would mean war between Yugoslavia and Italy. There was also some discussion of the feasibility of intervention by Britain or Hungary, but this was discounted since it was believed that passions would calm down once news of Papen's appointment was made known.[52]

Papen's appointment did indeed produce an 'enormous impression' in Rome, but not of the favourable kind which the Germans had expected. It meant, according to Aloisi, that Germany 'is not in any way drawing back. Defeated on the level of terrorism, she hopes to triumph through diplomacy. Papen, a clever man, is taking up a diplomatic post inferior to his rank as Vice-Chancellor of Germany. One is led to believe that he is destined to play the role of Vice-Chancellor of Austria.' For a time the Italian government pressurised Schuschnigg, Dollfuss's successor, not to accept Papen. But Germany regarded this as tantamount to diplomatic war, and Italy gave way.[53]

As regards the future of Austria, the French proposed setting up a council of ambassadors to meet in Rome to discuss how her independence could best be safeguarded. Suvich and Aloisi were in favour of the idea but hoped that it could be extended to create a general détente and thus offer Germany 'an honourable way out of the situation into which she had fallen'. German membership of the proposed council was especially desirable; moreover, 'it would mean the revival of the idea of the Four Power Pact'. There was a further consideration: German membership would also counteract attempts by members of the Little Entente to claim the same right of intervention in Austria as enjoyed by Italy. Effective intervention by Italy would, according to Aloisi, be greatly strengthened if British and French staff officers were attached to the Italian army in the event of its operating on Austrian soil. This is the first hint of the terms of a military agreement that was to be concluded between Italy and France in June 1935.[54] (See chapter 12.)

Many obstacles stood in the way of a collective guarantee of Austria. Only under force majeure would the Germans be induced to join. The British, too, were most reluctant to assume any commitments in Central Europe. The Little Entente held that, if Austrian independence were threatened, the matter should be brought to the Assembly of the League at its session in September. The alternative was an Italian guarantee of Austria, to which other powers could be invited to adhere. Despite reservations on the part of Suvich and Aloisi, Mussolini decided to put this proposal to Schuschnigg at a meeting to be held in Florence on 21 August. When the meeting took place Schuschnigg surprisingly gave the Duce no opportunity to raise the question of an Italian guarantee; the Austrian leader merely asked for a financial loan.[55] How is Schuschnigg's lack of interest in Italian military aid to be explained? The answer probably lies in the fact that he had far stronger legitimist and pan-German leanings than Dollfuss. The last thing he wanted was an Italian military presence on Austrian soil. He believed, moreover, that Austria was now in a better position vis-à-vis the Reich. With the Nazi extremists out of the way he could do business with the 'respectable' Nazis and the other varying shades of German nationalist opinion. After the meeting Mussolini was forced to revise his attitude. Instead of Italy's acting as patron of Austria, she would have to underwrite a general guarantee of Austria on an equal footing with Britain and France: a solution which Schuschnigg favoured.

After his meeting with Schuschnigg a change can be detected in Mussolini's thinking on Austria. He told Aloisi: 'It is no longer necessary to discuss the independence of Austria, she must fend for herself.' He now doubted whether even Starhemberg had any faith left in Austrian independence. There was 'little hope of being able to prevent an *Anschluss*, but only of delaying it'.[56] Negotiations dragged on throughout most of September, with the British even more reluctant than ever to commit themselves to the defence of Austria. On 27 September Italy, France and Britain merely reaffirmed their declaration of 17 February, in which they expressed the pious desire for the maintenance of Austria's independence and integrity.[57]

In the summer of 1934 European problems absorbed Mussolini's attention to such a degree that he informed his service chiefs on 10 August that plans for an invasion of Ethiopia must in no way jeopardise Italy's ability to maintain her status as a great power in Europe.[58] If war against Ethiopia was intended, Italy had first to secure herself on the turbulent continent of Europe.

7 The Marseilles Assassinations and their Aftermath

WHILE the negotiations for a guarantee of Austria were taking place, Italian – Yugoslav relations were moving towards a new crisis. Mussolini took the opportunity of Italian military manoeuvres in August 1934 for indulging his favourite pastime, sabre-rattling. In a harangue to Italian army officers that month, he said that war was 'not far off; it might well break out at any moment'.[1] Some authorities have taken this comment to mean that he was thinking solely of an invasion of Ethiopia. But this is not necessarily so. Two days after the speech Aloisi observed that the Duce 'all the time is inclined to the thought of war. He told me that, according to the latest news received from Yugoslavia (attacks in the press against us à propos the large-scale manoeuvres), this power would start a war.' The Duce would draw the attention of the Yugoslav government to the matter.[2]

On 1 September Mussolini learned from Galli, the Italian minister in Belgrade, that, although there was some pro-Italian feeling in Yugoslavia, the King was especially bitter against Italy. A rapprochement would be possible only if the problem of the Ustaši were finally settled. Mussolini refused to put into effect Galli's concrete proposals.[3] His continued hostility to Yugoslavia found expression in numerous ways. While difficulties were put in the way of Italian citizens wishing to visit Belgrade to promote goodwill between the two countries, General Balbo on 9 September made a provocative speech at Zara. It was applauded by the Italian 'optants', who were free to claim citizenship of Italy while living in Yugoslavia; but, not surprisingly, it was given an icy reception by the Serb nationals.[4]

Meanwhile it had been decided that King Alexander should visit Paris in the second week of October. Later Barthou, the French Foreign Minister, was expected to visit Rome, with the object of patching up the Italian – Yugoslav quarrel.[5] But the prospects for this were far from favourable. Early in October the Yugoslavs, it seems, turned down an Italian suggestion for a press truce. The upshot was a renewed attack against them, launched on 3 October in an Italian paper, the *San Marco di Zara.* Suvich rushed to Milan, where Mussolini was due to make an important speech on the 6th, and asked him to insert some conciliatory words about Yugoslavia.[6] Although in the speech he boasted of Italian military strength, the Duce did not breathe 'fire and slaughter' against his antagonists, as was his wont, but contented himself with requesting Yugoslavia to refrain from those polemics in the press which touched Italy in her most sensitive spot: her military record in the First World War.[7]

While Mussolini was speaking, Alexander (who was now much more pro-German) was already on his way to Marseilles. He and Barthou were assassinated there on 9 October.

The *Ustaši* had drawn up their plans for the murders committed in Marseilles from camps in Hungary and Italy. Official Italian complicity cannot be proved. But Paolo Cortese, head of the Croat Department at the Palazzo Chigi, mistakenly thought that, with the death of Alexander, the Yugoslav state would disintegrate within a day or two. Conceivably he knew what the *Ustaši* were up to.[8] He was soon to be disillusioned. The Duke of Spoleto, who represented King Victor Emmanuel III at the funeral, held on 17 October 1934, informed Rome that Yugoslavia was more solidly united than ever before.[9] Anti-Italian feeling in that country ran high and the Yugoslav press reported that the Italians were concentrating troops, especially in the area of Zara, for an attack on their country. It also accused the French police of 'incredible negligence' for failing to provide adequate security safeguards. It is not surprising therefore that Prince Regent Paul, who acted on behalf of the young King Peter, Alexander's son, was less anxious to continue the pro-French policy of the past. He had been educated in England, a country which he admired, and he hoped that Britain would be persuaded to co-operate with Germany for the protection of the territorial status quo in the Balkans and for the containment of Communism.[10]

State funerals, especially of monarchs, provide excellent occasions for diplomatic business. Göring, who represented Germany, stole the limelight and made Marshal Pétain of France look small. President Lebrun passed unnoticed. To the intense embarrassment of the Wilhelmstrasse, Göring informed Romanian diplomats that it was not Germany's intention to change the territorial status quo by force. There were loud protests from Budapest, sighs of relief in Belgrade.[11] Göring's aims were not concealed from the Italians. A German official, who on

10 October announced Göring's departure for the next day and who evidently belonged to his entourage, let slip a sinister comment to Major Renzetti. By April 1935, he said, Germany would have '500 bombers ready for service'. By that time France, 'a dying nation', would be 'of no account'. Meanwhile Germany's aim was to take advantage of the antagonisms among the various powers and rearm.[12]

In order to prevent Yugoslavia from falling completely into the German orbit, Pierre Laval, the new French Foreign Minister, had no option but to support Yugoslavia and her associates of the Little Entente in their quarrel with Hungary. But he put the blame squarely on the shoulders of Hungary: Italy was allowed to get off scot-free. Even Pavelić, after a short period under arrest, was allowed to remain in Italy, allegedly because under Italian law no provision was made for the extradition of political criminals.[13] Laval's attitude to Italy was not merely guided by motives of political expediency. He had fully approved the negotiations with Italy over the fate of Ethiopia during his premiership in 1931–2. In 1934 he had served as a colleague of Barthou as Minister of Colonies, in which capacity he would have been conversant with affairs in East Africa.[14] His appointment was warmly welcomed in Rome and, with some reservations, in Berlin.[15]

The French and Italian governments (especially the latter) feared that, in the confusion resulting from the Marseilles murders, Germany would once again try her hand at atempting an *Anschluss*. The Austrian Legion under its S.A. leader, Reschny, had not, as was promised after the attempted *Putsch* of 25 July 1934, left its camps in Bavaria. Despite protests from the Wilhelmstrasse, it continued vigorously to attack Schuschnigg's government.[16] In order to secure Austrian independence, Mussolini invited Germany to accede to the Three Power Declaration of 27 September and thus resuscitate the idea of the Four Power Pact. His policy was strongly supported by Gömbös, who on 8 November 1934 told Hassell that the 'Rome–Berlin Axis, which has been cracked, should be repaired'. But Mussolini in his attempts to restrain Hitler over Austria was cold-shouldered, and he sulked. It emerged from a meeting on 23 October with Hassell, who had just returned from his holidays in Germany, that Mussolini was apprehensive over 'German Policy', not only in Austria but in South-East Europe also. He was especially offended by the alleged attempts by Göring to make personal contacts with Yugoslav officials with the avowed aim of promoting German economic interests in the Balkans to the detriment of Italy.[17]

Mussolini certainly based his general policy towards Germany on a false premise. After the events of the previous summer he had reason to suppose that, to all outward appearance, Nazi Germany lacked stability. Renzetti had even warned Rome on 30 July 1934 that there was a danger that Hitler might at any time be assassinated and that every precaution should also be taken to safeguard the life of Mussolini.[18] But the evidence does not support the view expressed by General Fischer, the German military attaché in Rome, that Cerruti, backed by Suvich, was regularly reporting to Rome that, since 30 June, Germany could be discounted as a power factor.[19] In the middle of October Cerruti told Mussolini that Hitler's prestige had diminished, but he continued to exert full control over the armed forces. The intellectuals were against him but not the middle classes. Cerruti believed that in the autumn of 1935, when Germany would have at her disposal an army of 300,000 men, she would attempt to draw Hungary, Yugoslavia, Bulgaria and Turkey into her orbit, the aim being the annihilation of Czechoslovakia. In the meantime, the pre-1914 system of alliances would be reconstituted.[20] Cerruti, who certainly did not underestimate German power, would have been correct about Czechoslovakia had he added a year to the time-estimate for Germany's aims. But in 1934 Hitler was almost entirely preoccupied with winning full military sovereignty within Germany itself, which was denied to her by treaty; an attack on Czechoslovakia was not yet practical politics.

In the autumn of 1934, initial progress in Germany's rearmament was being made. Squadrons of the future *Luftwaffe* were already parading the skies, and both military and civilian airfields were being built all over the Reich except in the Rhineland.[21] There were certain difficulties in the training of personnel. After the breakdown of the Treaty of Rapallo in the autumn of 1933 German pilots could no longer receive their training in Russia. Surprisingly, Italy acted as an alternative, and in 1934 alone 160 German pilots were trained in Italy, mainly as crews for bombers. Göring and Balbo were on especially good terms with each other and the former had great respect for the Italian air force. But by the autumn of 1934 active co-operation between the two air forces had come to an end, with Italy's refusing to export to Germany certain aircraft which were already paid for; and German pilots were no longer invited to train in Italy.[22]

In other respects, however, cordial relations between the service chiefs of the two countries were maintained. General Roatta, head of Italian Military Intelligence, was especially well disposed towards

Germany, and on 19 November 1934 arranged for an interview between the Duce and General Fischer, the German military attaché, whose wife was pro-Nazi. Fischer was asked by Mussolini 'how things stood at present in Germany'. Assuming incorrectly that Cerruti and Suvich had given Mussolini the impression that Germany was weak, Fischer told the Duce that the *Reichswehr* was co-operating harmoniously in the national interest with the S.A. and S.S. But in a private covering letter to General Fritsch, commander-in-chief of the army, which was not to be shown to Hitler, Fischer had some other things to say. The Duce, he said, had expressed to him the hope that 'Colonel General von Blomberg and you, sir [Fritsch], are exercising a decisive influence with the Führer in major questions not only of a military but also of a political character. I naturally encouraged him in the view.' Fischer concluded: 'It may be that we soldiers can still contribute something towards a détente in the present situation.'[23] But by the end of 1934 the *Reichswehr* leaders had much less political influence than Mussolini (and the British also) had supposed.[24] For one thing, Göring – whom Mussolini still suspected – and not Blomberg was appointed to command the future German air force. Nevertheless personal relations between the Italian and German officer corps remained friendly.[25]

Political relations between the two regimes, however, went from bad to worse. Late in 1934 Mussolini was dismayed to learn that in February Germany had concluded a press truce in her polemics with Poland, yet sections of the German press were still unrestrained in hostility to Italy. More serious was the rumour that Rudolf Hess, the Führer's deputy, intended to follow up a recent visit by Ribbentrop to Paris in order to prepare the ground for a German – French rapprochement. This would mean Italian isolation on the continent.[26] The growth of German military power coincided with a renewed German smear campaign against Italy. The murder of Alexander had enabled the Nazi party pundits to get their own back for what they regarded as slanderous abuse from Italy against the so-called 'northern barbarians'. The Bavarian edition of the Nazi paper edited by Goebbels, the *Völkische Beobachter*, was not identical with the Berlin edition and was anti-Italian. The absurd situation therefore arose that it was read by Mussolini but not by the senior German diplomats, who regarded both editions as too vulgar for the tastes of cultivated persons.[27] Late in 1934, moreover, a book was published in Germany in which the Italians (like the Jews) were depicted as an inferior race.[28] Italian Fascism and

National Socialism, each of which boasted of a cultural or a racial superiority, were on this point mutually contradictory and locked in bitter conflict. Nazi propaganda, for the first time since 1933, was even causing serious unrest among the German minority living in the South Tyrol. Mussolini had no choice but to lodge a protest. On 5 December, in a state of high emotional stress, he received Hassell who had come to thank him for Italian services over agreement on the Saar. In the presence of Suvich, the Duce let himself go. He read, evidently from a prepared statement, the words: 'No war would be as popular in Germany as one against Italy.' He had, he declared, 'reliable evidence' that Bavaria was being prepared as a base for air attacks on northern Italy.[29]

Mussolini had no real cause for anxiety. The Alps were such a formidable barrier that, earlier in the year, Göring, when piloting his own plane to Rome, had difficulty in crossing them; the primitive German bombers in 1934, when loaded, were scarcely capable of flying at high altitudes and over long distances.[30] The 'reliable evidence' Mussolini referred to certainly did not emanate from Cerruti. Jens Petersen thus draws the conclusion that, since the protest was not based on official information, it cannot be considered as sound evidence.[31] That Mussolini possibly spoke of the German air threat as a pretext for doing a deal with France must also be taken into account. But he had not yet taken the final plunge of opening negotiations with Laval. One thing alone is certain. Mussolini frequently expressed his fears of a preventive war – it had become almost an obsession. At one time the would-be aggressor was France, next Yugoslavia, later still Ethiopia and finally Britain. From his experiences as a polemicist, he was capable of accepting 'careless talk' as news, and he almost certainly shared the general belief that 'the bomber will always get through'. It was Göring's deliberate policy in 1934 to exaggerate Germany's air strength. Might not one of his reasons for doing so have been to frighten the Italians whose newspapers early in December 1934 expressed real alarm on the expansion of German air power?[32]

Hassell was so taken aback by Mussolini's verbal onslaught of 5 December that the next day he contacted Suvich, who told him that the Duce was genuine in what he said. Neurath considered the question to be so serious that he informed the German War and Air Ministries. Mussolini had no choice but to seek to reduce the supposed threat posed by the Reich, and he accordingly redoubled his efforts in promoting good relations with the members of the German High Command.[33]

According to General Fischer, Germany had two irons in the fire, Italy and France.[34] It was open to Italy not merely to play the one power off against the other, but at least on one issue to act as the broker between them.

In August 1934 the Council of the League decided that, in accordance with the Peace of Versailles, a plebiscite in the Saar should take place on 13 January 1935. The inhabitants of this territory, rich in coal, could vote for the status quo (which meant administration by a high commissioner, appointed by the League), or for reincorporation into Germany, or for union with France. A solution to the problems connected with the policing of the Saar by a contingent of British, Italian and Swedish troops during the plebiscite was finally reached in Rome on 2–3 December 1934. Aloisi played a conspicuous part in the negotiations, winning the gratitude of Anthony Eden, then Lord Privy Seal.[35] Mussolini had every reason to be pleased, for the principles underlying the Four Power Pact were now being given practical application, at least in Western Europe. Admittedly, the French under Laval had threatened to send troops into the Saar to ensure good behaviour on the part of Germany. But as soon as this threat evoked a hostile German response, Laval climbed down and assured Germany that the Saar would not be touched. Laval now laboured under the illusion that the Reich would be on its best behaviour. He was wrong.[36] On 4 December Hitler, in an exhilarated mood, declared to members of his cabinet that Germany was once again a great power. 'The French', he said, 'have definitely missed the opportunity of a preventive war.'[37] Once the Saar was firmly in her hands Germany would be able (as Hitler was to demonstrate) to go ahead with rearmament with little or nothing to fear from an Italian–French or an Anglo-French alignment.

While negotiations for the plebiscite in the Saar were in progress, the main obstacle in the way of an agreement between Italy and France still lay in the Danubian area. Mussolini revealed his real intentions only to his own diplomats. On 16 November he instructed Aloisi to defend Hungary unconditionally in her quarrel with the Little Entente, which was to come up for review at the special session of the Council to be held at Geneva.[38] On 22 November the Yugoslav delegate submitted a damning indictment of Hungary and was backed, not only by the other delegates of the Little Entente and of France, but by those of Italy's old enemies, Greece and Turkey. Opinion of those League members not directly involved was at first sympathetic to Yugoslavia, but it changed early in December after the ruthless expulsion of innocent Hungarians from Yugoslav territory.[39] On 9 December, when feelings were running high, the Yugoslavs threatened to withdraw their memorandum and assume 'freedom of action' – which, in Aloisi's words, 'meant war'. This extremity was averted largely by the joint efforts of Aloisi and Eden. The latter, acting as rapporteur of the League, persuaded Hungary on 10 December to admit that 'certain of her officials' had carelessly issued passports to dangerous citizens.[40]

The quarrel between Hungary and Yugoslavia, which continued even after the compromise of 10 December, proved at this stage to be a more serious obstacle in the way of an Italian – French agreement than did colonial issues. Whereas Laval insisted that on his forthcoming visit to Rome (which was under discussion for some weeks) agreement with Italy could be concluded only if Austrian independence were guaranteed by the Little Entente, Mussolini obdurately pressed for an agreement with Austria and her neighbour, Hungary. Despite strong pleas by Aloisi and Theodoli for him to accept the French view, Mussolini, as late as 14 December, refused to budge. He maintained that opinion inside the Fascist Party was against sacrificing Hungary and conciliating Yugoslavia.[41]

As a result of Mussolini's high-handed policy during the crisis arising from the Marseilles murders, liberal opinion outside Italy was turning sharply against the Fascist regime. On 14 December he complained bitterly about hostile comment published in the *League of Nations Journal*. The same day, Haile Selassie appealed to the Council of the League to regard as a threat to peace the Wal Wal incident (soon to be famous) of 5 December. The incident occurred precisely at a time when Mussolini greatly feared German military power and when Italy's hands were tied by a major crisis in South-East Europe.

There has been, and still is, much discussion of the scale of Mussolini's plans in late 1934 in regard to armed conflict with Ethiopia. In the autumn of 1934 Italy had certainly sent troops to East Africa, but it is important to note that they were sufficient in number only for a colonial war, not for a national war, against Ethiopia. Mussolini's aim was a colonial war, and it was for this that elaborate plans were made.[42] It was not until late in 1935 that contemporary observers began to see the crisis arising from the Wal Wal incident as the crystallisation of a systematic plan, originating in the summer of 1934, for an all-out war of conquest.

This view is one of the myths of the history of the 1930s; unfortunately it still finds expression, even in recent scholarly monographs of exceptionally high value.[43]

8　Mussolini Decides on War

AFTER Hitler had launched his propaganda campaign against Austria in March 1933, Mussolini still sought to pursue a grandiose policy in Europe and could not devote his full energies to the *politica periferica* which in 1932 and 1933 was so popular among certain of his diplomats and Colonial Ministry officials (as we saw in chapter 1). After the collapse of the Four Power Pact consequent on Germany's leaving the League of Nations on 14 October 1933, Mussolini became thoroughly disillusioned with Europe as an arena for the deployment of 'Fascist dynamism' on behalf of Italian greatness. To deflect the minds of Italians from unemployment and apathy, the regime needed some dazzling success overseas. Rome had to be made once again a centre of world influence, with Italy renewing her 'civilising mission'.

It became an aspiration of the regime to make Italy a notable factor in the Islamic world, but Italy's standing here could be strengthened only if she healed the wounds inflicted before 1932 by Graziani's massacre of the Senussi in Cyrenaica. In 1932 Italian propaganda was still directed against the Arabs, for which purpose a special organisation was active in Addis Ababa as late as January 1933.[1] But by the end of that year there was to be a volte-face. In December 1933 over 500 students, mostly from Islamic, though not Arab, countries (Afghanistan, the Lebanon, Persia and India), were assembled in the Hall of Julius Caesar at the Capitol and addressed by Mussolini himself. With the full backing of the papal Congregatio de Propaganda Fidei, a Middle East Centre was soon established in Rome.[2]

Italy was now posing as an anti-imperialist power, and was ready to champion the cause of the Arab world. The second language of educated Arabs over the entire Mediterranean basin was French. To win their sympathy, the Italians in 1933 published books and later newspapers in that language. But Mussolini also wished to appeal directly to the Arab masses, most of whom were illiterate and who were discontented with their lot. He showed his genius as a propagandist by effectively making use of a new medium, the radio. From March 1934

Italian broadcasts from Radio Bari were no longer confined to Italian settlers, dispersed throughout the Mediterranean basin, but were addressed first to the Arabs in Syria, in order to put pressure on the French, and later to the Arabs in Palestine and eventually to those in Egypt in order to create difficulties for the British. The broadcasts could be heard from cheap Italian wireless sets bought by restaurant proprietors.[3] Propaganda slogans were interspersed by light Arab music and the programmes thus appealed to a wide audience.

But, despite the skill of Italian propaganda, certain contradictions did not pass unnoticed. Mussolini was encouraging the Arabs in Palestine to revolt and at the same time financing the settlement in that mandate territory of Jews whom he hoped to use for the promotion of Italian influence.[4] He was championing the cause of Egyptian and Tunisian nationalists, yet simultaneously demanding that the Italian settlers should be accorded a privileged status in both countries. But in 1934 the basic aim of Mussolini's propaganda was more to win the sympathy of the Arabs than to disrupt the French and British Empires. His major preoccupation was still in Europe: the security of the Brenner frontier, for which he needed the sympathy of the Western powers.

Mistakenly, as has been seen, he thought that the Rome Protocols of 17 March 1934, followed by Hitler's visit to Venice, would provide Italy with optimum security in Europe.[5] On 18 March, in the speech commemorating the Second Quinquennial of the Fascist regime (already referred to in chapters 1 and 5), he spoke about Italy more as if she were an island than a peninsula, and he emphasised that the Mediterranenan linked her with the East and West. The historical objectives of Italy had 'two names, Asia and Africa'. There was no question of 'territorial conquests' but of cultural, political and economic expansion. Italy was to take the lead in bringing the peoples of Africa, the Near East and the Far East into mutual collaboration. More especially, the peoples of Africa were to be brought more fully into the civilised world.[6] Although the speech was interpreted by Yugoslavia and Turkey as a strident statement of imperialism, no protests were lodged by Haile Selassie, who, because of the Ethiopian frontier raids into British and Italian Somaliland, could not at this stage afford a row with Italy.[7]

On 17 April 1934, when Mussolini again had reason, because of Austria, to suspect Hitler, the French under their Foreign Minister, Louis Barthou, rejected an Anglo-German compromise on disarmament. The next month the tortuous proceedings of the Disarmament

Conference were wound up. Italy, by virtue of her accumulated stock of weapons, either manufactured in Italy or captured from the Austrians in the First World War, and with her small but glamorous air force which was the envy of foreigners, could still pose as a great power.[8] But Mussolini was only too well aware that if an arms race began in earnest, Italy – lacking adequate natural resources – would soon be left far behind. The conclusions he drew from the failure of the Disarmament Conference were spelled out in an article, 'Verso il Riarmo' ('Towards Rearmament'), published in *Il Popolo d'Italia* on 28 May 1934 – the day before the Disarmament Conference ended. To all intents and purposes, he claimed, the League of Nations no longer commanded authority. There would thus be a reversion to the pre-1914 scramble for alliances in preparation for war. Italy, to survive, had no option but to rearm and to win quick returns in Africa before other states had rearmed. The whole emphasis in the article has been described as one of 'activism, militarism, combative nationalism'.[9] Mussolini, of course, had to conceal his specific intention in regard to Ethiopia. But planning had already made progress.

Before a war with Ethiopia could be attempted Mussolini had first to become master in his own house, which meant bringing under his direct control all the main organs of government. It has been seen that in July 1932 he became his own Foreign Minister; but he was still not free from the restraints imposed by his professional diplomats and other advisers. This situation he took steps to alter during 1933. In August of that year all matters pertaining to East Africa were transferred to the Colonial Ministry under De Bono, on whom Mussolini could rely to pursue an expansionist policy (see chapter 2). Nor was De Bono subject to undue interference from the service chiefs. According to a decree of 1927, the War Ministry, the chiefs of the Army, Naval and Air Staffs, as well as the head of the General Staff, were responsible for metropolitan defence only. They had merely to be kept informed of the political and military situation in the colonies, and were allowed to express an opinion on important questions relating to the movement and organisation of troops in the colonies, at least in so far as this affected metropolitan defence. But the Colonial Ministry could on its own initiative draw up operational plans and implement them.[10] General Gazzara, the cautious Minister of War, was likely to resent having to comply with directives emanating from De Bono. In July 1933 he was dismissed and Mussolini became his own War Minister. General Federico Baistrocchi, with a reputation for 'Fascist dynamism', was appointed Deputy Secretary of War.

In November 1933 Mussolini went a stage further in augmenting his own power. The redoubtable Italo Balbo, Minister of Air, had ambitions of his own. He was capable of speaking boldly to Mussolini, and the last thing he would tolerate was the transfer of the bulk of the Italian air force to De Bono's command in East Africa. Moreover, having flown the Atlantic in 1933, he was stealing the limelight from the Duce. In November 1933 both Balbo and Admiral Giuseppe Sirianni, Minister of Marine, were dismissed. The former was appointed to take Marshal Pietro Badoglio's place as governor of Cyrenaica and Tripolitania (united to form Libya in January 1934). Although Mussolini had removed one potential rival, he overlooked the possibility that Badoglio, hero of Vittoria Veneto in 1918, who as Chief of Staff had direct access to the King, might one day take over the government from the Duce himself. Badoglio was an ambitious, forceful character and a superlative organiser. He had no time for Fascism and his loyalty lay with the House of Savoy. But as a corps commander in the First World War he had been accused by his fellow-generals of being partly responsible for the disastrous Italian defeat at Caporetto in November 1917. To restore his tarnished reputation as a field commander, what better than if he, instead of De Bono, took personal command of the Italian forces in East Africa?[11]

It has been seen (chapter 2) that in letters to the Italian service chiefs De Bono had submitted the first plan for an invasion of Ethiopia on 29 November 1932, and had gained Mussolini's approval of it by the end of that year. But, because of unrest in Europe, nine months or so were to elapse before either Mussolini or his military staffs gave serious consideration to implementing the plan. In September 1933, however, at a time when it seemed that German rearmament would become an accomplished fact, Mussolini entrusted De Bono, who was still in Rome, with the practical preparations for an attack on Ethiopia. It was still planned to take place in October 1935. At first De Bono had to keep expenditure down to a level consonant with the limited resources of Eritrea alone. Only in April 1934 did he receive additional funds from the Italian government.

De Bono's plans on purely technical grounds stood open to criticism from the General Staff and War Ministry. And there were many able generals who did not think that he was the right choice as commander. General Alberto Bonzani, chief of the Army Staff, was a staunch

Piedmontese conservative with no liking for Fascism. Determined to use his authority to the utmost, he subjected De Bono's plans to devastating criticism. Bonzani's criticisms were forwarded to De Bono by Baistrocchi on 15 September 1933. According to Bonzani, the time needed to send 35,000 Italian troops (two divisions and one mountain brigade) to the assembly area would be far longer than the single month allowed for by De Bono.[12] In a second letter to Baistrocchi of 14 March 1934 (the day of the Rome Protocols), Bonzani stated his objections to the plan on political grounds. Reinforcing Eritrea would deplete the Italian peninsula itself of much-needed troops. Only after fortifications on Italy's frontiers on the Alps were completed, and after metropolitan forces were re-equipped with modern arms, could Eritrea (in Bonzani's view) be placed on a war footing.

Bonzani attached the highest importance to the role of Italy's hypothetical enemy, France. If that country could be won over as Italy's ally, Ethiopia, deprived of arms from the port of Djibuti, would virtually be at the mercy of Italy. If Italy, on the other hand, incurred French hostility, she would be compelled to send forces to Libya, where a French attack from Tunisia could be expected. Ethiopia, Bonzani feared, would take advantage of Italy's involvement in war in Europe to launch a preventive war and strike at her colonies which were dangerously exposed to attack.[13] (Surprisingly, Bonzani – no less than Mussolini himself – ignored Britain as a potential enemy.) In contrast to other commanders, he was also anxious to reinforce Italian Somaliland. Both he and Badoglio rejected the contention that the aim of the war should be to extend the frontiers of Italy's existing colonies: it should rather be the complete conquest of Ethiopia; hence operations should be on such a scale as to characterise the war not as a colonial but as a national conflict.[14]

Marshal Badoglio, whose role was ill-defined, together with Baistrocchi, took up many, but not all, of Bonzani's ideas and elaborated on them. In a letter of 20 January 1934, after his return from Libya, Badoglio had peremptorily reminded the Duce of the importance of Anglo-French interests in Ethiopia. But he concurred with De Bono's contention that, if Ethiopia were converted into a cohesive state with a modern army, she would constitute a serious threat to Italy. There was therefore no alternative for Italy but to launch a preventive war at a time of her own choosing.[15] Although it had already been decided at a ministerial meeting of 8 February 1934 (presided over by Mussolini, with Badoglio, De Bono and Suvich present) that operations should

start under De Bono's command after the end of the monsoons in
October 1935, preliminary preparations were almost entirely
neglected – perhaps because of the quarrel over Austria, which the
generals could use as an additional reason in favour of a postpone-
ment.[16]

Towards the end of March 1934 Badoglio, supported by Bonzani and
Baistrocchi, made devastating criticisms of the plans and asked
Mussolini whether Bonzani should not command operations instead of
De Bono, whom he considered too old for the task. On learning this De
Bono noted in his diary on 28 March: 'That swine Badoglio has tried to
get rid of me.' In his correspondence with Mussolini De Bono insisted
that the General Staff had no right to amend plans drawn up by the
Ministry of Colonies.[17] The only way to put a stop to this internecine
warfare would be for Mussolini to become his own Minister of Colonies
in addition to being Minister for War and Foreign Affairs; in this new
capacity he could give central authority to military preparations which
were vital if the war were to start in the autumn of 1935. But evidently
he was still too preoccupied with European affairs to make this step, and
the General Staff in April and May took the lead in operational
planning and quarrelled with the Colonial Ministry. Instead of the
20,000 men asked for by De Bono, Badoglio maintained that
80 – 100,000 should be dispatched from Italy. However, the number of
askari then in Libya (whose fighting ability Badoglio was inclined to
doubt) was to be reduced from 60,000 to 30,000 men. he was opposed to
the bombing of towns, which in any case were of little strategic
importance, because of the adverse effect this would have on world
opinion. Badoglio won Mussolini's approval for the idea that the
Italians should start fighting a defensive war and then, at a favourable
moment, switch to the offensive after the Ethiopians had massed their
forces – which it was estimated would take three months. At a further
meeting of military experts on 7 May, presided over by Mussolini, it was
decided to send an army corps of three divisions to Eritrea. But in the
event very few of these forces reached their destination before the end of
1934, and Italian planning remained hampered by controversy.[18]

On 12 May Badoglio implored Mussolini not to resort to war until
after three years and in the meantime to pursue a pacific policy in East
Africa. He returned to this argument, having studied a report of 29 May
by Colonel Viscount Prasca, a member of his staff who had just
completed a tour of inspection of Eritrea. Badoglio maintained that
military preparations, already started, should have two aims: first, to

curb any reckless thoughts Haile Selassie might entertain of his ability to win a preventive war; second, to assure Italy of victory if she were attacked by Ethiopia. In contrast to Bonzani, both De Bono and Badoglio agreed that, since the climate in Somaliland was allegedly too hot for the white man, operations in that theatre were of secondary importance.[19] By the end of June Badoglio, but not Bonzani, gave up all thought of removing De Bono. Bonzani pressed for legislation to repeal the law of 1927, but he no longer had the support of Badoglio and Baistrocchi. Bonzani was therefore dismissed.[20]

At a further meeting of Mussolini and Badoglio on 28 May, with Suvich and De Bono present, the marshal's proposals were accepted. Eritrea was to be placed on a firm defensive footing, but peace with Ethiopia was to be maintained for appearance's sake. Only after Italy was militarily prepared should Ethiopia be provoked indirectly into taking action against Eritrea so as to provide Italy with a valid pretext for going to war. A convincing incident was to be framed by Ruggero, military attaché in Addis Ababa. Italy's plans were not to be made known to either Britain or France.[21]

In the subsequent months of 1934, the technical and logistical problems confronting the Italians became even more pronounced. According to the Naval High Command, the number of troop-transports required was so great that it would severely hit the Italian economy. Eight months were needed for construction work at the port of Massawa. On 18 July De Bono asked for eight squadrons of bombers, with one reconnaissance and one fighter squadron to be sent to Eritrea within twenty-four hours. They were to resist an Ethiopian attack which he expected would take place that October, when Italy had to be prepared for war in Europe. De Bono was told by General Valle, Deputy Secretary for Air, that there were only a few machines in Libya capable of service in East Africa and that airfields in Eritrea could be built only after the monsoons in September.[22]

Mussolini had also to reckon with stubborn opposition from his officials in the Palazzo Chigi who knew little about the military plans. On 30 June, Raimondo Franchetti, an expert in railway politics in Ethiopia and a colonial adventurer, had an altercation with Aloisi. He said: 'The Duce wants to launch the *politica periferica* [the subversion of local chieftains] immediately.' Aloisi asked him why this policy had not already started. Franchetti replied that he was 'worried by the lack of liaison between the Foreign and Colonial Ministries'. (He did not mention the infighting between the War and Colonial Ministries.) But

Franchetti was right in stressing that, without strong central direction, 'nothing could be attempted'. Aloisi dismissed this objection and pointed out that without 'serious preparation in Europe an undertaking in Abyssinia could only end in disaster'. Evidently Mussolini had hidden from Aloisi his full intentions regarding Ethiopia. For Franchetti, and not the Duce, told Aloisi in confidence that, after accompanying the King to Eritrea in October, De Bono would remain there as governor of Italy's two colonies, but that Mussolini personally would probably assume the post of Minister of Colonies. Evidently Balbo, governor of Libya, and far more competent than De Bono as a soldier, wanted to conduct the campaign but he was reputed in the summer of 1934 to be on bad terms with the Duce.[23]

For military reasons alone Mussolini eagerly sought a deal with France, a power which, it has been seen, was in desperate need of Italian friendship in view of German rearmament. Having strengthened France's ties with her allies in Eastern Europe, Barthou originally intended to visit Rome in December 1934. From Mussolini's point of view this date was too late; anything could happen in the meantime.[24] Nevertheless the ground could be cleared for the meeting by negotiations between Italian and French professional diplomats on those complicated colonial issues which, for years, had bedevilled relations between the two countries. The major issues were: the frontiers of Libya; the cession of the area near Lake Chad to Italy, giving Libya access to the Atlantic through the Cameroons; and the status of Italians living in Tunisia. Of particular importance, according to Aloisi, was the Italian claim, made in 1919, on Djibuti which, 'on account of the numerous warlike plans manifest from all sides [in Italy] against Ethiopia, is a burning issue'.[25] Chambrun, the French ambassador, responsible for these preliminary negotiations from the French side, felt optimistic about their outcome. But he was frank enough to tell Aloisi on 20 July that Italy's claim on the region near Lake Chad would have to be dismissed for it would result in the dissection of the French Empire in West Africa. Aloisi's rejoinder was shrewd. Italy would be willing to allow France a free hand in West Africa in return for the right to round off her own empire in East Africa by the acquisition of Djibuti. Ever since the negotiations on these subjects in 1931–2 the French had continued to invest considerable sums on this port and on roads in French Somaliland. They were thus far from willing to hand over Djibuti to Italy.[26]

The Italian imperial dream in Africa was again to be eclipsed by events in Europe. It has been seen (chapter 7) how, after the assassination of Dollfuss, Italy became involved in a major quarrel with both Germany and Yugoslavia. In a directive of 10 August Mussolini peremptorily reminded De Bono and the Italian service chiefs that any enterprise in Africa which led to a reduction of Italian military potential was highly dangerous. The 1928 Treaty with Ethiopia must thus be observed. He decided to put a stop to all the 'chatter that Italy cherished aggressive designs on Ethiopia' which was already causing embarrassment in Rome. But this did not mean that Mussolini had abandoned all thought of war in East Africa. Reinforcements from Italy might have to be rushed to Eritrea to anticipate an Ethiopian attack. The fundamental aim was still 'to resist' an attack 'behind our defensive positions, and only after inflicting a decisive defeat on the enemy to pass over to the counter-offensive in whichever direction and towards whatever objectives were desirable in the situation at any given time'.[27]

In the autumn of 1934, no less than in 1932, the prospect of a dazzling feat of arms in Africa was jeopardised by crises in Europe. But there was a marked change in Italy's position. Whereas late in 1932 Mussolini had considered taking the initiative against Yugoslavia, by August 1934 he feared that Yugoslavia would attack Italy. Moreover there were other differences in his situation. Late in 1932 France stood squarely behind Yugoslavia; by the autumn of 1934, with the threat of an Italian march into Austria, Germany could compete against France for the friendship of Yugoslavia. The problems were thus more complex for the Italians who were now on the defensive in Europe and who feared that Ethiopia might take advantage of their weakness and attack.

Towards the end of September 1934 the date of Barthou's intended visit to Rome was brought forward. The French aim was to entice Italy into supporting Austria's independence in co-operation with the states of the Little Entente, especially Yugoslavia. Early on 9 October, before the news of the assassinations in Marseilles had reached Rome, Chambrun, again in an optimistic mood, discussed with Aloisi problems connected with Barthou's visit to Rome.[28] Unfortunately, neither the French nor the Italian documents have been published for this period, but it is evident from an Italian summary of French policy in 1935 and from British documents that Barthou was certainly ready to allow Italy to extend her influence in Ethiopia to an extent not yet defined in order to win Italian co-operation with Yugoslavia against Germany.[29]

Mussolini, who in any case believed that France would impose no insuperable barriers against Italian ambitions in East Africa, also considered that the principles underlying his agreements with Britain of 1925, concerning a possible partition of Ethiopia, still held good.[30] In these circumstances Aloisi and Suvich in a discussion of 2 October on the rumours of war, which Mussolini's directive of 10 August had failed to prevent, were more optimistic. They agreed that nothing should be done in preparation for war with Ethiopia until the international situation was more stable. According to Suvich, the Duce now reckoned on war in Ethiopia 'two years hence'; for this reason Suvich optimistically believed than an attack on Ethiopia might never take place.[31] Mussolini certainly did nothing in the autumn of 1934 to strengthen Italy's position vis-à-vis Germany and Yugoslavia, and he can hardly have given serious attention to Ethiopia after the crisis resulting from the Marseilles murders.

Italian involvement in Europe was most certainly known to Haile Selassie, but he did not just follow a policy of drift, hoping thereby that preoccupations elsewhere would prevent the Italians from an attack. In order to provide his country with maximum security two courses of action were open to him. He could either come to terms with Italy immediately, or else, having obtained the promise of support from foreign powers, throw down the gauntlet and take on his adversary before he was militarily prepared. He evidently tried each alternative. On 30 September he elicited the assurance from Mussolini that 'Italy does not have any intention that is not friendly to the Ethiopian government with whom we are bound by the Treaty of Friendship of 1928'.[32] He was to use this document to strengthen his hand later.

The same month Mussolini committed a blunder which Haile Selassie could not fail to take advantage of. Italian pilots were engaged in training the embryonic Nationalist Chinese air force, and in September 1934 the Italian legation in Canton was raised to the status of an embassy. The Japanese were highly offended. If Mussolini was embarrassing Japan in China, why should not the Japanese play the same game against Italy in Ethiopia? It is estimated that 80 per cent of Ethiopia's imports, which included textiles and opium, came from Japan. The Japanese, too, held in admiration a non-European independent kingdom with an ancient indigenous culture. In January 1933 it had been officially announced in Tokyo that the daughter of a Japanese prince was to be betrothed to a nephew of Haile Selassie.

There was such indignation in Rome that this picturesque romance had, under diplomatic pressure, to be called off. But Japanese imports to Ethiopia increased, and there were even reports that Ethiopia was being supplied with Japanese arms. Hence in March and again in July 1935 a violent press campaign against Japan was launched from Rome.[33]

Far more valuable to Ethiopia was support from European powers, above all Germany with whose diplomats Haile Selassie had been on good terms since his youth. On 28 October 1934, without consulting his professional advisers, most of whom were foreigners, Haile Selassie asked von Schoen, the German minister in Addis Ababa, who in late August knew that the Italians were planning for war, whether an Ethiopian representation might not be allowed to visit Germany to negotiate the purchase of arms, including aircraft.[34] Although he was given an evasive answer, the Emperor's appeal was not in vain. Neurath had been carefully studying Italian military preparations in East Africa, and he kept Hitler fully informed. Hitler personally replied to Haile Selassie in a letter dated 27 November, which unfortunately does not survive.[35] It was not delivered until a month later, after the Wal Wal crisis. The immediate question is raised: Why did Hitler delay a whole month before sending his letter? True, a German member of the Ethiopian section of the Somaliland Boundary Commission, Herr Beitz, had recently been murdered, which certainly caused anger in Berlin. But this is not the whole truth. In a memorandum for Hitler of 31 October, Neurath analysed with remarkable perception Italy's general political predicament. 'So long as France continues to play the role of protector of Abyssinia', he observed, 'it is scarcely to be assumed that an armed conflict will take place between Italy and Ethiopia. It is however just possible that Italy will try to reach a general political agreement with France by means of an adjustment of interests in Ethiopia.' If Italy succeeded in persuading France to write off Ethiopia, then the 'way would be open for Italian action. England would presumably remain neutral, and be repaid for this friendly attitude by an increase of Ethiopian territory as provided for under the Secret Treaty of 1906.' Germany, according to Neurath, should remain neutral and wait until a Franco-Italian agreement was imminent before defining her attitude. War, if it broke out, was expected by the German military experts to last for at least a year.[36] Hitler most probably acted on Neurath's advice and therefore adopted a waiting attitude.

But even if Germany decided to go to the rescue of Ethiopia she could do so effectively only if either Britain or France allowed the Germans to use their territory for the transit of arms. Haile Selassie in 1934 again made attempts to reach agreement with France, but they proved stillborn.[37] He next tried to win the support of Britain. In 1931 he had promulgated a constitution which provided his country with a representative government, at least on paper. His efforts to abolish slavery were also regarded by certain British liberals, such as Noel Buxton, as sincere. While he endeavoured to keep the local *rases* (chieftains) in order, he was careful to avoid provoking them to revolt by too many reforms. The ancient system of land tenure, for instance, above all in the south, which allowed the *rases* and the Church to enjoy intolerable privileges over the peasantry, was left untouched. Ethiopia in 1934 was more than ever subject to tribal warfare; but, provided that Haile Selassie was permitted by the great powers to consolidate his central authority, the country might acquire what the British always admired, 'a viable government' under which the Emperor would curb his unruly subjects. It was not known that Haile Selassie merely intended introducing reforms to strengthen his position as Emperor, not to use his office of Emperor to carry out reform.[38]

In Ethiopia and on its borders, Britain's colonial interests were at stake. After the economic crisis of 1930, Sudanese cotton, which was a primary product, was hit, with the result that the British were less interested in erecting a dam near Lake Tana than they had been a decade earlier. But, apart from the dam, there were a number of outstanding differences between Britain and Ethiopia, such as the demarcation of the Ethiopian frontiers with Kenya, the Sudan and British Somaliland. However, the British no longer took the view, held in 1925, that the disintegration of Ethiopia was imminent. Hence they hoped to secure their interests in the country with the consent of Ethiopia and not by a partition of the country with Italy.[39]

Haile Selassie was prepared to pay a high price for agreement with Britain, provided that he could thereby gain British support against Italy. One issue stood out. The Somalis were little concerned with international frontiers, and they resented lordship regardless of by whom it was exercised. They were in search of grazing-land, which fluctuated with the seasons, and above all, as in biblical times, of water needed by their flocks. The Haud Plateau, forming a triangular area about a hundred miles south of the Red Sea coast, was intolerably hot and arid.[40] To the north were the 359 water wells of Wal Wal and

Gerlogubi. Since the frontier between the Ethiopian province of Ogaden and Italian Somaliland had not been clearly demarcated, there was some doubt about the ownership of these wells. Under the Italian – Ethiopian Treaty of 1928 they lay on the Ethiopian side of a line running approximately one hundred and fifty miles inland, parallel with the coast in a north-easterly direction to the frontier of British Somaliland. In 1929 the Italians, while consolidating their rule in northern Somaliland, recognised Wal Wal as lying in Ethiopian territory. But the next year, after the dispatch of an Italian military expedition, the wells came under de facto Italian occupation and were fortified. In 1932 the Italians demanded that even the tribesmen protected under Ethiopian or British law should apply for permission in advance to use the wells. Haile Selassie, who in any case regarded most of Ogaden with its Muslim inhabitants as a liability, probably valued the wells less than the Italians and certainly less than the British.[41] There was sufficient water for Ethiopian troops and animals in the Harar mountains to the north, but should the Italians decide to invade Ethiopia, and since they were dependent on animal transport, the wells of Wal Wal might prove of value to them, for the nearest alternative supply of water for them was the Shebeli river over 150 miles south-west of Wal Wal.

The Italians however had to be dislodged by the Ethiopians primarily for reasons of power politics. On several occasions after 1932 Haile Selassie had tried to occupy Wal Wal, usually by employing mercenaries; in the event of failure official Ethiopian responsibility could thus be disowned. One Somali proved especially valuable to him: Omar Samantar who, it has been seen (chapter 2), had defected from the Italians in 1926.[42] Already bearing a grudge against the Italians, Samantar was evidently bribed by Haile Selassie in the summer of 1934 into making a demonstration with irregular troops near the frontier of Italian Somaliland. There was also early in 1934 an incident involving Italian citizens at Gondar which created ill-feeling. Early in November Samantar's armed bands were joined by regular Ethiopian troops under Fitauri Shiferra. On 20 November the total force, now amounting in all to approximately 1000 men, reached Ado, 30 miles north-east of Wal Wal. Although it is not known exactly what Shiferra's instructions were, a show of force certainly fitted in with a political plan then under discussion in Addis Ababa and Whitehall.[43]

Haile Selassie needed to improve communications within his own country in such a way that they could not be used by the Italians for military purposes. Of vital importance was a port under Ethiopian sovereignty through which arms could be imported. In 1928 it had been agreed with the Italians that, in exchange for facilities at the Red Sea port of Assab in Eritrea, the Ethiopian government should, with the help of Dutch engineers, construct within its own territory that part of a motor road linking Assab with Dessie some 150 miles north of Addis Ababa. The Italians stalled over concessions to Ethiopia at Assab; and Haile Selassie, realising that this road, if constructed, could be used by the Italians to penetrate into the heart of his country, did not even allow work to start on it. Besides, only 10 per cent of Ethiopia's trade was with Eritrea. At the same time, dependence on the goodwill of the French at Djibuti, through which it is estimated that 65 per cent of Ethiopian trade passed, was most precarious. Towards the end of 1934 Senegalese troops were sent to French Somaliland for the defence of that small colony against raids by desert nomads. There was always the risk that the French colonial officials might collaborate with the Italians and allow goods to reach Addis Ababa only on their own terms.

Members of the British Colonial Office, backed by Sir Sidney Barton, British minister at Addis Ababa, proved more accommodating. Approximately 20 per cent of Ethiopia's trade passed from Gallabat in the Sudan across a mule-track to the centre of the country which was cut off from the capital during the torrential season. By 1934 a motor road had also been constructed from Dira Dawa on the Addis Ababa – Djibuti railway, well within the Ethiopian frontier, connecting the capital with the port of Berbera in British Somaliland. But only 5 per cent of Ethiopia's trade passed through this route. There was a relatively good road linking Addis Ababa and Jimma, in the fertile area of the south-west.[44]

In 1932 Haile Selassie had approached Sir Sidney Barton on the prospect of Ethiopia's obtaining the lease of Zeila, a second port in British Somaliland, together with a corridor linking it with Ethiopian territory. The Colonial Office disliked the idea of a lease and suggested instead the outright cession to Ethiopia of the territory in question. In return the British could demand territorial compensations on their long frontiers with Ethiopia. After much discussion within Whitehall, in which the service chiefs were involved, Barton was instructed on 21 March 1934 to raise the issue again with the Emperor.[45] A month later, to Barton's surprise, Haile Selassie (who had failed to get concessions from the French) showed himself disposed to give the proposal careful consideration. In return for Zeila, Ethiopia was prepared to transfer to

Britain territory in a triangle enclosed by a line running from Ji-Jigga in the north to Wardair and Ferfer in the south and then turning east to Damot. The extension of the frontier of British Somaliland, known as the 'Red line', would have placed under British control a considerable area of Ogaden, including Wal Wal (but not Gerlogubi, already occupied by Ethiopian forces in May 1934).[46] The Foreign Office was aware that the Zeila proposal was likely to meet with opposition. In February 1934 the French had been disturbed at British moves in Addis Ababa seeking to divert Ethiopian trade from Djibuti to Berbera and to Aden. The Italians were likely to be much more headstrong. News of the Zeila proposal was leaked to them towards the end of December 1934. Although accepted by the Ethiopians early in 1935, the British dropped the proposal as it was likely to involve them in a quarrel with Italy.[47] (The notion was not to die, however, as we shall see in chapter 12.)

The Zeila proposal was under discussion at a time when an Anglo-Ethiopian boundary commission, having surveyed the existing frontier between Ethiopia and British Somaliland, proceeded into Ogaden to study the migratory movements of the tribesmen. Colonel Clifford, the British commander of the commission, was accompanied by a small escort, sufficient in his opinion to protect the survey team. On his arrival at Ado on 22 November 1934, he was surprised to meet the force led by Fitauri Shiferra who told him that he would act as the main escort. Both groups then went on towards Wal Wal.[48]

Sir Eric Drummond, British ambassador in Rome, had unofficially informed G. Guarnaschelli, a leading official in the Italian Ministry of Colonies, that the commission would arrive at Wal Wal. However M. Rava, the Italian governor at Mogadishu, never received the message. It is highly unlikely that the Italian colonial authorities deliberately kept their officials in Somaliland in the dark in order to create an incident. The Italian Colonial Ministry, except for De Bono, believed that Haile Selassie's intentions were peaceful and they were constantly upbraided by Mussolini for their lack of interest in the *politica periferica*. Perhaps Drummond's message was not sent because of an administrative oversight. Roberto Cimmaruta, the Italian commander at Wardair, having no instructions, wanted to avoid an incident; but he viewed the arrival of the boundary commission, accompanied by such a strong escort led by Shiferra, as a threat. He accordingly sent a plane over the Anglo-Ethiopian commission's camps to frighten them off.

The commission itself withdrew out of harm's way to Ado, but Shiferra's escort, together with Samantar's irregulars, remained. For the next ten days about a thousand Ethiopian and 500 *askari* troops menacingly faced each other. Although the commanders of both sides showed remarkable restraint, a shot was fired from the Ethiopian lines in the hours of darkness on 5 December, when Italian aircraft could not operate effectively. The next day, after a fierce battle, the Ethiopians were routed.[49]

The evidence suggests that the Wal Wal incident was not staged from Rome. In fact, the kind of incident which Mussolini frequently spoke about and intended to use as a pretext for military action was to have been staged, not in Somaliland (which was virtually depleted of Italian troops), but in Eritrea. It was to be planned by Colonel Ruggero, the Italian military attaché in Addis Ababa. Because of the crisis in Europe no time was less favourable for an Italian punitive expedition against Ethiopia than December 1934.

The Italians were taken by surprise. Immediately after the incident Mussolini ordered aircraft and armoured cars to be rushed to East Africa. Those *askari* troops who were serving in Libya, and had been earmarked for Eritrea, were now to be sent to Somaliland. They were to be joined by one metropolitan division, the *Peloritana*, consisting of southern Italians, who could withstand the heat.[50]

The Italian military documents substantiate the verdict of the Politis Commission of 3 September 1935: Italy was not responsible for the actual Wal Wal incident. But the Italian claim, that Haile Selassie was responsible, could not be proved by the Politis Commission.[51] Had he been firm in his resolve to dislodge the Italians from Wal Wal by military action, Haile Selassie would not have allowed Shiferra to wait ten days, by which time the Italians would have received reinforcements for an attack. Besides, Shiferra, according to the British, was a discreet man of a peaceful disposition. Most probably Haile Selassie hoped that Italian-led *askari* would be persuaded to evacuate Wal Wal when confronted by an Ethiopian force twice its size. The presence of British officers near Wal Wal would enable Shiferra to act with greater authority. Once in de facto possession of the wells, Haile Selassie would have something substantial to offer the British in return for Zeila.[52]

After the incident Haile Selassie thought that he stood on firm legal ground. Mussolini's reaction has been compared with that over the Corfu incident in 1923. On 8 December he demanded a formal apology, a high indemnity, recognition of Italy's right to occupy Wal Wal by a salute to the flag, and the surrender of defectors (including Samantar) to the Italian authorities. At this stage Haile Selassie was dissuaded from an appeal to the League by Sir Sidney Barton. Instead, on 9 December, he invoked article v of the 1928 treaty with Italy, which had recently been renewed. Mussolini refused, on 14 December, to negotiate on the basis of this treaty. Later that day, this time with British approval, Haile Selassie brought the Wal Wal incident to the notice of the League of Nations. On 3 January 1935 he formally invoked article XI of the Covenant which provided for conciliation, but not sanctions.[53]

Mussolini had just been attacked in the *Journal* of the League, an institution which he detested, by anti-Fascists. He was now determined to punish Ethiopia for two acts: resorting to the League, and intriguing with a foreign power, Britain. On 20 December he drafted a directive for an invasion of Ethiopia.[54]

De Bono and Vinci, the Italian minister in Addis Ababa, probably summoned by Mussolini, spent Christmas in Rome. Both were anxious to receive clear instructions as soon as possible. On 24 December De Bono commented: 'The Abyssinians are becoming arrogant and are being backed by the British'; three days later: 'We are mobilising in Somaliland and partially also in Eritrea. Time is needed. The principle should not be one of stringency; we need aircraft and armoured cars. For the good of Italy I hope that the crisis quietens down.' De Bono's words strongly suggest that Italy was not ready for war.[55]

Aloisi's job was to deal with the Ethiopian protests delivered to the League on a political level. On 24 December he contacted the Ministry of Colonies, which denied that Italian troops had advanced against the Ethiopians. The ministry, however, claimed that the *rases* wished to dethrone the Emperor who personally was opposed to 'a large-scale action against us'. Aloisi next rejected the Ethiopian claim that Italy was responsible for the attack; the reverse, he said, was true. He was authorised by the Duce to inform the Italian embassies in Paris and London about the true course of events, since diplomatic support was expected from both capitals.[56] The Italians probably believed that they were the innocent party.

On Christmas day 1934 Aloisi again contacted the Duce who told him that everything would be settled after he, personally, had taken over the Ministry of Colonies. Mussolini added that 'the Abyssinian affair would ripen after we have concluded an accord with France', and that 'it is now necessary to get things moving fast'.[57] But an agreement with France required a complete about-face in Italian policy. On 14 December Mussolini had resisted pressure from France to come to terms with Yugoslavia. But by 29 December he agreed to drop Hungary and instead to co-operate with the Little Entente under the auspices of the League to defend Austrian independence. On 30 December it was learnt from intercepted messages from Paris that Laval was demanding the highest possible price for agreement during his forthcoming visit to Rome. Nevertheless, Mussolini was now ready to negotiate.[58]

Meanwhile Haile Selassie's appeal to the League of 14 December had proved abortive. The Council had adjourned on 10 December after a heavy session. The British and the French governments did not want to forfeit Italian goodwill, which they needed for the forthcoming Saar plebiscite and to check German rearmament. The Wal Wal incident was still regarded by them as an African, not a European, issue. Their point of view was strongly supported by Joseph Avenol, the Secretary General of the League, himself a Frenchman. To avoid friction with the League, Mussolini agreed to drop his demands for an apology and to submit the dispute for arbitration under the 1928 Treaty.[59]

Before the crisis came to a head the Emperor enlisted support from a quarter which may have made him all the more obdurate. On 26 December 1934, when an agreement between France and Italy seemed imminent, Hitler's personal letter of the previous month was at last delivered to the Emperor by Willy Unverfehrt, the German chargé d'affaires in Addis Ababa. No foreign adviser was present. Haile Selassie 'expressed his thanks and stressed the flourishing and friendly relations between the two countries'; Germany was Ethiopia's only 'sincere friend'. Hitler must have held out some sort of promise, for the Emperor gave Unverfehrt a memorandum supplementing the previous memorandum which von Schoen, the German minister, had taken with him for negotiations in Berlin. It contained Ethiopia's detailed requirements for arms, including material for chemical warfare. If the German reply were favourable a special representative would be sent to Berlin. Unverfehrt reminded the Emperor that 'there could be no question of any official German agencies being concerned with the delivery of arms'. In order to deflect the Emperor from the arms issue Unverfehrt suggested that Germany might use her diplomatic influence on behalf of Ethiopia – both among those states with whom Germany had friendly relations, and with those who belonged to the League – in an attempt to find a solution to the Wal Wal dispute. The next day the Wilhelmstrasse instructed him that the Reich would 'observe the strictest neutrality' in an Italian – Ethiopian conflict and that it could not act as mediator because of 'Germany's attitude to the League'. The 'greatest caution' was to be used on the question of the supply of arms. No mention was made of those unofficial agencies in the Reich, of which there were legion, or of the Emperor's personal contacts in Berlin.[60]

The Ethiopian honorary consul-general in Berlin, Major Hans Steffen, was an international arms dealer and an expert in Middle East affairs. Having acted as adviser to Feisal of Iraq and Ibn Saud of Arabia, he had in the 1920s won the 'full confidence' of Haile Selassie. Possibly having learned from Schoen what Haile Selassie's needs were, he was ordered to Addis Ababa. But he acted under the instructions, not of the cautious Wilhelmstrasse, but of Rosenberg's Party Office for Foreign Affairs which late in 1934 was violently anti-Italian. Steffen was ordered to use 'all possible means' to promote war in East Africa in order to bring about a relaxation of political pressure on Germany in Europe.[61] Steffen left Berlin late in December; the Rome Agreements were, as will be seen, concluded on 6 January 1935. Thereafter his mission assumed far greater importance. On 18 January he advised the Emperor, in a discussion on the general strategic situation, 'à attaquer et prévenir l'ennemi avant que ses préparations soient finies'. To achieve this goal Steffen promised him that Germany would provide Ethiopia with all necessary arms. For 11 million Reichmarks three Ethiopian armies could be equipped with heavy weapons. Germany was to be repaid from the produce of Ethiopian agriculture, which was now organised by a German company, to be paid in ten-year instalments. The Germans were later even offered land for settlement in Ethiopia.[62] Although the Italians had an excellent intelligence service both in Addis Ababa and in Berlin, and were later to publish details of Steffen's activities,[63] there is no evidence that in December 1934 Mussolini suspected that Germany intended sending arms to Ethiopia and that he therefore decided to attack the country for this reason. (The development of Ethiopia's arms contacts with Germany is traced in chapters 10 and 12.)

Mussolini was much more worried at this time by the German threat north of the Brenner. Cerruti later wrote that, on being recalled to Rome early in December 1934, he was asked by the Duce how long it would be before Germany was capable of attacking Austria. The ambassador replied, 'less than two years'; upon which Mussolini remarked: 'Now we will have to finish the war in Ethiopia and afterwards return and adopt an attitude of absolute intransigence with regard to an *Anschluss*.'[64]

Mussolini was now ready for action. On 30 December he distributed in five copies his draft directive of the 20th to the service chiefs and Ministry of Colonies. Evidently the Palazzo Chigi never knew even of its existence. And at all costs its contents had to be kept from the French. Since the directive has now been made available in English, it needs only to be summarised here. The Duce claimed 'time works against us'; it was therefore necessary to solve the Ethiopian problem as soon as possible, before Haile Selassie had time to modernise his army with the help of foreign experts. It was already well-equipped with portable arms. A force of 100,000 combatants, backed by *askari*, should be ready to march by the beginning of October 1935, at the end of the wet season. The aim was to be 'the destruction of the Abyssinian forces and the total conquest of the country'. The air force, by making use of chemical warfare, was to play a conspicuous role. No complications were expected at least for two years in Europe. Yugoslavia was too divided internally to threaten Italy, and German rearmament would not be completed before 1937. Moreover, Germany was still rent by internal dissension and could be kept in check by an agreement with France for which Mussolini was now prepared to pay the highest possible price. The interests of Britain and France in East Africa would be respected so as to maintain their neutrality.[65]

Mussolini had severely miscalculated on several counts. He later claimed that one of the objectives of the campaign was to cut the Djibuti—Addis Ababa line. But this operation could be achieved only by a flagrant violation of France's economic interests. Mussolini never expected that Germany would in fact provide arms to Ethiopia and he shut his eyes to the prospect that there might be trouble from the League of Nations, the supporters of which were already critical of Fascist Italy. He mistakenly believed that, at the end of the war, equipment could be returned in good condition to Italy and used to maintain her status as a world power.[66]

Mussolini's improvised decision to launch a national and not a colonial war against Ethiopia not only marked an important stage in a chain reaction leading to the Second World War: it was also to cause a major upheaval in tropical Africa. His decision can be considered either as the last great venture of European imperialism or, after a further examination of the evidence, as a significant step towards the de-colonialisation of Africa and the Middle East.

9 The Mobilisation of Italian Troops

LAVAL was given a tumultuous reception on his arrival in Rome on 4 January 1935. However, the subsequent bargaining between the French and Italian diplomats proved such heavy going that for a time it seemed the negotiations would have to be called off. But after a private meeting between Laval and Mussolini on the evening of 6 January, the Frenchman told the representatives of the two delegations: 'C'est fini.'[1] Next day eight agreements were concluded; four of them were made public, four kept secret.

The 'public' agreements concerned Central and Eastern Europe. France and Italy would, within the framework of the League, consult on measures to be taken if Austrian independence were threatened. Austria and 'other interested states' – which were to include her neighbours (except Switzerland) and perhaps Romania and Poland – would be invited to conclude a reciprocal convention for non-intervention in each other's domestic affairs.[2] The Italians tried, but (on 28 January) failed, to win Germany over to this plan. And the Hungarians took particular exception to the inclusion of Yugoslavia. On lodging an official protest shortly after the agreements were signed, they were told by Mussolini that, had Italy not supported Hungary during the crisis at the end of December 1934, it would have been a walk-over for the Yugoslavs, who would have marched on Budapest.[3] Within a few months Hitler was to have little difficulty in taking up the cause of Magyar revisionism and, when it suited him, in diverting it towards Czechoslovakia instead of Yugoslavia.[4] For a time early in 1934 (as we saw in chapter 5) Mussolini had considered clinching a political agreement with Yugoslavia. But he failed to do so, which had grave consequences later.

In a secret protocol on disarmament, France and Italy in the Rome Agreements agreed to consult if Germany should 'modify by unilateral action her obligations in the matter of armaments'. This clause was designed to meet a situation if the Saarland were ceded to Germany on 1 March, as a result of the plebiscite to be held on 13 January.[5]

There was no knowing what Hitler would do next. Could he be tamed, or would he embark on a fresh venture? Simon's aim at the end of 1934 was to win Germany back into the League and to reach a general agreement with her.[6] Laval evidently hoped that agreement with Germany could be reached with the collaboration of Britain. But Mussolini, unknown to Laval, had to take into account the possibility of a German invasion of Austria and even of the South Tyrol while Italy was still engaged with the bulk of her forces in Ethiopia.[7] From the French point of view, the reintroduction of conscription in Germany might be accompanied by her reoccupation of the Rhineland.

Since neither France nor Italy could depend on assistance from Britain, the question of future military staff talks was tentatively raised in the Rome discussions.[8] Although the initiative in this was evidently taken by Mussolini, the idea had first been adumbrated by Aloisi during the previous August. The Italian General Staff may also have pressed for a military convention with France in order to secure success in Ethiopia. The French General Staff regarded a military agreement with Italy as highly desirable. It would enable them to move approximately 14 divisions from the frontiers with Italy in Europe and North Africa to their exposed frontier with Belgium; they could also concentrate naval forces in the North Sea instead of in the Mediterranean. The French were suffering from a special and serious handicap: as a result of the decline in the birth rate during the 1914–18 war, the number of recruits to the French army was reduced from approximately 230,000 in 1934 to 118,000 men in 1935. The problem was so grave that the service chiefs were seriously interested in the possibility of the new rapprochement's leading to the deployment of Italian forces on French soil. The presence, in an emergency, of Italian troops in the more defensible areas of France's perimeter would permit a stronger concentration of the available national manpower in more vulnerable areas.[9] (The subsequent history of this remarkable notion is related in chapter 12.)

By far the most controversial of the secret agreements was that concerning Ethiopia. France was prepared to forgo those economic interests in that country which she had enjoyed under the 1906 agreements, except in the zone adjoining the Djibuti–Addis Ababa railway (of which, even so, 7 per cent of the shares were to be acquired by Italy). To the gratification of his diplomats, Mussolini verbally elicited from Laval France's 'désintéressement politique' in Ethiopia, and there is no doubt that Laval used the expression a 'free hand' in

regard to Italy's activities there. It is, however, highly unlikely that he
acted on his own initiative in this. The promise had to be made in such a
way that it could not be disowned by him or by his successors. Léger,
Secretary-General at the Quai d'Orsay, most certainly knew that his
predecessor and Laval had in 1931–2 advocated such an arrangement
(as we saw in chapter 1). But Mussolini still had to pin the French down
by a written undertaking on this point.

In a note of 4 January 1935, Laval agreed that France would seek no
advantage for herself in Ethiopia, 'even in the event of a modification of
the status quo', apart from upholding her economic interests in the
country as defined in the agreements. Britain's interests in Ethiopia had
also to be respected.[10] This letter can be considered as conclusive
evidence that Laval had no objection either to the Italians' organising a
coup against Haile Selassie or to their annexing Ethiopian territory by
force. But his insistence on upholding French economic interests in the
Harar and Shewa regions, through which the Djibuti – Addis Ababa
railway passed, ruled out France's complicity in a total conquest of
Ethiopia. On this issue Laval was misled. Mussolini's aim now was
indeed the conquest of Ethiopia; and the interception of the
Djibuti – Addis Ababa railway was one of his main strategic objectives
(see chapter 15). Laval, and later the British service chiefs, seem to have
reckoned that the Italians would, at most, take advantage of internal
unrest and follow the example of the famous Marshal Lyautey who,
after a long guerrilla war lasting from 1912 to 1934, had conquered
Morocco and converted it into a French protectorate.[11]

Minor frontier rectifications were also agreed to in Italy's favour
between Eritrea and French Somaliland, and between Tunisia and
Libya. It was to be open to children of Italian parents, born in Tunisia
after 1945, to choose Italian citizenship; those born after 1965 were
automatically to become French citizens. Although Mussolini was
accused by Italians living in Tunisia of selling them to the French, he
was given ample time to repudiate this arrangement if the French were
to let him down.[12]

While in Rome Laval visited the Pope. It is often overlooked that he
was the first French statesman for seventy years to be granted a papal
audience. Pius XI, always an advocate of Italian – French friendship,
presented the ex-Socialist with a rosary of coral and gold in exchange
for three handsome calf-bound volumes published in the seventeenth
century. The meeting was of political significance. The Vatican was
extremely concerned at the encouragement Hitler was giving to the

National Socialist neo-pagans in Germany, and also at the recent rising of miners in Spain led by Anarchists and Militant Socialists. It is not known whether the subject of Ethiopia was raised at Laval's Vatican audience. The *Osservatore Romano* so far had supported the Italian point of view over the Wal Wal incident, and the Pope was greatly appreciative of the French Republic's sympathetic understanding of the 'mission of the church'.[13]

Italian missionaries, under the strong influence of the Jesuits, were remarkably tolerant towards the Fascist regime and later many of them supported the war in Ethiopia. There was much rivalry between them and the French missions. Already in 1930 the Italian missionaries were using the Ethiopian College at Addis Ababa as a base with the aim, not of converting adherents of the Ethiopian Coptic Church to the Latin form of Christianity, but of detaching them from their administrative head, the Coptic patriarch of Alexandria, and of bringing them as a 'Uniate Church' into allegiance with Rome. A very limited success in this direction had been achieved in Eritrea, with the establishment there of a small Uniate Coptic Church.[14] While it is almost certain that the Pope knew nothing of Mussolini's military plans for Ethiopia, the establishment of an Italian protectorate over that country might prove advantageous to the Roman Church, strictly provided that it did not lead to war. The leaders of the Coptic Church, for their part, recalled their predecessors' success in previous centuries in resisting the influence of the Franciscans and later the Jesuits. There was now a new organisation to which they could turn in resisting renewed Roman Catholic pressure. Already by 1935 League of Nations Unions, backed especially by the non-Roman Catholic Churches, were active in Britain and in other liberal – democratic states. Appeals from Ethiopia to what is loosely termed 'world opinion' were not to fall on deaf ears.[15]

But in the early stages of the dispute over Wal Wal, the Ethiopian representatives at Geneva made little or no headway with the permanent League officials. Ethiopia's fresh appeal of 3 January 1935 for the quarrel to be submitted to the Council under article xi of the Covenant was side-tracked by Joseph Avenol, who followed with alacrity the advice of Massimo Pilotti, his Italian deputy. According to Avenol, the Council was not 'automatically' obliged to take cognizance of the appeal. Instead he enjoined Italy and Ethiopia to settle their differences under article v of the 1928 Treaty. Mussolini agreed to this on 19 January.[16]

Despite danger signals, the issue of Wal Wal had so far caused only friction, not a quarrel, between Italy and Britain. On 26 December 1934 Vansittart warned Barton at Addis Ababa that colonial interests 'should not at this stage be allowed to react in a way upon the relations between Italy and the League and thus affect the European situation'. But Britain's attitude (which is dealt with more fully later in this chapter) was not consistently maintained.

Sir Eric Drummond in Rome had been kept in the dark on colonial issues, and he told Mussolini that no negotiations had taken place between the British and Ethiopian governments on the Zeila Plan. Mussolini knew through his own excellent Intelligence Service that the opposite was true. He could hence accuse the British of duplicity, which caused Drummond acute embarrassment. Vansittart in a letter of 27 December 1934 attempted to enlighten Drummond on his government's real intentions. Apprehensions in the Egyptian Department of the Foreign Office concerning leakages of the Zeila proposals in Addis Ababa led to a considerable tussle with the Colonial Office. Barton was accordingly not only warned by Vansittart to proceed very cautiously with the Zeila Plan, but also told that it might be necessary to drop it altogether. ' . . . I must tell you in strict confidence that we have been confronted with great difficulties in the whole matter, owing to the pronouncedly anti-Italian attitude of the Colonial Office'. He admitted that its apprehensions had some foundation. Apart from renewed Italian 'cultural' activity in Malta, which was much resented by the Colonial Office, it was feared that, once in occupation of Wal Wal, the Italians would next deny use of the wells to British-protected nomads. It was generally believed by the native inhabitants over 'wide stretches of the African continent', Vansittart continued, that Italy 'intends sooner or later to smash Ethiopia, paying scant attention to the rights of other countries'. An attack on Ethiopia, unopposed by Britain or France, would lead to a very definite loss of British authority over the tribes. Regardless of the truth behind such allegations, ' . . . We are not helped by frank statements made recently by Vitetti [the Italian chargé d'affaires in London] to the effect that Abyssinia provides the only region in Africa open to Italian politico-economic exploitation'.[17] Although Vansittart, who was given considerable responsibility for the day-to-day decisions on foreign policy, firmly believed that the defence of Austria must take absolute precedence over that of Ethiopia, he yet had no desire to encourage the Italians. Mussolini was thus not altogether wrong in his belief that the best course open to Italy was 'to let sleeping dogs lie'.[18] Mutual recriminations between Italy and Britain were exchanged on other matters. Mussolini complained that British officers at Wal Wal were aiding and abetting the Ethiopians. On 14 January Eden lodged for the second time a protest about the obstacles Italian officials had put in the way of British-protected nomads seeking to use the wells. According to Drummond, the situation was now 'threatening'.[19]

From Mussolini's point of view the Wal Wal issue was only of secondary importance. On 23 January, having agreed to the compromise of the 19th and to staff talks with France, he took the momentous decision which, according to Aloisi, might 'jeopardise the whole future of the regime'. Practical preparations for war against Ethiopia were to start immediately. He was in an extremely bellicose mood. 'I wish', he said on 24 January, 'to make an army of soldiers and workers. Relations between nations are founded on force of arms.' And later: 'A nation to remain healthy must have a war every twenty years.'

The conquest of Ethiopia had now become an 'idée fixe' with Mussolini, and he neglected other important matters of state. On 1 February he planned for the Fascist militia to be integrated with the army.[20] Already Minister of Colonies, after the departure of De Bono to Eritrea on 16 January, he decided on other ministerial changes. Alessandro Lessona became Under-Secretary for Colonies but with no real power. Since Aloisi was far from enthusiastic about his leader's gamble, Mussolini wanted him posted to Paris. But Italy also needed the services of an experienced diplomat and brilliant lawyer at Geneva. So Aloisi's job was now to get the major powers to revert to an earlier plan for solving the Wal Wal dispute by means of a Commission of Conciliation and Arbitration, as provided for by the Italian–Ethiopian treaty of 1928. The commission was to continue with its investigations until October, when the monsoons came to an end; military operations could then start. Such was the Italian plan.[21]

Now that Mussolini's own diplomats knew that he was in earnest, and determined on war, Britain could no longer be held in suspense. On 29 January Vitetti, on instructions from Rome, told Simon 'in an informal way' that Italy, having concluded economic agreements with France on the future of Ethiopia, would be quite prepared to negotiate with Britain as 'seemed suitable for defining more precisely the extent of our respective interests in connection with the Tripartite Agreement of 1906'. Simon, according to the Italian account, ended the conversation by remarking that Italy would surely be as much averse as other powers to regarding Abyssinia as an area to be absorbed by European states. Grandi, who personally shared Simon's view, had no desire to follow up the interview with further enquiries as to Britain's attitude, and he received no clear-cut instructions to do so. Later both Grandi and Simon were taken to task for having failed to define their respective government's position towards each other with greater precision.[22]

Mussolini took no notice of Simon's veiled warning. On 10 February the nucleus of an army corps of two to three divisions was put in a state of readiness to depart to East Africa.[23] The world press gave a most hostile reception to this news. On 27 February the British cabinet for the first time discussed the Ethiopian question and later set up an interdepartmental committee, headed by Sir John Maffey (later Lord Rugby), to review British interests in that country.[24] Earlier in the month both Simon and Vansittart attempted, through Grandi, to dissuade Mussolini from embarking on war in Ethiopia. The British could not honourably refuse an Ethiopian request to import war material, purchased from foreign firms, to pass through British Somaliland. On 27 February Vansittart bluntly told Grandi that the 'Italian military preparations appeared disproportionate to the nature of the controversy', and added: 'Italy must not form illusions on the attitude of British public opinion, which is hostile to the idea of war in Africa as elsewhere.' But Mussolini, despite warnings from Grandi and his diplomats, persisted in thinking that 'Ethiopia could be considered as an object of the colonial policy of the three powers concerned and not one of international [i.e. League] policy'. He was well aware that British imperial interests in East Africa were not so important to London as security in Europe, and he believed that the 1925 agreement was still in force.[25]

He was not altogether mistaken in his interpretation of the British attitude. Vansittart took the view, which was widely held in the Foreign Office, that the energies of both Nazi Germany and Fascist Italy should be allowed some outlet. This, it was envisaged, was to be achieved by peaceful penetration in Africa, not in Europe where the danger of war was greater. But so long as Simon, who had the lawyer's aversion to unnecessary initiatives, remained Foreign Secretary, there could be no question of Britain's deliberately offering Italy Ethiopian territory unless war between the powers were imminent. Certainly, Vansittart's aim was to win Italian support for the containment of Germany. But he was at cross-purposes with the Duce. The latter acted on the assumption that Italian forces would first overwhelm Ethiopia and then return to Europe before German rearmament was complete. For their part, Vansittart and certain members of the cabinet believed that, if Italy embarked on a colonial war which would prove a long affair, she would render herself useless as a power factor in Europe.[26] Even so, despite the fundamental differences of view, there were still in April 1935 no indications of an open rupture between Britain and Italy over Ethiopia. Far more serious in the eyes of Mussolini and his diplomats was British policy in Europe.

An election was due in Britain later in the year. Nothing was more likely to keep the predominantly Conservative 'National Government' in power, so Mussolini thought, than some British confidence-trick in foreign policy—such as recognition of German rearmament within well-defined limits and, above all, the enticement of Germany back into the League. Mussolini's apprehensions were not without foundation. He had at least one good reason to suppose that Germany might even prove more dangerous to Italy if she rejoined the League than if she remained an outsider. He was apprehensive not only of German military power but also of a German appeal to the principle of self-determination, which was so popular in League circles. He was thus anxious that the Saar plebiscite should not result in an overwhelming majority in favour of union with Germany (which in fact happened) and he did not conceal from the British his dislike of plebiscites.[27] He may well have feared that after the Saar plebiscite Germany would rejoin the League only to demand plebiscites in Austria and even in the South Tyrol.

Moreover, Mussolini may have exaggerated the personal conflicts between the decision-makers in London far beyond their true proportions. Vansittart, for example, was allegedly opposed to Simon and on bad terms with Eden, Lord Privy Seal. Although Eden did not share Vansittart's view that the League was an ineffective instrument for preserving peace, the two men worked tolerably well together and, Eden especially, found the atmosphere in Geneva congenial. They had repeatedly told Grandi that an Italian attack on Ethiopia would have serious consequences.[28] Assuming that, in a last analysis, Mussolini was reasonable, they felt assured that he would not attempt any act likely to endanger the peace. But a study of the available Italian military documents suggests that the British statesmen might have had as mistaken a notion of Italian intentions (which was to prove no less unfortunate) as the Italians had of the British.

The reception given by the generals to Mussolini's directive of 30 December 1934 was far from favourable; and, in spite of Baistrocchi's demand that the plans of all three services should be co-ordinated, there was almost total confusion. General Valle, Deputy Minister of Air, wanted the air force to conduct a war on its own. Totally disregarding a previous plan for constructing airfields on the Eritrean plateau, he proposed the construction of new airfields in the sweltering heat on the plain adjoining the Red Sea coast, 100 kilometres distant from the bases from which the army would operate. His aim was twofold: to infuse a 'healthy terror' into the enemy by destroying urban centres (of which there were none!); and to prevent an Ethiopian invasion in the south by setting ablaze the scrub in Somaliland.[29] He even wanted the air force to dispose of its own ships for the transport of the dismantled parts of machines by sea. The naval high command was no less jealous of its autonomy. It reckoned that four-and-a-half months would be needed to transport to Massawa the number of men, material and animals (as estimated before the plan had been extended to 30 December). Instead of co-ordinating the plans of all three services, Badoglio on 19 January told Mussolini that, because of the insuperable logistical problems (including the transport of wood for huts, which was in fact unnecessary), the campaign should be postponed for two years.[30]

De Bono, now on better terms with Badoglio, was bewildered by Mussolini's new plan. On 3 January he complained: 'In military matters the chief is an amateur. He wishes to send almost the whole army, the air force and navy [to East Africa] without considering how they are to be transported there and be supplied.' To his chagrin, General Graziani – the ruthless desert warrior who was a by-word for brutality in the war against the Senussi, and whose personal loyalty lay, not with the crown, but with the Duce – had been appointed commander in Somaliland. After the Wal Wal incident this theatre had been reinforced at the expense of Eritrea. De Bono had learned from Graziani that Mussolini would not 'permit anyone else [except himself] to steal the limelight. If there is to be glory that glory must redound to the Duce alone. He is too much persuaded that the regime is in need of military glory.'[31]

G. Rochat and G. W. Baer, together with those Italian historians who accept a priori the primacy of internal over external policy, rightly lay emphasis on Mussolini's thirst for personal glory.[32] But they go further than this, and claim that, since the economic crisis hit Italy later than other countries, Mussolini intended to cut unemployment and also solve Italy's demographic problem by a dazzlingly successful colonial war. The evidence, however, that the economic crisis hit Italy first in 1932, and that recovery had started in 1934, carries considerable weight, and when Mussolini issued his directive of 30 December 1934, no explicit or implicit reference was made to internal discontent.[33] There is a further consideration. If Mussolini for domestic reasons wanted war, why did he wait for several weeks after the Wal Wal incident before ordering the attack? Did he issue the directive of 30 December in order to rouse the Italian people from their flagging enthusiasm for the regime, or did he want to humiliate Ethiopia? In the course of the crisis, the more he was castigated by Britain and the League, the greater was his resolve to avenge himself on his intended victim and, by the same token, to win prestige for the regime. No clear-cut distinction can thus be drawn between the external and internal stimuli which were both goading Mussolini to war.

No doubt Mussolini was also spurred on by the fear, expressed on many occasions (notably in his directive of 30 January), that after Haile Selassie had modernised his army he would use it to attack the Italian colonies. Fear of being put to shame by a barbaric African kingdom gradually gave way to Caesarian delusions of grandeur and, with them, a recklessness in the conduct of policy. On 30 December 1934 he still assumed that Haile Selassie's intentions towards Italy were hostile. But on 26 February, in the middle of the international press campaign against Italy, he wired De Bono: 'Since we can now say that the Negus has no intention of attacking us, we are thus able to take the initiative ourselves.' On 8 March he was more specific: De Bono was to have 300,000 men, 300 to 500 aircraft and 300 vehicles. 'You asked me for three divisions by the beginning of October. I intend to send you 10, I say ten. Five from the regular army, five from formation of Black Shirt volunteers. These Black Shirt divisions will prove that the enterprise has popular consent. . . .' The implication of the last sentence is that the party and its leader were to be as much involved in the venture as the army and its king. By the middle of March De Bono recognised that the campaign had assumed a radically new character. On 16 March he noted: 'While at first it was considered that a defensive action could be converted into a spirited counter offensive, today it is considered necessary for us to assume decisively the offensive.'[34]

Badoglio – who drew up a detailed plan of campaign on 8 March in which he stressed the importance of the battle of annihilation, to be won by the commitment of the air force – again warned Mussolini that 'an all-out war against Ethiopia represents without doubt the most difficult undertaking assumed by a European nation in Africa'. Fully aware of the logistical problems, he reminded Mussolini that the road between Asmara and Massawa could not carry double the existing traffic until the middle of October 1935. The Duce had no choice but to give way, and to reduce the size of the monthly contingents of troops due to reach Massawa. He rejected, however, Badoglio's assumption that the Somaliland front was of 'secondary importance'. Hence 100,000 men were to be kept in Italy to feed either front.[35]

At the end of March De Bono unexpectedly learned from several sources that the Ethiopians intended an offensive towards Assab. In a state of near-panic he immediately asked Mussolini for more aircraft and vehicles. He was not to be disappointed. The first units of the *Gavinana* division soon arrived at Massawa where there was inadequate transport to convey them to Asmara. After the Italian troops had landed in Eritrea on a large scale in May 1935, Mussolini had committed himself to a policy of war.[36] The alternative of accepting a compromise peace would mean sending thousands of troops and their equipment back to Italy. Such an expensive and senseless move would make Italy the laughing-stock of the world and would impose on her a humiliation greater than the Fascist regime could bear.

10 The Stresa Interlude

MEANWHILE, as a result of the plebiscite held on 13 January 1935, by which an overwhelming majority of the inhabitants voted in favour of union with Germany, the Saarland reverted to the Reich on 1 March. Although Aloisi was congratulated by Hitler for his skilful handling of the problem, neither he nor Mussolini could now hold on to their former illusions about the rate of German rearmament. Among many causes of friction between Italy and Germany, that of Austria remained paramount and 'prevented the possibility of discussion of other international questions both in Europe and abroad'.[1]

The British had agreed with the French at a meeting in London on 3 February to consult with the other powers if Austria's independence were threatened or if Germany by unilateral action repudiated her disarmament obligations. They also took up an idea, originally proposed by the French, that Germany should be invited to participate in reciprocal agreements with the other Locarno powers for assistance in the event of air attacks. Hitler accepted with alacrity the idea of an air pact; and, although he did not wish to be inveigled into negotiations for a general agreement on arms limitation as a substitute for Part v of the Treaty of Versailles, he gave way and accepted Simon's condition that the subjects for future Anglo-German negotiations should be treated as an 'indivisible and integral whole'. On 20 February it was agreed that Simon should visit Berlin on 8 March. The British were optimistic about the outcome.[2] On learning the news, Grandi immediately sought a meeting with Simon. In masterly, vituperative prose he described the meeting in a private letter to Mussolini:

One of the results of the Rome and London meetings has been to give Germany a very precise feeling of her own isolation. Experience shows that this is the only way with any possibility of bringing the Germans back to their senses. And now these lunatics of Englishmen, instead of working on the natural German apprehension at seeing the allied bloc revived for the first time since Versailles, rush off to Berlin simply as a result of their wretched and completely wrong-headed electoral machinations. . . . And thus, once more . . . as inconsistent as their fog, the English will have helped to hasten on the time of war, instead of having helped the cause of peace.

Grandi had already contacted Corbin, the French ambassador in London, on many occasions since the Rome Agreements. In spite of their combined protests, 'Simon's answer was and is always the same. . . . I [Simon] see Lloyd George point to me with his finger: "It is your fault because you rejected Hitler's offer of conversations . . .".' Simon tried, but failed, to inveigle Grandi into a discussion about postponing the dispatch of the two Italian divisions to East Africa.[3]

News of Simon's proposed visit to Berlin reached Rome at a time when Germany was still on probation, waiting for the return of the Saarland before committing her next offence. The Italians rightly feared that the Anglo-German flirtation would continue even after a new fait accompli, the nature of which could not be predicted.[4] Hitler in fact wanted to meet Simon only after he had achieved a position of strength from which to bargain. Using as a pretext a British White Paper on the need for accelerated rearmament, in which reference was made to increased German expenditure on arms he caught a diplomatic cold and the visit was postponed. On 5 March the *Luftwaffe*, the existence of which the British dreaded, was officially established as a third branch of the armed forces. On 16 March a law was promulgated in the Reich for the reintroduction of conscription. Although the French reaction against Hitler's decisions was, at first, much stronger than the Italian, Mussolini was chagrined to learn that the British rejected a proposal that there should be an immediate meeting held in Italy to discuss steps for preventing future unilateral action by Germany.[5] Still worse, Simon, instead of cancelling the visit to Berlin, decided to go there in late March. His aim was to make a final bid to induce Germany to recognise prescribed limits in her armaments, and (to the horror of Mussolini) to try to win her back to the League of Nations.[6]

Suspicious of Britain and violently angry with Hitler on account of Germany's reintroduction of conscription, Mussolini declared on 23 March in a speech commemorating the foundation of the Fascist movement that the 1911 age group would be called up.[7] It has been contended that he merely used events in Germany as a pretext to raise more troops for the invasion of Ethiopia.[8] But the Italian documents suggest that his primary aim still was to play the strong man in Europe and frighten Germany. He afterwards told Aloisi: 'I know the Germans only too well. By this method alone, namely a show of force, can they be convinced.'[9] He would also have in mind the fact that Italy would soon be depleted of some of her best army units; he needed therefore to deploy sufficient forces at home to guard the Brenner while the war in Ethiopia was in progress.

News of the meeting between Simon and Hitler was described by Mussolini as 'absolutely disastrous'.[10] In fact Simon and Eden were 'electrified' to learn from Hitler, who was lying, that Germany had attained air parity with Britain; and while Hitler still refused to budge on the question of Germany's return to the League, he was yet prepared to start negotiations for a bilateral naval agreement with Britain. The door for a general Anglo-German rapprochement thus remained open.[11]

Mussolini was angry with Britain not only because of her policy in Europe but also because of certain indications that she was collaborating with Germany in Africa. On 4 March Drummond was given accurate details by Suvich of the arms deal concluded between Steffen and the Emperor[12] (mentioned in chapter 8). Perhaps this served as a warning for, earlier in the year, Grandi had been told in London that Colonial Office officials in British Somaliland could not refuse foreign firms the right to transport arms to Ethiopia through British territory.[13] But the German government had to take the full brunt of Italian protests. On 27 March, after his return from a visit to Paris and on instructions from the Duce, Suvich complained to Hassell not only about Steffen's activities but also about a démarche allegedly made by Kircholtes, the newly appointed German minister to Ethiopia. The day before he presented his credentials, Kircholtes gave Haile Selassie 'comprehensive assurances' that Ethiopia could rely fully on German support 'diplomatically and in practical matters'. It was believed in Rome that arms, including aircraft and material for chemical warfare, would be despatched, and German instructors seconded to train the Ethiopian army and air force. With utmost urgency a courier was sent on 28 March from Berlin to Rome with a statement prepared by Bülow, denying flatly that there was any substance in Mussolini's charges.[14] In fact the Ethiopians in the spring of 1935 were so certain that League states would support them with arms that they apparently failed to follow up the contacts previously made with Berlin.[15] (In chapter 12 we shall trace later developments in German – Ethiopian arrangements over arms.)

Of no less concern to Rome was the distinctly pro-Ethiopian and anti-Italian comment in the German press. In a talk with Rust, German Minister of Education, on 11 April – the day the conference of British, French and Italian leaders opened at Stresa – Renzetti complained that certain members of the Nazi Party were not taking instructions from their Führer but were hoping to subordinate him to their own will. He proposed that these fanatical persons, responsible for pro-Ethiopian propaganda, should be 'driven into concentration camps'. Renzetti's conclusion was that Hitler wanted better relations with Italy, but was not yet fully in control of the Reich.[16]

Even more serious for Italy than German aid to Ethiopia were fears of a German drive towards the south – fears substantial enough to cause the Swiss government earlier on to lodge a protest in Berlin.[17] On 26 March in response to the war scare, Hassell found it necessary to remind Suvich that 'No sensible Italian could believe that we are planning a coup against Austria or an attack on Italy . . .'. Suvich replied that Germany's willingness to negotiate with the Western powers (meaning Britain) had caused such a surprise that many Italians feared a 'sudden German decision'. After a further meeting with Suvich on 29 March Hassell, describing the general atmosphere in Rome, reported that Italy was gradually slipping away from her traditional ties of friendship with Britain and merely accepting directives from Paris. Although no mention was made of Italian – French staff talks, 'Italy', he claimed, 'is constantly subject to powerful political and military pressure from Paris . . .'. Even in the Italian Foreign Ministry a 'military clash' with Germany in the near future was considered inevitable. Since Mussolini was 'expected to take action against Ethiopia within twelve months', he was opposed to 'warlike developments in Europe'. But there was 'no other way out', Hassell concluded, 'unless Germany changes course at the eleventh hour'.[18]

The Germans also regarded Italy as a potential enemy. By the end of March, on the eve of fresh staff talks between the Italians and French, German military and naval planners were assuming that France and Italy were 'determined to attack us'. They expected that the French fleet, reinforced by an Italian squadron, would operate in the North Sea.[19]

The war scare at the end of March coincided with renewed diplomatic activity by Ethiopia against Italy. On 16–17 March, just after Germany had reintroduced conscription, the Ethiopian government, in an appeal to articles xi and xv of the Covenant, claimed that 'in consequence of the mobilisation ordered by the Royal Italian government and of the continued despatch of troops and war material to the Italian – Ethiopian frontier there now exists between Ethiopia and the Royal Italian government a dispute likely to lead to rupture'.[20] It would be interesting to establish whether Haile Selassie was in fact, as is suggested by the Italian documents, making simultaneous approaches openly to the League and secretly to Germany. At this stage Mussolini found it increasingly difficult to champion the League in Europe against Germany and defy it in Africa. On 22 March he denounced the Ethiopian appeal as 'inaccurate and inappropriate', but once again called for direct negotiations. The Ethiopian government (represented at Geneva by Teckle Hawariat), realising that Mussolini was playing for time, appealed to Avenol to have the issue placed on the agenda at the forthcoming session of the Council to be held in the middle of April. Hawariat was told that the Council itself would have to take the decision, which meant that responsibility lay with Britain and France. On 10 April, on the eve of the Stresa Conference, Mussolini took a further step to render intervention by the League virtually unnecessary. He now agreed to the nominating of a commission of arbitrators.[21]

It has been argued that he was pursuing a skilful and systematic policy of isolating Ethiopia step by step in order to gain time before the date of the attack.[22] In certain respects this is true. Aloisi, for example, despite Mussolini's ham-handed interference, managed Italy's difficulties with the League with consummate skill. But the Duce did not give Italian policy towards Ethiopia that central direction with which he is often credited, for all that, on 4 April, he established a Department for Ethiopian Affairs under the old stalwart of the *politica periferica*, Guariglia.[23] Before taking office, Guariglia had thoroughly familiarised himself with the terms of the Rome Agreements with France and Mussolini's motives for signing them. He was also aware of Grandi's warnings of the growing hostility of British opinion towards Italy's aggressive policy in Africa. But his task was not easy. Apart from the Foreign and Colonial Ministries and the General Staff, the Press Department was involved. Its head, Galeazzo Ciano, Mussolini's son-in-law, was intriguing against leading Italian diplomats, such as Suvich, and also against the Vatican. It is evident from Drummond's reports that the average Italian was, to say the least of it, far from enthusiastic about the Ethiopian *impresa*, and 'propaganda preparation' for it was to be expected. But it is more than probable that Ciano's

Press Department presented Mussolini with accounts of the state of Italian opinion favourable to a war of conquest in Ethiopia. This department also drew the Duce's attention to material in those British newspapers (such as the *Daily Express*) and magazines which were taking a favourable line towards Italy, and were less concerned to give commensurate coverage of hostile British comment.[24] Believing that Britain was capable only of moral grunting, Mussolini evidently did not think it necessary to raise the matter of Ethiopia at Stresa. But Suvich, having discussed the matter with Guariglia, persuaded him at the last moment to take with him his East African expert, Guarnaschelli.[25]

According to De Felice, the French were mainly responsible for keeping the discussions at Stresa in April 1935 free from embarrassing questions on Ethiopia, on the grounds that such questions would be likely to jeopardise efforts towards establishing a united front against Germany.[26] But France and Italy were not alone in responsibility for deciding what was to be discussed at Stresa. For reasons precisely opposite to those of Italy and France, the British government was intent that the subject of Ethiopia should not be placed on the main agenda. It fully realised how ruffled Mussolini was over the visit of Simon and Eden to Berlin at the end of March, and it believed that relations with Italy could only worsen if awkward enquiries were made about Italian aims in Ethiopia. British policy in Europe also diverged seriously from that of France and Italy. On 8 April the cabinet had decided to reject an invitation, which was expected to be made by the other two powers, for Britain to form part of a united front against Germany. Instead, its intention was to make one more attempt to persuade the French and Italians to co-operate with the British in attracting Germany back into a system of collective security under the auspices of the League and with the aim of disarmament. Moreover, Britain was as anxious as ever not to assume new commitments – as, for instance, preventing the Germans from acquiring Memel from Lithuania, or taking over Austria.[27] Grandi realised that the British intended to sweep under the carpet complications arising over Ethiopia, and insisted that there should be frank discussion. At the last moment he persuaded Vansittart to take with him to Stresa Geoffrey Thompson, the British expert on Africa.[28]

When Ramsay MacDonald, Simon and Vansittart, but not Eden (who was suffering from air sickness) conferred with Mussolini, Flandin and Laval, accompanied by their respective experts at Stresa from 11 to 14 April 1935, the main proceedings – not surprisingly – were almost entirely confined to European problems. Germany's repudiation of her disarmament obligations was condemned; Britain and Italy reaffirmed their obligations under Locarno; all three powers agreed to consult on the steps necessary for the maintenance of the independence of Austria.

But Ethiopia was not overlooked. While the principal negotiations were being held on the island of Isola Bella, Thompson on the mainland, in the course of four conversations, learned from his opposite number, Guarnaschelli, that Italy could not 'exclude the possibility of solving the Ethiopian question by force'. Thompson regarded this revelation as of the highest importance and immediately informed Vansittart. He was asked late on 13 April to discuss the question with Simon at breakfast the next day. Vansittart and Simon, before learning from Thompson about Italy's hostile intentions towards Ethiopia, had already drawn up the text of the final communiqué according to which the three powers 'working within the framework of the League . . . find themselves in complete agreement in opposing by all practical means any unilateral repudiation of treaties which may endanger the peace of Europe'.[29] In fact, Simon left for Isola Bella without consulting Thompson, who had to eat his breakfast alone.

It has been held that Vansittart bears the major responsibility for having failed to warn Mussolini that the Ethiopian question would soon prove more than a matter of friction between Italy and Britain, and actually bring these powers to the brink of war. The subject of Ethiopia was not, as is generally believed, by-passed at Stresa. But Stresa has given rise to a myth. In the summer of 1935 Mussolini told Flandin and others that at the last moment he had secured the addition of the qualifying expression 'of Europe' to the word 'peace' in the communiqué. Vansittart in his memoirs adopted Mussolini's account, and even the most recent authorities have accepted this at its face value. In fact, the British had themselves drafted the communiqué the night before it was signed, which perhaps deluded Mussolini all the more into thinking that they would not oppose him over Ethiopia.[30] The next two months were to show that he had gravely miscalculated.

11 Towards a Détente with Germany

NEVER had Mussolini's prestige stood higher than after Stresa and the Council meeting of the League which followed immediately afterwards at Geneva, on 15–17 April, 1935.[1] The vote of censure cast against Germany for repudiating her obligations under Part v of the Treaty of Versailles was, Aloisi remarked, 'an impressive manifestation against Germany, due solely to the energetic attitude of Mussolini who had imposed his point of view on the other two powers'.[2] Certainly the Duce, along with Vansittart, was accused in Germany of having taken the lead in establishing the League's anti-German front. On 20 April Hassell delivered to the Italian government the protest to the League powers in which Germany declared that she refused to recognise the discrimination shown against her at Geneva, and would reserve the right to define her attitude to it. Aloisi was told by Mussolini to 'consign that document to the archives'.[3]

Two related developments were soon to cause additional animosity between Italy and Germany. On 24 April news reached Rome that Britain had asked the government of the Reich to send a mission to London to conclude a naval agreement. Once again the Germans sought to confront Britain with a fait accompli, for they had already launched twelve submarines. The prospect of Germany's becoming a naval power again finally put an end to one vexed issue in Italian–French diplomatic haggling over many years: naval rivalry. France would now concentrate her fleet against Germany. Staff talks took place on an official level after Stresa, and Italy and France were soon to draw so closely together that a strategic alignment emerged. On 13 May they concluded an Air Convention.[4]

Mussolini's main motive in committing Italy to France was certainly his concern to defend the Brenner frontier, a subject on which Hassell had frequently warned his government.[5] Even before the Stresa meeting he had maintained that it would still be possible to prevent Italy from throwing in her lot wholeheartedly with France, provided that the government of the Reich were to declare publicly that it intended neither to annex Austria nor to interfere in the internal affairs of that country. Italy's main concern, Hassell claimed, was still fixed on the old Roman *acies occulorum*, with anxiety over the incursion of the 'Cimbri and Teutons' from the north, and a 'forcible solution of the Austrian problem'. That Mussolini's repeated requests for a German assurance over Austria were treated coldly was understandable, he admitted; but the blank refusal in Berlin even to consider them wounded the Duce in his most sensitive spot, amour-propre. Neurath brushed aside Hassell's remonstrances. There was little point in offering the olive branch to Italy at a time when 'hysterical outbursts' in the Italian press were made against Germany, and when military measures were taken in Italy as a response to the reintroduction of conscription in Germany. Mussolini's fears of a German invasion of Austria were attributed by Neurath to the 'extremely faulty Italian intelligence service'.[6] Yet there was still little or no control exercised by the Wilhelmstrasse over party agencies in Bavaria, which continued to hurl abuse against their favourite target, Fascist Italy. So indignant was Mussolini at reports of these continued attacks that, early in May, he told Pittalis, the Italian consul in Munich, that from now on 'all bridges with Germany are broken. If she wishes to co-operate for the peace of Europe, so much the better; otherwise we will crush her, for in future we stand completely on the side of the Western powers.' Hence he desired better relations, not only with France, but also with Italy's old antagonist, Yugoslavia.[7]

However, Hitler soon had an opportunity for inserting a wedge between Italy and France. After the conclusion of the Rome Agreements on 6 January 1935, Laval and Mussolini continued to promote the idea of a Danubian pact, according to which Austria's principal neighbours (if possible including Germany) would pledge themselves to a policy of non-intervention and non-aggression in regard to Austria. The option was to be left open to any member of the pact to go one stage further and conclude a treaty of mutual assistance. Hitler viewed with suspicion the formation of an Italian – French condominium in South-East Europe; and when Germany was again invited to take part in negotiations he hedged, using as a pretext his preference for bilateral, as opposed to collective, undertakings. But the French for their part did not want to be too dependent on the support of Italy. On 2 May, after prolonged negotiations, Russia and France concluded a Treaty of Mutual Assistance; and on 16 May Russia agreed to support France if that country fulfilled its obligation to aid Czechoslovakia in the event of an unprovoked German attack.[8] Henceforward Hitler's wrath was directed primarily against Czechoslovakia. Indeed, between late March and early May 1935 he had under consideration a preventive war against that country.[9] With German interest deflected elsewhere, the question of Austria was to recede into the background. And Rome, too, was greatly disturbed by the Franco-Soviet Treaty.

Antagonism to Communism did not, as we have seen, prevent Mussolini from making an agreement with the Soviet Union in the shape of the Non-Aggression Pact of 2 September 1933, when this seemed to be a useful device for bringing Germany to heel. But he shared with Hitler a deep antagonism to the Soviet Union and to its 'competitor' totalitarian creed. He feared that if Russia were brought fully into the European system she would – in addition to throwing her weight against Italian expansionist aspirations and notably in the quarrel with Ethiopia – use her new treaty arrangements to spread Communism, not only among the French but also among Italian workers in France. He was very uneasy, despite boasts to the contrary, about the possibility of anti-Fascism's gaining ground in his own country.[10] Nor had he any sympathy with Czechoslovakia, a country where parliamentary institutions on the whole proved effective, and which allegedly acted as a link between the Comintern and the League. There were, moreover, many Austrians who sought the protection of Prague rather than that of Rome.

Another cause of friction between Italy and Germany had yet to be removed. The success of an Italian expedition against Ethiopia depended to a large degree on depriving the Emperor of arms. Although Neurath had assured the Italians early in April that not 'a single rifle or cannon' had been sent to Ethiopia from Germany, they continued to believe that German citizens were enlisting for service under the Lion of Judah and that two missions would be sent from the Reich to Addis Ababa, the first to deal with technical, the second with military, matters. The main Italian anxiety was over the possible dispatch of aircraft manned by German crews.[11] On this score their fears were soon to be allayed. According to a report of 10 May to the Foreign Ministry from the Ordnance Department of the German army, the only arms to have reached Ethiopia from Germany were of minor importance, such as hand-grenades. There was a ban on the export of artillery and machine-guns. It had not, however, been possible for the *Luftwaffe* to check whether German aircraft were being smuggled into Ethiopia via other countries.[12]

There was also a new complication of world-wide import. Italian claims on Ethiopia had thrown open the question of a repartition of Africa, and this afforded Hitler an opportunity for raising the question of the return of German colonies with Simon and Eden during their visit to Berlin at the end of March. As we have seen (chapter 3), under the 'gentlemen's agreement' of April 1933 Germany and Italy were obliged to consult if either party negotiated with a third on the redistribution of colonial territory. Both parties could now accuse each other of breaking this agreement. It was feared in Rome, and also in Paris, that Germany would use an independent Ethiopia as a base to extend her influence in East Africa. It was later feared in Berlin that the British and French would bribe the Italians to desist from the Ethiopian venture by the gift of territory elsewhere in Africa – probably at the expense of Portugal, whose colonies were coveted by Germany also. Certainly, the Portuguese and the South Africans were well aware of the Italian threat: mere talk of a repartition of Africa was bound to provoke anti-European unrest among their native African subjects.[13]

While Hitler's ultimate aim was expansion in Europe, not Africa, he had first to break up the Stresa front – which meant setting Italy at loggerheads with her partners in Europe. The quarrel between Italy and the League provided him with a 'heaven-sent chance' which he was determined to exploit for all it was worth.[14] He could exert or relax pressure on Italy as it suited him, provided that neither course proved detrimental to German interests. The success or failure of future German policy depended on whether he could exacerbate the quarrel between Italy and the League.

Before the Stresa conference met, the option was still open to Ethiopia to submit her differences with Italy over the Wal Wal incident to the Council of the League. Italy had agreed on 19 January 1935 to allow the quarrel to be settled under article v of the 1928 Treaty, but she had taken no practical steps to implement this decision on the grounds that direct negotiations between the two parties should first be tried. The Ethiopians were becoming impatient with Mussolini's dilatory tactics. On 17 March they had again appealed to the League, this time under articles x and xv. Between 10 and 14 April Mussolini tried to undermine Ethiopia's case for an appeal to the Council, at its next session on 20 May, by agreeing in principle to nominate two Italian representatives for the Commission of Conciliation and Arbitration.[15] But no action was taken.

On no account could the British cabinet allow Mussolini to stall indefinitely and thus provide Ethiopia with a valid pretext for appealing to the Council. If Haile Selassie had his way, Britain would be placed in the intolerable dilemma of having to choose between Italy and the League. This perhaps explains why at the secret meeting of the Council on 15 April Simon unexpectedly invited the governments of Ethiopia and Italy to give the Council an immediate assurance that 'the conciliators on both sides should be appointed before the May session of the Council and that the terms of reference of the Commission should be fixed in advance'. The Ethiopian delegate readily accepted the proposal, provided that military preparations undertaken by Italy were called off. Aloisi, speaking for Italy, said that his government would do its utmost to see that the procedure of conciliation and arbitration was set in motion as soon as possible; but, strongly backed by Laval, he refused to give a pledge that Italy would comply with what she considered to be a British ultimatum. Simon used even stronger language with Avenol after the meeting.[16]

Senior Italian diplomats were at this stage far more concerned about Britain's attitude than was Mussolini himself, who was not present at Geneva. The British had not replied to the Italian hint of 29 January that they should state what their imperial interests in Ethiopia were, and the Maffey committee of Colonial Office experts examining the question was far from finished with its tedious work. Guariglia received a report on 16 April giving the impression (which was true) that Britain was more concerned with securing her imperial interests than with upholding the Covenant. The British General Staff, so the report ran, was calculating on an Italian – Ethiopian war of such duration that at the end of it, when a crisis was expected in Europe, Italy would not militarily be in a position to confront Germany in Europe. In the meantime, Britain would try to profit from the conflict by securing her own long frontiers with Ethiopia. There was all the more reason, according to Suvich and Guariglia, to keep London through Grandi fully informed of the scope of Italy's intentions.[17]

Grandi responded with alacrity to instructions. In a talk with him at the end of April, Vansittart brushed aside the contention that Britain had ulterior motives for demanding a solution of the Wal Wal problem by means of a commission of arbitration. On the contrary, the British aim was to remove the dispute from the atmosphere of Geneva and to have it settled by direct negotiations. Grandi replied that Italy 'foresaw in the near future a new conflict in Europe. It was thus necessary for her first to secure her frontiers in East Africa', which she considered to be threatened by Ethiopia. After defeating Ethiopia, Italy could then transfer her forces and stand up to Germany. Vansittart reminded him that causes of friction between Italy and Britain in East Africa could be resolved with little difficulty. However valid the Italian case might be, the crux of the matter was that 'British public opinion would be decisively against Italy' and could not be controlled by the government. Simon later confirmed in more general terms Vansittart's statement of the British position.

Soon after, on 4 May, Mussolini told Drummond that it was necessary for Italy to solve the Ethiopian problem by whatever means were open to her in order to win freedom of action in Europe. But Drummond did not warn him in forthright terms of the dangers involved. He even went so far as to tell Suvich on 14 May that, if the French aim was to restrain Ethiopia, the British would follow suit. Drummond was subsequently called to London where he was informed of the gravity of the situation.[18] The day before (3 May) his meeting with Drummond, Mussolini asked the British government through Grandi whether it was prepared to give Italy the same free hand in Ethiopia as had been given by the French in January. The cabinet discussed Mussolini's démarche at meetings held on 8, 15 and 17 May. It came to the conclusion that support for the League against Italy would 'greatly compromise Anglo-Italian relations'. What was worse, the European situation would 'be most seriously affected' and it would be 'hard to imagine a state of affairs which would be more welcome to Germany'. On the other hand, if the British government failed to take a stand in support of the League, it would lay itself open to strong public criticism. Later in the crisis the British defined more clearly the full implications of betraying the League. It would, Simon told the cabinet on 17 July, amount to nothing else but 'a heavy blow' at the 'whole of the Pacts and Agreements on which the post-war system of Europe had been built up'.[19] Mussolini had placed Britain in a position over Ethiopia not unlike that of the Inquisitor with Joan of Arc. How could a suitable formula be found to save Ethiopia's soul without having to burn her body?

But there was one significant change in the British attitude. Before Stresa the British tried to coax Italy into accepting the idea of a rapprochement with Germany: a country with whom she had a fierce quarrel. By the middle of May the British feared that Italy would on her own initiative come to terms with Nazi Germany.

At a time when the British were hedging on what their future attitude should be, the whole issue of Ethiopia assumed a menacing character. On 7 May one regular and two Blackshirt divisions were put on a war footing and more age-groups were called up. On the same day Lessona, Under-Secretary for Colonies, declared to the Italian chamber that the time had come for Italy to resolve once and for all the Ethiopian problem.[20] On 14 May, speaking to the Senate after Lessona, Mussolini himself gave full publicity to the Italian aims. But he chose his words carefully so as not to antagonise Britain. He denied that Britain or France had made a démarche in Rome on account of Ethiopia, and laid the blame for recent Italian military measures squarely on the shoulders of the Ethiopian government which had started mobilisation. He spoke emphatically of Italy's role in continuing to maintain peace in Europe.[21]

His next move was to deny the Ethiopians a pretext to resort to the Council of the League which was due to meet on 20 May. In accordance with British demands on 19 May he named the Italian members of the Commission of Conciliation and Arbitration. Drummond returned to Rome on 19 May with verbal instructions from London. He told Mussolini on 21 May that the quarrel over Ethiopia must not be allowed to undermine the authority of the League. Drummond posed to the Duce the dangerous question: whether Italy would be satisfied if she were enabled to enjoy in Ethiopia a status analogous to that of Britain in Egypt. Mussolini expressed interest in the idea.[22]

Until the important meeting of the Council of the League in May 1935, the whole question of Ethiopia was viewed within the context of European affairs. It was asked in London and Paris how Hitler would exploit Anglo-Italian differences for his own ends. His Reichstag speech of 21 May was a diplomatic masterstroke, which threw the Stresa front into disarray. Although he alluded to a 'legal element of insecurity' which France's alliance with Russia had introduced into the Treaty of Locarno, Germany would continue to recognise that treaty. This pleased the French. Hitler also said: 'Germany neither intends nor wishes to interfere in the internal affairs of the Austrians . . . to annex Austria or to conclude an *Anschluss*.' The words were spoken precisely at a time when the Austrian government was soliciting support from Rome. They could not have been better chosen to allay Mussolini's personal suspicions of Hitler's intentions. But Hitler added a rider which has frequently been overlooked. In rather confused words he claimed that the Germans of the Reich and Austria were people of the same 'descent' who must be allowed that right of self-determination which was accorded to nationals of other states. Whereas the Germans living in Switzerland were contented with their lot, the same could not be said of the Austrians. By implication Hitler was demanding the right to achieve an *Anschluss* by consent, while at the same time regretting the tension caused by the Austrian question in German – Italian relations.[23] Hitler's ambiguous words gave rise to protest in the Italian press. On 25 May, to Bülow's later regret, the German press was ordered to refrain from further propaganda 'not only concerning the Ethiopian question but on all matters concerning Italian policy as a whole'. Two days later Mussolini learned with gratification that Göring had prohibited the export of aircraft to Ethiopia. The first step towards a German – Italian détente had been taken.[24]

From the Italian point of view, the press truce with Germany could not have occurred at a more favourable time. Towards the end of May the real duel was no longer, as Aloisi noted, between Italy and Ethiopia but between Italy and Britain, behind whom were ranged all the supporters of the League.[25] Mussolini was certainly prepared to accept the British challenge, but he still could not afford to convert wild words into deeds. He had to take into account the skilful tactics employed by Teckle Hawariat and Gaston Jèze (a Frenchman by birth), the two delegates of Ethiopia at Geneva. On instructions from the Emperor, Jèze informed Geneva late in May that his government would invoke article xv of the Covenant only if Italy either refused to agree to arbitration on all questions of dispute (including the demarcation of frontiers), or failed to give a clear promise not to resort to force.[26]

There has been much speculation on why the Emperor gave precedence to arbitration over action under the Covenant. He certainly had every reason to suppose that Italy feared arbitration. According to Guariglia, if the Commission of Conciliation and Arbitration decided that Italy was in the wrong, she would have to pay Ethiopia an indemnity. If, on the other hand, Ethiopia were proved to be in the wrong, she might have to make territorial concessions to Italy which would be certain to fall short of the latter's desire. However the verdict went, Italy would be deprived of a convincing pretext for going to war and would be forced to frame a new incident to achieve her purposes.[27] But if Italy feared arbitration, for Ethiopia there were dangers in resorting to the League. Ethiopia's own record was not unstained. From previous experience Haile Selassie was very well aware of the role of

Avenol, the League's Secretary-General, in manipulating the complex procedure of the Council in Italy's favour. Avenol had, in fact, kept up his sleeve a subtle plan, later disclosed to Theodoli (see chapter 12), for turning the tables against Ethiopia at Geneva: one which would enable Italy to act as the accuser. Under this plan Ethiopia was to be condemned as a bad neighbour who, in violation of the 1906 and 1928 treaties, had allowed armed bands to cross her frontiers into Italian, French and British Somaliland. She had subjected her Galla and Negro inhabitants to all manner of indignities, including slavery. While Avenol did not go so far as to suggest that Italy could win sufficient support to have Ethiopia expelled from the League, yet he believed that she should, as a member of the Council, co-operate with the French in undermining Ethiopia's position.[28]

But Mussolini was not yet ready to fall in with Avenol's subtle stratagem. Instead he instructed Aloisi to negotiate directly with Laval and Eden on ways of keeping the quarrel outside the competence of the League. Mussolini rejected an Ethiopian proposal that neutral observers should examine the military situation on the spot, claiming that Italy's military preparations should not be subject to scrutiny by representatives of the Council. He also turned down an Anglo-French proposal that Italy should renounce all resort to force. On 25 May, after the toughest bout of bargaining Eden had so far had to endure, a compromise was reached. Italy and Ethiopia agreed to submit the dispute to conciliation and arbitration under article v of the 1928 Treaty, the Italians hoping to gain more from conciliation, the Ethiopians from arbitration. The arbitrators, who could include one non-Ethiopian citizen on the Ethiopian team (a concession made by Italy), were to deal with all frontier disputes but not the question of sovereignty over Wal Wal. If arbitration failed the dispute would be settled under the Covenant. The proposal, as G. W. Baer points out, gave the Council the option at the end of August to become party to the dispute.[29]

The same day on which Mussolini agreed to compromise he spoke to the Italian Chamber. The emphasis of his speech was much less on Italy's obligations in Europe than it had been on 14 May. With Hitler's recent assurances over Austria in mind, he addressed himself to those who would like 'to fossilise us on the Brenner, to prevent us from moving the army in any other part of the world'. All European problems 'had to be viewed in relation to what may happen in East Africa'. He stated emphatically that the test of Italy's attitude to any given power would be exclusively determined by whether it supported or opposed Italy over Ethiopia. But he made no threats and the tenor of the speech was far from defiant.[30]

But Mussolini's mood was soon to change. News that the press in Britain greeted as a British victory Italy's acceptance of arbitration threw the Duce into a state of outright fury. He now seriously considered defying world opinion by both denouncing the Treaty of 1928 and withdrawing Italy from the League.[31] Acting through Lessona, he even proposed translating wild words into deeds by creating an incident as a pretext for an immediate attack. He also decided to mobilise three extra divisions to make up a total of eleven for the campaign. Aloisi warned him that precipitate mobilisation might expose Italy to counter-measures by the states supporting the League; it would be preferable to raise the necessary number of troops in stages. His diplomats were so appalled that, supported by the generals (especially Graziani), they presented him with a note on the adverse results which his intended repudiation of international obligations would have. By 31 May Mussolini had no choice but to climb down. Italy would abide by the Treaty of 1928 and remain in the League, but the pace of mobilisation was to be stepped up.[32]

Committed to war, Mussolini decided on a new plan for the future of Ethiopia.[33] He now set about studying the country's political and religious history. Having abandoned the idea of supporting the claim of Lig Yasu (deposed in 1916 and still alive), it was now his aim to have Victor Emmanuel III proclaimed Emperor. Guariglia, assisted by Astuto, an official of the Colonial Ministry, set to work on a 'scholastic monograph' on the problem entailed. The King of Italy was to be proclaimed Emperor by an assembly of *rases* and without reference to the Patriarch of the Coptic Church in Alexandria, who alone had the right to appoint the Abuna, the Egyptian head of the Ethiopian Church.[34]

Since Mussolini was determined on outright annexation, proposals for a compromise were considered solely in terms of tactical expediency. The first plan for a territorial compromise came from an unexpected quarter. On 7 June, when feeling was running so high in Britain against Italy as to cause Vansittart great uneasiness, there was a cabinet reshuffle. Baldwin took over the premiership from MacDonald, Sir Samuel Hoare replaced Simon as Foreign Secretary, and Eden was appointed minister responsible for League of Nations matters. The confusion resulting from these changes and the divergence in aim of the new policy-makers should not be exaggerated. One thing is certain: the new cabinet had to make urgent decisions. Its first major task was to continue negotiations with Ribbentrop for a Naval Agreement with Germany. This was concluded on 18 June. Germany was permitted to build a fleet just exceeding one-third of the tonnage of the British.[35] Indignation over the Naval Agreement was not as great in Italy as might have been expected: Britain was simply playing the foul game expected of her. But, despite advance warning, to which the French cabinet took no exception, there was an outcry in the French press over what commentators regarded as official recognition by Britain of Germany's repudiation of her obligations under the Treaty of Versailles. Moreover, having done a deal with one totalitarian state, the British government found it more difficult in future to act in accordance with high moral principles to another totalitarian state. Much of its support from the League came from the Scandinavian countries, who objected both to the prospect of German naval domination in the Baltic and to the high-handed manner in which Britain apparently tolerated treaty violations. But in a memorandum dated 17 July the British stated their case in a convincing manner and they thus did not lose the support of the Scandinavian states.[36]

Shortly after the conclusion of the Naval Agreement Hitler decided to follow up the truce of 25 May 1935 in press polemics against Italy by a new move to improve relations with that country. He personally placed considerable value on good relations with Italy. But there was the obstacle of his dislike of Cerruti (whom he had tried to persuade Mussolini to sack late in 1933). In a conversation lasting for one hour with Major Renzetti on 21 June, he admitted that every nation had the right to send whatever person it considered suitable as its representative to Germany. 'I too have the right . . . to speak truthfully only to those representatives who defend, and are obliged to defend, the interests of their own country.' But regardless of whether they were 'anti-German or anti-Nazi', Hitler said, he was interested only in whether they faithfully and accurately recorded his own words. Most ambassadors in Berlin, he claimed, fulfilled these requirements. There was one exception, the Italian ambassador – 'namely Cerruti'. He went on to say that, should the case arise that Mussolini even hinted that he was not content with Hassell, he would within twenty-four hours send any other person as ambassador – with the exception of Ribbentrop (who, as signatory of the Naval Agreement with Britain, was thoroughly unpopular in Rome).[37]

Renzetti's report was evidently read by Mussolini, who immediately took action. Cerruti was to be transferred to Paris, and Bernardo Attolico, a party man, was to move from Moscow to Berlin. But the services of Renzetti, who was most unpopular with both Italian and German professional diplomats, were no longer needed. Later in the month he was appointed Italian consul-general in San Francisco. Before leaving for Paris there was still work for Cerruti to do. On 21 July the Duce told Aloisi that, since a coup d'état by the *Reichswehr* could be expected at any moment, it was necessary for Cerruti to remain at his post.[38] The appointment of Attolico was to bear fruit only after several months. Mussolini still trusted Hassell, and it was not until 19 February 1936 that he contemplated asking for his recall.[39] But we can see that by June 1935 the two dictators had started in effect to intrigue against their own accredited diplomats, a process which culminated with the dismissal, first of Suvich in June 1936, then of Hassell in November 1937, and finally of Neurath.

In the summer of 1935 Mussolini was seeking all manner of ways of keeping open the possibility of improving Italy's relations with Germany, with the intention of putting pressure on Britain. He was to be disappointed. The day on which Renzetti met Hitler (21 June) an informant in Rome suggested to Hassell that an *intesa* (understanding) between Italy and Germany should be reached whereby Italy be allowed a free hand in Ethiopia and Germany be given back her former colonies. But the officials of the Wilhelmstrasse, who were more contemptuous of Italians than Hitler was, poured scorn on the proposal.[40] Cold-shouldered by Germany late in June, Mussolini had no alternative but to turn once more to France.

12   The Confrontation with Britain, June – July 1935

No sooner had Baldwin formed his cabinet on 7 June 1935 than the Defence Requirements Committee, established in 1934 (not to be confused with the Committee chaired by Sir John Maffey), came to the conclusion that Germany would be capable of launching a war in January 1939. With Japan waiting on the sidelines, 'enigmatic and disturbing', the best course open to Britain, in the cabinet's view, was to continue the policy of a rapprochement with Germany. But Baldwin was determined that Britain should step up her rearmament. Fear of Germany was the driving force behind British policy.[1] It became especially prominent in late June when the option seemed to be open to Italy to come to terms with Germany. By that time a diplomatic crisis was assuming a more pronouncedly military character.

Coinciding with angry attacks against Britain in the Italian press and rumours that Mussolini might turn to Germany, it was reported in London that many Italian troop-transports were on their way to the Red Sea. Italy was now actively preparing for war against Ethiopia regardless of Britain's attitude. The intensification of the crisis coincided with ministerial changes made by Baldwin, the new Prime Minister, and this enabled Vansittart to exert even greater influence on the formulation of policy. The new Foreign Secretary, Sir Samuel Hoare, had worked well with the Italians, including Mussolini, after their defeat at Caporetto in November 1917, and he was even more prepared than Simon had been to follow Vansittart's lead. On 8 June the latter bluntly told Anthony Eden, now Minister for the League of Nations, that Italy would have to be 'bought off' – otherwise 'Ethiopia was going to perish and so would the League'. Vansittart therefore revived the idea of ceding Zeila, with a corridor through British Somaliland, to Ethiopia. But this time Italy, not Britain, was to receive compensation in the form of a large stretch of territory in Ogaden. As we shall see, the cabinet sanctioned this proposal on 19 June.[2]

Meanwhile, the interdepartmental committee reviewing British interests in Ethiopia, under Sir John Maffey's chairmanship, had

completed a draft report by 18 June, the essentials of which were to be
accepted by the cabinet early in August. A first reading of its
conclusions indicates that Vansittart was right: 'No vital British
interests exist in Ethiopia', so the report reads, 'or in adjoining countries
sufficient to oblige His Majesty's Government to resist a conquest of
Ethiopia by Italy.' In certain respects, an Italian occupation of that
country would render it easier for Britain to rectify her frontiers and
secure her interests near Lake Tana. The report's findings were based
on the assumption that, after the conquest of Ethiopia, Anglo-Italian
relations would remain friendly. It was not foreseen that Mussolini
would throw in his lot with those so-called 'dynamic states', Germany
and Japan, which had already defied the League with impunity.

The Maffey Committee had not been invited to state its views on the
effect Italian expansion would have on the broader and graver problem
of imperial defence which became more pronounced later in the crisis.
Only by implication was this problem dealt with in the report: 'From
the point of view of imperial defence, it would be preferable if Ethiopia
remained an independent country.' In developing this argument, the
officials of the Foreign Office observed in a memorandum for the
cabinet of 5 August: 'It might not be an excessive exaggeration to
suggest that Italy harbours the long-range ambition of uniting her
North African territories with those of East Africa.' She was already
edging her frontier in Eritrea in a north-westerly direction towards
Libya, the frontiers of which had been enlarged earlier in the year. With
land communications established from Libya through the Sudan to
Eritrea, and from Eritrea to Somaliland, Egypt would be 'in a pocket',
and Italy would have direct, continuous access to the Indian Ocean,
Mussolini's ultimate dream.[3]

The Foreign Office and the Admiralty were becoming increasingly
aware that, parallel with his plans for the conquest of Ethiopia,
Mussolini had more far-reaching imperial aims. They were to be
proved right. In return for the demilitarisation of bases in the
Mediterranean he later demanded extravagant concessions for Italy.
Already in 1934 Italy had spent a vast amount on building up her navy
and had militarised naval and air bases in the Dodecanese from which
pressure could be exerted on Turkey to allow favourable conditions for
access through the Straits to the Black Sea, one of Italy's main trading
routes (especially for oil from Romania). From the Dodecanese the
Italians could also threaten Britain's sea communications in the eastern
Mediterranean. Negotiating from a position of strength, Mussolini

would be able to demand that Italy should have equal trading rights with Egypt and that the Constantinople Convention of 1888, governing traffic through the Suez Canal, should be revised in Italy's favour. Moreover, since 1934 the Italians had developed Massawa and other naval bases to be in a state of readiness to service warships, including submarines, which could prey on enemy shipping in the narrow waters of the Red Sea. Britain, Mussolini realised, would be at a severe strategic disadvantage if Italian ships took up their battle positions in the Red Sea before the Suez Canal was closed.[4]

In Italy's general confrontation with Britain, Mussolini had of course to take into account the pacific temperament of his own people who, on the whole, were favourably disposed towards Britain. But there was no need for him to use his outstanding talents as a propagandist to change their attitude.[5] He told Hassell early in August that he was spurred on to action by hostile comment in the British press, which he described as 'a whip necessary to wake up the broad masses'. It dispelled their 'timorous mental reservations' about his warlike policy. The Italian clergy were now on his side and were giving gold generously to defray some of the cost of the great military enterprise.[6]

The British cabinet had no choice but to continue to take its stand on those moral principles which infuriated Italians and made Mussolini all the more headstrong. On 27 June 1935 the results of the famous Peace Ballot in Britain were published. From this it appeared that 94 per cent of those voting agreed that, under the auspices of the League, economic and non-military sanctions should be imposed on an aggressor; 74 per cent favoured military sanctions. According to its critics, the League of Nations Union, which organised the ballot, failed to state clearly the precise nature of the action the League could take. It was presented as an effective organisation with an executive of its own to which Britain would merely contribute a military contingent. The League, it was implied, would uphold Britain, not Britain the League. It was not made sufficiently clear to the voters that Britain herself would have to do the work of the League almost single-handedly. Voters were also opposed to Britain's fulfilling her obligations to either side under the Treaty of Locarno; but they were not asked what their attitude would be if their country's vital interests were at stake.[7] Whatever the cabinet's collective opinion of the wisdom or reliability of the Peace Ballot, the outcome of this new form of mass-consultation certainly did nothing to weaken its conviction that the only option open to it was to steer a middle course between upholding the principles of the League and giving satisfaction to Italy within the frontiers of Ethiopia.[8]

Having taken stock of the situation, Hoare, Vansittart and Eden decided on 15–16 June on a plan which can only be described as a self-denying ordinance. Vansittart's proposal to revive the Zeila Plan – first mooted in 1932 (see chapter 8) – was endorsed by Hoare and Eden, in the new 'pro-Italian' form he had developed. Ethiopia was to be allowed the port of Zeila, with a connecting corridor of territory carved out of British Somaliland. In return, Ethiopia was to be made to cede most of Ogaden in the south to Italy and allow Italy economic concessions within the rest of the empire. On 19 June Eden was instructed by the cabinet to present this new Zeila plan to Mussolini on a visit to Rome.[9]

Before leaving London, Eden received a letter, dated 13 June, from Avenol, who had learned from General Prasca, a prominent member of Badoglio's staff, that Italy was militarily prepared for a defensive war only. Conditions at Massawa were described as chaotic. Prasca had asked Avenol to use his influence to allay Italian fears (which might well have been genuine) of possible Ethiopian aggression. Avenol, having discussed the matter with Prasca, proposed to Eden that Italy should expose all her grievances against Ethiopia at a meeting of the Council of the League. In Avenol's mind was the calculation that, in so doing, Italy could outwit Ethiopia and deny her a monopoly of world sympathy. Eden, who was mainly concerned with the new Zeila plan, gave Avenol an evasive answer but admitted that there was a faint ray of hope opened by these proposals.[10]

Avenol had also to persuade Mussolini to adopt a more moderate pro-League line. Before Eden's arrival he discussed the crisis with Albert Theodoli, chairman of the Mandates Committee of the League. France, he claimed, could exert her influence over the British government only if an abrupt change could be brought about in British public opinion, which so far had been hostile to Italy. After the Conciliation and Arbitration Commission had completed its work, Italy, he claimed, should produce substantial evidence at Geneva proving that Ethiopia had violated her Treaty of Friendship with Italy of 1928 and had subsequently acted as a bad neighbour, unworthy of League membership. Suvich, having studied Avenol's proposals, believed that they afforded a possible solution but that only after the lapse of some two years could they bear fruit. It would be impossible for Italy to wait for such a long time. Drummond was also informed of

Avenol's conversation with Theodoli, which he reported to Hoare. Although Avenol's proposals were most probably known to Mussolini before Eden's visit, they did not at first carry much weight. Drummond, who informed Suvich of the forthcoming visit on 19 June, was reminded of Mussolini's 'unmovable determination'.[11]

Eden, accompanied by Strang, a Foreign Office official, left London on 20 June and first visited Laval in Paris. Their aim was to assuage French anger over the Naval Agreement, and no mention was made of the Zeila Plan. This silence has been rightly described as 'a most serious and deplorable error'.[12] Djibuti, held by France, would be rendered virtually of no value in the Zeila Plan were implemented. For her part, Italy made very strong objections to the Ethiopian acquisition of Zeila. Communications from this port to the interior of Ethiopia could be cut only by an Italian advance from Eritrea across the French-controlled railway from Djibuti to Addis Ababa, thereby violating French economic interests which Italy had promised to respect. Moreover, the corridor to Zeila lay within a British sphere of influence and was in striking-distance of a possible British attack. If Ethiopia had to be given a port, it should, in Mussolini's view, be one within easy grasp of the Italians; and this could be none other than Assab.[13]

Eden met Mussolini in Rome on 24-5 June. The Duce was given full credit by his own diplomats for his extraordinarily patient response to the British proposals which, if put into effect, would have converted Ethiopia into a maritime power and have enabled her to import arms.[14] In return, Italy would acquire yet more large tracts of useless desert. While categorically rejecting the proposal, and perhaps influenced by Avenol's plan, the Duce demanded the cession of all the non-Amharic areas of Ethiopia in the north and south, and a virtual protectorate over the rest of the country. If these claims were not granted, Mussolini (borrowing words from Crispi) declared that Ethiopia's 'name would be wiped off the map'. Eden was surprised to learn from him that in January Laval had given Italy a political, not just an economic, free hand in Ethiopia.[15]

There were many influential Italians, such as Grandi in London, who recognised that, once the principle of dismemberment had been accepted, Italy might gain what she wanted without resort to war. Since the French were already working on a more radical solution to meet Italy's needs, by which Ethiopia would for all intents and purposes be converted into an Italian protectorate on the model of Morocco, Italy was in a strong bargaining position. Could not the gap between the French and British proposals be closed and Mussolini's minimum demands be satisfied? But no such compromise could be reached unless League opinion in support of Ethiopia were first rendered impotent. Before Eden's departure Avenol's plan was accepted by Aloisi. At the opportune moment Aloisi would, as suggested by Avenol, launch an oratorical attack on Ethiopia at Geneva. France and Britain would then seek to persuade the Council to refer the problem for solution by the two remaining interested powers: France and Britain. A precedent had been set by the Chaco affair.[16] With the Council adopting this procedure, the British public would be persuaded that the prestige of the League had not been jeopardised.

Eden did not play into Aloisi's hands. At a cabinet meeting on 3 July he reported that his visit to Rome left no doubt that Italy, contrary to her obligations under the Tripartite Treaty of 1906 and those of the Covenant, intended an invasion of Ethiopia. This would leave members of the League with the simple alternative either of honouring their commitments or of allowing the post-war European settlement to collapse. After the meeting Baldwin, in face of determined opposition from the service chiefs, was still 'firmly in favour' of action, provided that the French agreed to support Britain.[17]

Baldwin had every reason to be concerned. After the rejection of the Zeila Plan, the Italians started secretly to mobilise their fleet and to stir up trouble among the Egyptian nationalists.[18] In one respect, this hostile display had revolutionary consequences for British foreign policy. Hitherto the French had had to beg the British for support in Europe, which was never forthcoming. Now the shoe was on the other foot; the British were now dependent on the French and were compelled to ask them for military support to uphold their imperial interests.

A revision of strategic planning had, in fact, made the French less dependent on British support. Whereas early in 1935 it was still their aim (at least in theory) to occupy Belgium as a prelude to an attack on Germany, after April 1935 the French service chiefs switched over to a purely defensive strategy. An occupation of Belgium was now considered necessary only for the defence of the industrial areas of northern France.[19] The Italians could enable them to find the necessary manpower better than the British. No sooner had Eden left Rome than Gamelin arrived. On 28 June a military agreement was concluded by which France undertook to send an army corps to serve as a 'sandwich' between the Italians and Yugoslavs on the Austrian frontier; Italy, in return, was to send a corps for co-operation against the Germans in the relatively safe area of Belfort. The military convention was to come into full force only within the framework of a general political agreement, still to be concluded.[20]

When approached on 2 July over the question of supporting Britain, Laval (now French Premier) stood on relatively firm ground. He declared that he was too absorbed with the budget to give adequate attention to the problem of Ethiopia. He went on to say that France would take no action which would result in Italy's withdrawal from the League. Because of the French delay, Hoare merely reminded Grandi that Mussolini's summary rejection of the Zeila Plan might mean that opportunities for future discussion would be lost.[21] With France restraining Britain, Mussolini had every reason to suppose that Ethiopia was isolated.

Ruling a country which was in the throes of an economic crisis, Laval did all in his power to have the Ethiopian crisis solved out of court by the signatories of the 1906 treaty.[22] If the Covenant had to be invoked there could be no doubt in his mind that it should act strictly on the lines suggested by Avenol. After Eden submitted the Zeila Plan, Laval still had reason to hope that it was open to France to support both the League and Italy. Only later in the crisis did it become apparent that she had to choose between them.

Despite his military agreements with France, Mussolini tried to maintain the links, established late in December 1934, between members of the German High Command and senior Italian officers, led by General Roatta, head of the Italian Military Intelligence. Roatta was evidently on good terms with his opposite number in Germany, General Stülpnagel (chief of German Army Intelligence) and with General Fischer (the General military attaché in Rome). Soon after Gamelin's visit, Roatta told Fischer that military agreements, but not a binding alliance, had been concluded with France for the defence of Austria. In September Roatta (as will be seen in chapter 14) was to meet Admiral Canaris (chief of German Armed Forces Intelligence) on the possibility of German – Italian co-operation against communism.[23]

With Mussolini's keeping a line open to Berlin, Laval could not afford to antagonise the British. In the last analysis, a binding and political alliance with Italy depended on whether this would leave him with no alternative but to abandon all hope of British friendship. Gamelin stated the issue clearly: while Italian support was 'desirable' that of the British in the long run was 'essential'.[24] There was yet some prospect that Italy and Britain could after all compose their differences, which would rescue Laval from an intolerable dilemma.

By 5 July the Commission of Conciliation and Arbitration, which had started its work on 6 June, had reached deadlock, allegedly on account of Ethiopian insistence that the question of the sovereignty over Wal Wal fell within its competence. On no account could the Italians afford to allow the Council, as agreed on 25 May, to place the entire dispute on its agenda at the meeting planned for late July. The Council's competence, so the Italians insisted, should be confined to choosing an arbitrator, selected from non-Italian members, who would act as a fifth member of the Commission. The closing date would then be 25 August by which time, so the Italians hoped, the Council would have taken no action.[25]

After the Commission's work broke down, the British cabinet was brought face to face with the problem of what it should do in the event of sanctions being invoked. Eden proposed at a ministerial conference on 15 July that the time had come for plain speaking: 'Laval should be told that His Majesty's Government would be prepared to fulfil their obligation under the Covenant if others did the same.' Eden's proposal was turned down. Instead, Hoare made every endeavour to give Mussolini what he wanted in Ethiopia provided that force was not used. He even told the House of Commons on 11 July that His Majesty's Government had always understood Italy's desire for expansion.

Aloisi did not conceal his gratitude. 'The British cabinet,' he noted, 'under attack from all sides, had decided to stop inciting the League against us', and he perceived in the words used by Hoare in the House a 'change of front' in Britain's attitude.[26] The British government's desire to avoid a confrontation with Italy was almost certainly due mainly, as will be seen, to the very serious apprehensions of the service chiefs, especially of the Admiralty. On 15 July Mussolini, taking advantage of Britain's evident change of attitude, announced the mobilisation of one additional army corps and one Blackshirt division.[27] The world now waited to see whether Haile Selassie, if left in the lurch by the League, would continue to stand up for the independence of his country.

With his country's treasury virtually empty, and his military forces lamentably ill-equipped with arms, the Emperor made an attempt, but failed, to win support from the United States.[28] He now had no alternative but to strengthen his links with another power outside the League: Germany. One of the most trustworthy of his political advisers,

D. Hall, was half-German. On 17 July Hall arrived incognito in Berlin and met Dr Prüfer, former German minister in Addis Ababa. In the name of the Emperor, Hall asked Prüfer whether Germany could provide Ethiopia with 3 million Reichmarks for the purchase of arms. The Emperor, according to Hall, was taking this step for no ulterior motive of self-interest, and was aware that Germany would warmly welcome a weakening of Italy's hold over Austria. Prüfer informed Bülow, who discussed the matter with Neurath. Although Bülow feared that an agreement with Ethiopia could have undesirable consequences in the event of its becoming known, he was against giving Hall a blank refusal. In view of the extraordinary importance of the Ethiopian conflict for future German policy, Bülow asked Neurath for a decision from Hitler himself. Hitler agreed to meet Hall's request; thereby he covertly reversed Germany's policy of neutrality.[29]

From a special fund at the disposal of the Foreign Ministry, Prüfer duly paid the Emperor's envoy. Afterwards Major Steffen was entrusted with the purchasing of war material, including Orliken guns made in Switzerland. The cargo was loaded at Lübeck on board a British ship, the *Santa Maria*, to which Hall, for security reasons, gave an Arabic cover-name. Later Steffen acquired thirty 3·7 cm anti-tank guns, with appropriate ammunition. These arms, originally intended for the German army, were purchased for Ethiopia, on Hitler's personal orders, from the Rheinmetall-Borsig firm. Every precaution was taken to ensure absolute secrecy. After the name plates of the manufacturers had been removed, the guns were put on ship at Stettin, a duty-free port, under the supervision of a retired *Luftwaffe* officer.[30] The *Santa Maria*'s final destination may have been Berbera, from which port local British officials were allowing arms from foreign firms to be sent to Ethiopia. The Italians certainly believed in late July that Britain was still permitting the transit of arms through her territory and, suspecting that Germany was a major source, continued to lodge protests at the Wilhelmstrasse. On 3 August Hassell assured Mussolini that Germany remained neutral. On 10 August Bülow put Funk, state secretary in the Foreign Ministry, fully in the picture, with the information that the dispatch of arms was, in fact, only then about to begin and that at no cost should this leak out to the press.[31] In the autumn a shipment of arms, presumably carried by the *Santa Maria*, was sent via Norway and Belgium to a port convenient for Ethiopia. No doubt knowledge of this shipment strengthened Haile Selassie's resolve to fight. The situation thus arose that, precisely at a time when the League powers were imposing an arms embargo on Ethiopia, the Germans were doing the opposite.[32] (Towards the end of September, however, Hitler – for reasons to be discussed in chapter 14 – decided not to extend his arms commitment to Ethiopia.)

The Emperor also won support from another unexpected quarter. It has been seen (chapter 8) that in 1933–4 Japan showed sympathetic interest in Ethiopia's predicament. Given her position in world affairs by 1935, it would not have been surprising to find her at this time turning away from the weaker partner in a conflict whose interests were gaining increasing support within the League. Like Germany, Japan had left the League in 1933. She was well pleased to see Britain at loggerheads with Italy at Geneva. Moreover, Sujimura, the Japanese ambassador in Rome, did not disguise his personal admiration of Fascism. He declared in the second half of July that his government would adopt a policy of neutrality in the Ethiopian dispute. However, anti-Western feeling was deeply rooted in Japan, and the Ethiopians' parlous plight as a 'coloured' people struggling against a European power aroused popular emotion, and also gave political circles an opportunity for serving Japanese world-interests. Sujimura's statement was disowned by the Foreign Ministry in Tokyo. This resulted in an Italian campaign, launched with 'great violence', against Japan.[33] Anti-Italian feeling in Japan was correspondingly intensified. So marked was the bitterness there against 'European imperialism' that in September, when Daba Birru, the Ethiopian chargé d'affaires, was received in Tokyo, he was given full diplomatic honours. Some 2000 students, belonging to the ultra-nationalist Black Dragon Society, were gathered to greet him, carrying placards with the slogan 'Down with Italy'. Later in 1935 a group of Japanese officers attempted to raise funds for a detachment of volunteers for service in Ethiopia.[34]

By the summer of 1935 Haile Selassie had proved himself in his relations with foreigners a very good propagandist; and, in contrast to Mussolini, he had won more popularity abroad than he had at home. On many occasions he or his advisers were capable of outwitting the more legalistic Italians who were working against him behind the scenes at Geneva. It is one of the myths of the period that Mussolini had systematically outmanoeuvred him step by step on the diplomatic terrain and that the subsequent campaign was a walk-over. In fact, Haile Selassie played his cards very well. He won material and moral support (for what the latter was worth) not only from members of the League but also from countries outside it. Germany promised – and sent – war material; and Japan offered something more than moral sympathy. Moreover the 'Third World' of the day, including Egypt and China, condemned Italian policy towards Ethiopia. Aid expected from abroad, even if it arrived late, enabled Haile Selassie to fight, although not to win, a war in which troops levied by feudal landlords were flung against a modern army and bombed by modern aircraft.

Germany's role in the crisis was perhaps as significant as Britain's. Manfred Funke, who has brought to light certain unpublished documents on Hitler's policy, draws the conclusion that Hitler intended assigning to the Duce a role in the Ethiopian war similar to that which Franco was later to play in the Spanish Civil War. For Hitler was not to wish Franco a 'hundred per cent victory', the continuation of internal conflict in Spain being in Germany's interests. Some qualification needs to be made, however, in a comparison between the Spanish and the Ethiopian conflicts. In the latter, Hitler at first tried to get both contestants, not just one side, to start fighting. His policy towards the Ethiopian question was bipartisan; it fluctuated, and he was not just the 'grinning spectator' who watched the opponents quarrel. That Hitler should want to exacerbate the quarrel between Italy and Ethiopia is not surprising. It was clearly in his interests for Italian attention to be diverted from Austria and from the issue of German rearmament. And, after Stresa, he had very strong reasons for wanting to make it difficult for Italy to uphold the status quo in Europe in co-operation with France.[35]

13 The Anglo-French Compromise of August 1935

THE concentration of Italian forces in East Africa and the construction of military bases, though not complete, were sufficiently far advanced by late July 1935 to make Mussolini all the more determined on action. In an article with the title 'The Irrefutable Fact', published in *Il Popolo d'Italia* on 30 July, he announced to the world that there could be no turning back. But on this occasion he laid far less emphasis than previously on Italy's 'civilising mission', and he did not mention the superiority of the white races. He concentrated instead on the vital need of the Italian people for more living-space and on the supposed military threat posed by a predatory neighbour in Africa. Ethiopia, he declared, tied down Italian forces needed for the defence of the Brenner frontier. He left his readers in no doubt that there would have to be a 'total solution . . . with Geneva, without Geneva, against Geneva'. A compromise was out of the question.[1]

In the second half of July the Ethiopian government requested that neutral observers should be sent by the League to investigate the build-up of forces on both sides of the frontier, and that articles XI and XV of the Covenant should be invoked to settle the quarrel. Avenol side-stepped the issue with the suggestion that the dispute should not come before the Council but be settled, to the exclusion of Ethiopian representation, by the signatories of the 1906 Treaty. But the Ethiopian delegates in Geneva did not press their case, for they knew that the only result would be open rupture with Italy and that country's withdrawal from the League.[2] On 24 July, after the Italian–Ethiopian Commission – established to settle the question of responsibility for the Wal Wal and subsequent incidents – had again reached deadlock, the Ethiopian delegation proposed anew to Avenol that the special meeting of the Council should be convened, as had been agreed to on 25 May. Avenol this time could not ignore the appeal, especially as Maxim Litvinov, the Soviet delegate and currently chairman of the Council, was more than anxious that Ethiopia should be given a fair hearing.

The Council was due to meet at the end of July, and the world waited anxiously for Britain to show her hand.[3]

The cabinet in London had of course to take into account the pro-League lobby, represented in the House of Commons as well as in the League of Nations Union which was organised on a nation-wide scale. But it would be a mistake to assume that most members of the cabinet, or their advisers in the Foreign Office, regarded the League as the sick man of Europe to whom lip-service had to be paid in order that a general election should be won. In August Vansittart even feared that, in defence of the League, Baldwin might involve Britain in war with Italy.[4] The general view in Whitehall was that the League was a useful instrument of conciliation (but not of coercion) through which Britain could make her voice heard in those specific disputes in which her own vital interests were not at stake. The League could also serve a more general purpose. On 29 July, before the Council met, Clerk, the British ambassador in Paris, was reminded by the Foreign Office that 'if the League failed to do its duties, the moral leadership of Britain and France would end'. As a result the 'countries of Central and Eastern Europe' would, out of 'apprehension of Germany', be drawn into the orbit of that country.[5] In other words, the League was an essential instrument for the maintenance by peaceful means of the balance of power in Europe against Germany.

The French, on the other hand, while valuing the League, took a different view of the role it should play. Admittedly, Laval strove for a direct understanding with Germany, but after the Anglo-German Naval Agreement of 18 June, Léger, Secretary-General of the Quai d'Orsay, persuaded him that, since Germany's position was now much stronger, she was no longer in such dire need of the friendship of France.[6] As the only alternative to a direct understanding with Germany, the French system of alliances, concluded within the framework of the League, had to be strengthened and used – albeit only in a last resort – by force so as to contain Germany within her frontiers. As regards Italy, there was also by August a more marked difference of emphasis in the attitudes of the British and French. The British aim was to uphold the League, without thereby incurring the hostility of Italy; the French sought, for military reasons, to cultivate Italian friendship, hoping that in so doing they would not have to choose between Italy and the League. Domestic considerations also heightened the differences between the two countries. In contrast to Britain, in France the extreme Right and the extreme Left were both powerful. A collapse of Fascism in Italy, occasioned by military defeat, would probably have the result of barring the French Right from power and of opening the way for the Left. Laval precariously stood in the centre. He could not rely for a majority in the Chamber on the moderate Right alone; he needed the support of those Radicals, led by Herriot, who favoured the League. It has rightly been contended that Laval was trying the impossible; to support both the League and Italy.[7]

Baldwin was not faced with so painful a dilemma. His aim was to convert the Labour Party to the cause of rearmament, and the Conservatives, if possible, to the Covenant. Had Laval from the start stated where France stood, Baldwin's task would have been immeasurably easier. For even if France declared she would support Italy and not the League, Baldwin would have been provided with a convincing reason, which he could use in an election campaign, for not taking action under the Covenant.[8]

Because of the worsening situation at the end of July, both countries had to review their strategic position. The major preoccupation of the British High Command was metropolitan defence against air attacks by German bombers. It also had to pay due attention to a danger in a more remote part of the world. At the end of 1934 Japan had repudiated the Washington and London Agreements for the limitation of naval armaments. Should war break out in Europe there was, so the British Admiralty thought, a real danger that Japan, taking advantage of her growing naval strength, would seize some of the rich territories in South-East Asia. Since American intervention for the protection of British imperial interests had to be ruled out, the Admiralty had no alternative but, in the event of war, to abandon Hong Kong. Singapore (the development of which as a naval base had been interrupted, to be completed only in 1937) could, it was thought, be held with some difficulty. Certain that the Royal Navy could not take on Germany and Japan simultaneously, the Admiralty decided that, while a small nucleus of naval forces should be retained for defensive action in home waters, the main body of the fleet should in an emergency be sent to the Far East, whence, having defeated Japan, it would later return to meet the challenge from Germany.[9]

Nothing was more vital than free and unrestricted access through the Mediterranean to the Suez Canal and the Red Sea. Although the need for rearmament was recognised in 1932, it was only in the spring of 1934 that the cabinet belatedly accepted proposals for giving immediate effect to a programme to repair deficiencies. But the Treasury, according to its critics, was spellbound by pre-Keynesian principles of political economy; it slashed the programmes for expansion which the Admiralty and, more particularly, the Army General Staff, had submitted for cabinet approval. As an alternative to the ten-year rule governing British defence strategies, plans for war against Italy, as well as the United States and France, were, as late as July 1934, excluded.[10]

The Ethiopian crisis made nonsense of the Admiralty's plans. In the first week of July alarming reports were received in London that the Italians had secretly started to mobilise their fleet. The Admiralty, therefore, on its own initiative began on a small scale to reinforce its Mediterranean Fleet, the aim most certainly being the protection of British imperial interests from a 'mad dog act'.[11]

After the breakdown of the Italian – Ethiopian negotiations on 5 July 1935, the service staffs were invited to examine the military prospects of war with Italy. They left no doubt that the imposition of sanctions, no less than the interruption of Italy's communications with Ethiopia, would lead 'almost inevitably to war': a war in which the co-operation of other sea powers would be vital. The one power they had in mind was France. Not only did France possess a formidable fleet of her own, but she could put at the disposal of an ally two excellent bases, Toulon and Bizerta, capable of accommodating and refitting capital ships. By using their air force in conjunction with that of Yugoslavia, the French could bomb the industrial towns of northern Italy and prevent the much-vaunted *Regia Aeronautica* from bombing Malta – the only British base in the Mediterranean with adequate docking facilities for capital ships.[12] The French could also be of invaluable assistance in a war on land. For example, should Mussolini decide on a move against Suez from Libya, he certainly possessed a force numerically far superior to that of the British. Senior Italian officers, moreover, were well-trained in desert warfare. But as the construction of the famous coastal road, the *Littoranea*, connecting Tripoli and the frontier of Egypt, was started only in February 1935 and not completed until April 1936, the Italians, before reaching Suez, would have to cross several hundred miles of open desert.[13] A French attack on their rear from Tunisia could prove catastrophic to them. When the Admiralty was ordered to prepare for a possible war with Italy, it reminded the cabinet that Britain needed two months to get her fleet ready, and stressed that the 'assured military support of France' was vital. That the French could not be expected to render assistance to Britain, so soon after concluding vital military agreements with Italy, can hardly have escaped the notice of British planners.[14]

The British cabinet and professional diplomats cherished the illusion that, in spite of his tendency to make bellicose noises, Mussolini was fundamentally a flexible and experienced statesman who would shrink from upsetting the peace of the world for the sake of Ethiopia. But the British had to use stronger language in seeking to restrain him than they had employed earlier in the summer. They also gravely miscalculated on the extent to which patriotic fervour had gained a grip inside Italy itself. By the late summer of 1935 it was too late to offer the Italians free access to raw materials and food in Ethiopia. National prestige now mattered more than pomegranates: it was generally felt that the time had come for Italy to fight, not to bargain. Towards the end of July, Guariglia and his colleagues in the Italian Foreign Ministry noticed a stiffening in the British attitude, and attributed this almost exclusively to cynical considerations of national self-interest and not to a resolve to uphold the Covenant. They even suspected that Vansittart, in his desire for a crusade against Germany, was striving to set the League in motion by testing it against Italy in order that it could later prove fully effective against Germany. The Italians also drew the conclusion that the British were beginning to have grave doubts about the value of Italy as a potential ally on the grounds that, irrespective of the outcome of a war in Ethiopia, the effect would be detrimental to Britain's interests and to her interpretation of international well-being. Should Italy triumph after a quick campaign, new ambitions in Africa, such as the conquest of the Sudan, would deflect her attention from Europe and convert her into an imperial rival of Britain. Should the campaign prove to be a long-drawn-out affair (as was expected by most military experts, including the Italian generals themselves), Italy would cease to be a power factor in Europe worthy of consideration; and this would upset British calculations of power-balance. If, on the other hand, the Ethiopians were in the end to triumph, not only would European domination in Africa and the Middle East be undermined, but the Fascist regime, already under financial strain, would fall and something more sinister would take its place.[15]

On the eve of the Council meeting late in July, Eden proposed that Mussolini should be given a strong private warning, but he was overruled by the cabinet and, instead, presented Laval with his government's written proposals. There was much muddled thinking behind the reasons advanced in the British proposals for avoiding a conflict over Ethiopia, and mention was made of diverting Italian expansion to other parts of Africa. To his later regret, Laval handed this too-revealing document to Aloisi who in turn sent it to the Duce. The phraseology in which the document was couched was so tactless that its authors left themselves open to the unwarranted accusation that they were deliberately trying to pick a quarrel with Italy. On reading it Aloisi noted: 'This is terrible for us. It spells out completely the intention of the British cabinet towards us. London, which treats us like little fools, is uneasy for the League, for its colonial empire, and will prevent us at all costs from our making war.'[16]

When the Council of the League duly met at the end of July it could not have gathered in less propitious circumstances. It was agreed that the Conciliation and Arbitration Commission, set up on 25 May and consisting of two Italian and two Ethiopian representatives, should resume its work, with the addition of a fifth member representing a power not involved in the dispute. The question of sovereignty over Wal Wal was not to fall within its competence. It was also agreed, on Avenol's advice, that Britain, France and Italy, to the exclusion of Ethiopia, should try, as signatories of the 1906 Treaty, to reach a general settlement among themselves without resort to the League. On 3 August, before the Council adjourned, it agreed, to the satisfaction of the Ethiopian delegation, that it should review the entire issue on 4 September.[17]

Mussolini left the negotiations to his diplomats and turned his own attention to preparations for war. In a letter of 6 August to Victor Emmanuel III (who was spending his holidays at Santa Anna di Valdieri in Piedmont), the Duce stated that Italy would have to prepare for war with Britain. The King immediately replied that he 'ardently' desired to avoid an armed conflict with Britain which, because of the uncertainty of support from France, would prove 'particularly grave' for Italy. 'We are bound to take into account the fact that, if faced with the choice of friendship with ourselves or with England, France in the end would choose the latter.' The King thus warned Mussolini, but took no action to stop him from following what could be regarded as a suicidal policy.[18] Mussolini remained resolute. He told Suvich on 9 August: 'I do not want agreements unless they give me everything, including the head of the Emperor.' The aim was not 'to gain time'.[19]

On 13 August Badoglio, on orders from Mussolini, conferred with Admiral Cavagnari (representing the navy), General Valle (air force) and General Baistrocchi (army). Cavagnari and Valle declared categorically that the Italian fleet and air force were absolutely unprepared for war against Britain. Baistrocchi was more optimistic of the army's prospects on account of the speed with which Italy could mobilise and the weakness of Britain in a war on land. Instead of sending Mussolini a plan of action, Badoglio on 14 August lodged a letter of protest. It read: 'Our fleet has no battleships; it has fast cruisers, with little or no defences; it has good destroyers, good submarines. It is thus able to engage in little more than what can be described as guerilla warfare at sea. . . . Given the conditions of manifest inferiority, our fleet could disturb, but not prevent, attacks attempted by the British fleet on our cities and on our industrial installations on the coast.' Italian aircraft had already deteriorated from many years of wear and tear. True, Italy possessed a few modern machines, but because of the need to recall and train 2000 pilots, the bulk of the air force would be out of action as soon as hostilities started. Badoglio laid the main stress on a relatively new arm. Britain had six aircraft-carriers which constituted a mobile base for approximately 220 machines. This base, escorted by warships, could move to any point in the Mediterranean. With Britain master of the seas and the air, Italian supremacy on land meant next to nothing. Ships carrying men and reinforcements from Italy to Africa could simply be intercepted by the British. Although Badoglio admitted that there was real indignation in Italy against Britain, he told Mussolini: 'It is, I repeat, my strict duty to declare to Your Excellency that I consider the situation now confronting us to be by far the most serious which our country has ever had to face in its long happy history of unification and national consolidation.' Mussolini summarily dismissed Badoglio's protests. On 13 August he informed De Bono that two additional Blackshirt divisions were about to embark; they duly left Naples three days later.[20] More units of the Italian fleet were also made ready for war and some were sent to the area where British shipping was most vulnerable to attack, the Red Sea.

Mussolini's warlike preparations were made at a time when the political situation was sharply deteriorating. Early in August it had been decided, on promptings from Laval, that Mussolini's old enemy and Haile Selassie's friend, Nicolas Politis, the Greek Foreign Minister, should act as the neutral arbiter rather than Nicolas Titulescu, the

Romanian who was much favoured by certain Italian diplomats. Laval evidently believed that, provided Italy could prove that she was the victim of 'continued' Ethiopian 'aggression', she need have no fear of League action. The Commission resumed its work on 19 August, at first without Politis.[21] But the question of responsibility for the Wal Wal incident had by now receded into the background. The independence of Ethiopia was at stake.

On 11 August, before Aloisi departed for the meeting with the French and British due to be held on 16 August in Paris, he was briefed by Mussolini. The Duce stridently declared: 'I want to see you leave with great defiance. You must act as a fighter rather than as a diplomat, as a Fascist rather than as a negotiator. Even if I am given everything I prefer to avenge Adowa. I am prepared.' Aloisi proposed that, until 4 September, Italy should stall and thus throw into disarray expected opposition from the League. Mussolini in his determination told Aloisi to speak 'frankly' to Laval and promise him that Italy would concert her action with France for the protection of the Danubian area. She would consent to a treaty, and even go as far as to conclude an alliance with Yugoslavia, 'provided that France supports us in this affair. . . . If this is so we will set up a barrier against German expansion in Europe.'[22]

For military reasons Laval had a hold over the British and could, it seemed, comply with Italy's wishes. On the eve of the negotiations the British service chiefs, backed by Vansittart, earnestly requested the cabinet to 'keep in step with France'. On the other hand, Britain enjoyed a political advantage over France. Avenol had just told Eden that almost every delegate to the Council, including those from countries allied to France, had been instructed by his government to follow the lead given by Britain. France, having thus lost the moral leadership of the League, had no choice but to draw closer to Britain.[23] In the negotiations of 16 August, Laval thus adopted an intermediary position between Eden and Aloisi, but he did not go sufficiently far to meet Mussolini, who wanted all or nothing. According to the French proposals, the League was to entrust Britain, France and Italy with the right to introduce reforms into Ethiopia. The former two powers should leave this task solely to Italy who thereby would be granted a virtual political protectorate over the country. The emphasis of the British plan, on the other hand, was on economic concessions, political control being granted to outside powers only if the Emperor gave his consent. Although 'frontier rectifications', similar to those suggested by Eden in June, were to be discussed, the independence and sovereignty of

Ethiopia were to be respected. Since the British proposals were far more likely to meet with League approval than those of the French, Eden had little difficulty in persuading Laval to accept them.

On 17 August, after its submission to Rome, Mussolini defiantly rejected the Anglo-French plan as 'absolutely unacceptable from any point of view'. Ten months earlier the proposals would have been 'open to discussion'. But since then Italy had dispatched 280,000 men to East Africa and had spent 2 million lire for the defence of her colonies against Ethiopia, who now (supposedly) deployed a force of 450,000 men.[24] Mussolini, adopting tactics already used by Hitler, now hoped that he could present Britain with a fait accompli. On 21 August he proposed advancing the date for the attack on Ethiopia to 10 September. For logistical reasons this proved impossible. The British and French were thus given additional time to work out a political solution.[25]

Mussolini considered that Laval had not given Italy the degree of diplomatic support expected of him: there had been too much hobnobbing with the British. Was it not open for Italy once more to seek to improve her relations with Germany? On 19 August, the day after Mussolini had rejected the Anglo-French proposals, Attolico (who had not yet presented his credentials to Hitler) had his first interview with Bülow. He complained about the isolation of his embassy and the difficulty in finding German press comment favourable to Italy. Bülow replied: 'We do not wish to have anything whatsoever to do with the Italo-Abyssinian conflict.' The new ambassador tried later to improve his relations with members of the Nazi hierarchy. He agreed, for instance to attend the Nuremberg party rally in September.[26] But the Germans, emphasising their strict neutrality, showed a chilly indifference to Mussolini's quandary. Guariglia even complained that during the summer of 1935 the absurd situation arose whereby anti-Fascist Italians for very different motives co-operated with German officials with the aim 'of exacerbating the animosity between Italy and England'.[27] Rebuffed a second time by the Germans, Mussolini had no alternative but to remain on good terms with Laval. He allowed flattering references to appear in the Italian press on Laval's constructive qualities as a statesman, and he pledged his word that he would remain loyal to Stresa – which meant that, if German troops moved into Austria or the Demilitarised Zone, he would co-operate with France.[28]

By the end of August the military agreements between France and Italy began to bear fruit. The French started to move some of their ten divisions, facing Italy on the Alps, to the north-east.[29] The Italians were enabled by the agreements to withdraw troops from the French frontier and to transfer them, partly to the neighbourhood of Tarvis in north-east Istria, but mainly to the Brenner frontier where, in the last week of August, manoeuvres were ostentatiously held.[30] The aim of this redeployment of Italian forces was twofold: to deter Germany from attacking Italy before the meeting of the Council of the League on 5 September; and to enable Italy to put pressure on either Britain or France by threatening to withdraw these troops and thus leave the way open for a German invasion of Austria.[31] (Mussolini, all the same, was still genuinely concerned by the German threat, and his expert on problems connected with the South Tyrol, Ettore Tolomei, had gone so far as to submit to him a plan for expelling the German farmers in Italy's Alpine region and resettling them after the war in the highlands of Ethiopia.)[32] Military co-operation between Italy and France was again discussed on 6 September when Badoglio paid a return visit to Gamelin. Both generals were anxious that the military agreements should come fully into force but that Italy should seek a compromise over Ethiopia.[33]

After the break-down of the negotiation in Paris, Mussolini, feeling militarily secure, informed De Bono by telegraph that the tripartite conference had failed. Since no results could be expected from the Council of the League, the diplomatic situation was exhausted. 'You can draw the conclusion.' Mussolini even refused to discuss the question of Ethiopia with British diplomats and must have learned with considerable relish from Aloisi that, in Vansittart's view, everyone must reconcile himself to the inevitable – which to the Duce could only mean 'our war with Abyssinia'.[34]

Following the failure of the Paris talks, Baldwin interrupted his holiday at Aix-les-Bains to attend a meeting of the cabinet held on 21 and 22 August at which Sir Ernle (later Lord) Chatfield, First Sea Lord, was present. The most important decision taken was that sanctions against Italy would be applied only collectively, which meant in concert with the French. But it was also decided that the Home Fleet, instead of leaving bases in the United Kingdom for its annual short-distance cruise, should instead concentrate at Portland on the 29 August and be ready to sail at short notice for Gibraltar. It was agreed that, because of the lamentable state of Malta's anti-aircraft defences and the discontent incited there by Italian agents, the Mediterranean Fleet should make its way, as inconspicuously as possible, from Malta to the eastern

Mediterranean, its eventual destination being Alexandria. The decision to withdraw ships from the commanding position of Malta greatly impaired Britain's prospects in an offensive war in the Mediterranean. Desiring at all costs to avoid an encounter with Italian warships, the cabinet decided that the arms embargo against both sides should remain in force, despite the pleas of the Ethiopian government. To prevent alarmist conclusions from being drawn at home or abroad from news of naval dispositions, an Admiralty proposal for calling up naval reserves was turned down.[35]

Both Chatfield and Admiral W. W. Fisher, commander-in-chief of the Mediterranean Fleet, were convinced that the British were more than a match for the Italians. Professor Marder, the naval historian, rejects as totally unfounded the accusation that the failure to take a strong line against Italy is attributable to pusillanimity on the part of Britain's navy leadership. Apart from the shortage of ammunition, there was an especially compelling reason for seeking to avoid war with Italy. The Admiralty estimated that, even if Britain emerged victorious from a naval war with Italy, there were bound to be losses, even of capital ships. The balance of strength in the Far East would thereby be tilted in Japan's favour; and even in home waters Germany, who now possessed fast pocket-battleships of the *Deutschland* class as well as submarines, stood to benefit. If, however, war with Italy could not be avoided, hostile action on her part should, in Fisher's opinion, be met within twenty-four hours by a concerted move of the Home Fleet, concentrated on Malta, and the Mediterranean Fleet from Alexandria. Chatfield informed him that such offensive plans had to be dropped on the insistence of the cabinet, because of French refusal to co-operate.

It is true that the British had potential allies, other than France, in the Mediterranean. Mussolini's blustering diplomacy and open support for terrorist organisations had made Italy very unpopular in Yugoslavia, Turkey and Greece. Admittedly, these powers were so preoccupied by their own internal problems, and other potential enemies, that they paid only lip-service to collective security under the League; and their armed forces, with the possible exception of Turkey's, were far from modernised. Even so, these countries could at least place at Britain's disposal useful bases. For instance, in August the Admiralty considered using Navarino (Port x) on the western coast of Greece, allegedly as an advanced base for a counter-offensive, but in fact to deflect the Italian air force from Malta. Meanwhile, the fleet was to remain at Alexandria. Although Alexandria was well situated to cut Italian sea communications through Suez to East Africa, the channel leading from the harbour to the open sea was so narrow that ships sheltering there could easily be trapped by an enemy (as the Russians had been at Port Arthur in 1904). Moreover, due to the varying levels of the water caused by the influx from the Nile, it was at Alexandria difficult to use the Asdic apparatus for detecting submarines. The redistribution of British naval units had begun on a small scale before the Council of the League met on 4 September. The fact that they were undertaken at all meant that the subsequent quarrel between Britain and Italy was to assume a strategical as well as a political character.[36]

On 28 August, at a time when the British were most anxious to win French support for the League, Laval held a cabinet meeting. Certain that the imposition of sanctions meant war, he declared that the aim of French policy was to exercise a moderating influence on Britain and, with this end in view, to persist in working out a compromise over Ethiopia. Laval was strongly backed by Jean Fabry, Minister of War, who, together with the service chiefs, was extremely anxious that military co-operation with Italy, provided for by the promising agreements of May and June, should be maintained. But there were dissenting voices within Laval's cabinet. Herriot, the leading Radical, declared at the 28 August meeting that he was in favour of negotiations on the future of Ethiopia, 'but, if the time comes when we must choose between Great Britain and Mussolini, I shall not hesitate for ten seconds: I am with Great Britain'. Laval could not ignore the strong pro-League stance taken by liberal-minded men in France and abroad. On 30 August he accordingly informed Mussolini, through Chambrun, that France could not betray the League, and that it would be advisable for Italy to accept a compromise.[37] Meanwhile Laval and Avenol were working on the plan, broached by the latter some months before, whereby Italy should turn the tables on Ethiopia and assume the role of accuser. The French Premier laid emphasis on Ethiopia's unworthiness of League membership: Avenol, on the ill-treatment of the minorities within Ethiopia.[38]

Laval might have been persuaded to drop the Franco-Italian alliance provided he could be sure of future British support against German aggression in Europe. On 2 September, before the Council met at Geneva, he asked Eden to give France 'the assurance that Britain would be as firm in upholding the Covenant, to the extent of sanctions in Europe in the future, as she appeared today in Abyssinia'. Laval made it clear that he was thinking of 'deliberate military aggression' which amounted to a violation of the Covenant and 'not merely a repudiation of treaties', which would arise if Hitler violated Locarno or attempted an *Anschluss*. Eden, on instructions from the cabinet, replied that it would be 'impossible' for his government to promise unconditional support for France in Europe, but that Britain's obligations to uphold the Covenant would be increased if it were enforced now, and decreased if it were violated with impunity by Italy.[39] Having failed to win vital assurances from Britain, Laval was left with no alternative but to do all in his power to give Mussolini satisfaction in Ethiopia and thus avert war.

14 Towards the Outbreak of War

MUSSOLINI in his propaganda certainly intended that the coming war should strengthen the vaunted monolithic structure of the Fascist regime; and he hated haggling round a conference table. But his boast that his government, unlike those of Britain and France, spoke with a single voice needs qualification. He certainly monopolised the key offices of state, but this did not mean that his subordinates, who were experts in their own spheres, were incapable of placing obstacles in his way if they thought his policy would endanger the security of their country. Administrative efficiency, so needed in time of war, was also badly impaired because of the vicious feuds, encouraged by Mussolini himself, among rival state and party hierarchies. There was virtually no liaison between the Italian Foreign and Colonial Ministries, and between them and the military authorities. Aloisi did not even know whether the attack would take place before or after the Council met on 4 September.[1] Indeed, so serious was the duplication of work among all the Italian authorities concerned with Ethiopia that it is a wonder that in the end Italy triumphed.

Badoglio certainly realised that Mussolini's policy might lead to disaster but he did not, as Rochat claims, leave everything pertaining to diplomacy to Mussolini's 'genius'. He had approached Avenol, as has been seen, through Prasca earlier in the summer. That he did so without, it seems, informing Suvich seriously impaired the effectiveness of his action.[2] Nor did Badoglio establish a much-needed organ to co-ordinate the plans of the three branches of the armed forces in Rome with those of the subordinate commands in East Africa where there was bitter rivalry.

Graziani in Somalia was not content with the 3000 motor vehicles allocated to him by Mussolini personally earlier in the summer. Without consulting De Bono, who was in over-all command in East Africa, he had pestered the War Ministry for radio equipment, tanks and caterpillar troop-carriers. His proposals were rejected by Baistrocchi and by Badoglio.[3] But Graziani found two valuable allies in Rome.

Lessona, Under-Secretary of Colonies, felt ignored, not only by De Bono in Eritrea and by Balbo in Libya, two men who were his seniors, but also by the service chiefs in Rome. Joining forces with Suvich late in July, he advocated a plan, which was anathema to Badoglio, for strengthening the southern front. Lessona contended that a spirited Italian thrust into Ogaden should be attempted, for it would be supported by the predominantly Muslim Galla and Somali inhabitants of the area, who bitterly resented rule from Addis Ababa. An offensive in the south, he argued, would also enable the Italians to reach the fertile highlands of Harar, where Europeans could be settled. Suvich, for an additional reason, supported Lessona: Harar lay within striking distance of forces in British Somaliland which must be stopped from reaching the town first.[4] Unlike De Bono, Lessona and Suvich failed to appreciate the full political implications of an offensive in the south. The French regarded Harar as lying within their economic sphere. Any move towards that town or – even worse – to intercept the Addis Ababa – Djibuti railway would gravely jeopardise the delicate Italian – French partnership. When the Italians seriously considered carrying the war to this area in December 1935 and January 1936, French resentment was to prove so strong that it contributed to the fall of Laval.[5]

Italy's diplomats were to cross swords not only with their rivals in other departments of government but with Mussolini himself. One issue overshadowed all others: the diplomats wanted either a compromise peace or active British and French support. They made much of reports from Grandi in London emphasising the view of the pro-Italian Beaverbrook press, which regarded war in Ethiopia as inevitable. Preferably it should break out before 4 September, in which case there would be a sigh of relief.[6]

But Haile Selassie was already getting the better of Italy in the battle for world opinion. On 25 July the archbishops of Canterbury and of Uppsala, on behalf of most of the non-Roman Catholic churches, had urged the British and other governments to give firm support to the League.[7] Trade union opinion was no less adamant. The Second International denounced Fascist aggression; and on 25 September the Third International in Moscow enjoined its members to co-operate in resisting this aggression with those social democrats affiliated to the Second International.[8] The Ethiopian crisis thus gave a strong stimulus to the formation of popular fronts which were later to change the whole complexion of international politics.

Haile Selassie also tried again to win something more from the United States than pious words of sympathy. In Ethiopia, as in China, the American government sought, because of its economic interests, as far as possible to uphold the principle of the 'open door'. But so strong was the isolationist lobby in Washington that President Roosevelt had to tread warily. Late in August, under pressure of events in Europe, the first Neutrality Act had to be rushed through Congress. This measure, signed by Roosevelt on 31 August, enabled the President to declare when a state of war existed and to prohibit the export of 'arms, ammunition and implements of war' to all belligerents. According to the presidential proclamation defining 'implements of war', oil was not included. Although the law was acceptable to the isolationists, Roosevelt hoped that it would operate in favour of Ethiopia. For Italy was in a position financially to purchase arms in the United States: Ethiopia was not. Haile Selassie most certainly reconciled himself to the inevitable and he realised, even before the Neutrality Act was passed, that Ethiopia could not obtain arms from the United States.[9]

He still hoped, however, to put his country on a war footing by attracting American capital. He found a valuable ally in an Englishman, Francis W. Rickett. On 30 August, the day before the Neutrality Act was passed, Rickett had evidently persuaded the Emperor to assign a petroleum concession to an American firm, granting it a seventy-five-year exclusive lease for the exploration and development of large areas in the eastern half of the Empire. After the terms were published on 31 August, the Italian and French press drew the conclusion that the British were trying to consolidate their position in Ethiopia under cover of an American firm. The French press was to remain anti-British for several months.[10] It is thus possible to speak of an Anglo-French, as well as of an Anglo-Italian, quarrel. To avoid aggravating Italy, the British immediately persuaded the Emperor to issue a denial, to the effect that the British government was neither 'directly nor 'indirectly' involved in the Rickett concession. The President in peacetime exercised very little control over the American economy, which was based on private enterprise. However – albeit with considerable difficulty – the administration managed to persuade representatives of the Standard Vacuum Oil Company (the firm involved) to decline the Rickett concession. The American and British decisions were published on 3 September but they were soon overshadowed by events.[11]

On 3 September the Commission of Conciliation and Arbitration, having called in Politis as its neutral chairman at the end of August, pronounced its long-awaited judgement on the Wal Wal and subsequent incidents. While Italy was certainly not held responsible, no case against Ethiopia could be proved. Aloisi misconstrued the words used in the verdict (which were in fact remarkably objective) as meaning that Italy was held to be 'responsible for everything'. Politis, he claimed, 'has betrayed us'. It would now be less easy to accuse Ethiopia of being a bad neighbour. But Aloisi took consolation in the fact that the original cause of the conflict was now only of secondary importance.[12] He still hoped to turn the tables against Ethiopia at Geneva.

The next day, when the Council met, Aloisi launched the long-planned attack on Ethiopia (which Laval described as 'clever'), and he submitted a document drawn up with the greatest care over a long period, replete with hair-raising photographs of acts of barbarism committed in Ethiopia. The text of the document need only be summarised here. Aloisi claimed that, by her conduct, Ethiopia had placed herself 'outside the framework of the Covenant' and had rendered herself 'unworthy of that trust' placed in her when she joined the League. It was Italy's duty, 'peacefully if possible, by force if necessary, to correct this intolerable situation'. Italy had every right to defend her 'security, her rights and dignity', as well as to uphold 'the prestige of the League of Nations'.[13]

Many delegates most certainly knew that it was part of Italy's deliberate policy to foment chaos in the country as a prelude to an Italian invasion. They were also aware of a contradiction in the Italian thesis. If Ethiopia was in reality so badly organised as to be described as a barbaric state 'whose signature could not be trusted', what truth could there be in Mussolini's previous complaint that she possessed a large well-trained army, organised under European advisers? Yet there was some substance to the Italian charges. According to an American journalist writing in 1935: 'There is no country save America where negroes are more deeply despised than in Ethiopia.'[14] Eden, too – who had previously condemned Liberia at Geneva for allowing slavery to persist – knew only too well that similar charges could with some justification be made against Ethiopia. But many delegates present realised that Italy, however good her case, was not justified in taking the law into her own hands.[15] The Covenant itself provided the means for dealing with a recalcitrant member state which had failed either to live up to its international obligations or to provide justice for its own citizens. Litvinov, the Soviet delegate, fearing that a precedent would be established by which his own government could be censured because of its domestic policy, strongly supported Ethiopia; and he was backed by the delegate from Mexico. Mussolini lodged a vehement protest to the Soviet government, and Italy was to remain on bad terms with Russia. In general the Italian charges made no impact but 'fell into a void'.[16]

Next day Gaston Jèze, the French-born delegate representing Ethiopia, defended the charges against the country of his adoption. So strong was his language in condemnation of Italy that Aloisi and other members of the Italian delegation felt constrained to leave the chamber. His speech, noted Aloisi, amounted to an 'explosion of hatred emanating from the world of Freemasonry and anti-Fascism. All the champions of anti-Fascism are assembled here.' Later he declared that he would not in future take part in negotiations at which an Ethiopian delegate was present.[17]

On the Council's recommendation, a Committee of Five was set up on 6 September comprising representatives from Britain, France, Poland, Turkey and Spain. Salvador de Madariaga from Spain was appointed chairman. Since Italy herself was a contending party she was not permitted to be represented on the committee. An Italian objection that Britain should likewise be excluded was ruled out, for the smaller states refused to act without Britain. While not voting against the proposed committee, the Italians reserved the right to ignore its conclusions.[18] On 9 September, the day before the Committee of Five started work, the Assembly of the League met and elected Beneš, whom Mussolini disliked personally, as its president.

Behind the scenes Hoare and Eden met Laval and discussed means for putting the mechanism of collective security into operation in such a way as not to jeopardise peace. Hoare had just been told by Drummond in Rome that in 'their present mood both Signor Mussolini and the Italian people are capable of committing suicide if this seems the only alternative to climbing down', and that Rome was 'full of rumours of an impending declaration of war' against Britain. Hoare wished at all costs to avoid an armed confrontation with Italy, and he was backed by the British High Command. Not surprisingly, Hoare and Laval agreed to work for a negotiated settlement. Only limited economic sanctions, imposed 'cautiously and in stages', could be considered. The risk of war was so great that military sanctions, such as the blockade of Italy and closure of the Suez Canal to her shipping (which alone, according to the Admiralty, would bring Italy to her knees) were absolutely ruled out. Hoare and Laval not only sought to avoid the risk of war: they both admired Mussolini and frequently expressed the fear that his downfall would lead to chaos and the victory of Communism in Italy.[19]

Hoare had brought with him the text of a speech, drafted with the help of Chamberlain and Vansittart, and approved by Baldwin. He hoped that by delivering it at the Assembly he could infuse 'new life into the crippled body of the League'. He also knew that units of the Home Fleet were about to leave for Gibraltar. News of their arrival, so soon after his speech, would put new heart into those members of the League whose co-operation was vital to Britain, and make Mussolini think twice before invading Ethiopia.[20] Hoare's trenchant denunciation of Italy on 11 September has given rise to much discussion. It is now known that he omitted from the draft text a phrase, proposed by Vansittart, to the effect that Britain would stand by her obligations under the Covenant in Europe no less than in other parts of the world. With this important passage deleted, the speech can thus be interpreted as a challenge to the French no less than to the Italians.[21]

Laval took immediate advantage of the speech. That same day he told Aloisi that he had had a long talk with Hoare. From Laval's mendacious account the Italian drew the conclusion that 'England had exerted strong pressure on France and had evidently obtained her support over sanctions against us in return for the promise that she would be on France's side if she were engaged in war against another country.' If France refused to support Ethiopia, Britain might be compelled to leave the League and take unilateral action against Italy. Having informed Aloisi of Britain's determination, Laval added: 'As I always have said, my task remains the same: to minimise the measures which the English now wish to take against Italy' and 'to try and satisfy as far as possible your demand'. Aloisi took careful note of Laval's words and described Hoare's speech as 'calm, moderate and profound'.[22] It was, he thought, addressed not only to the British electorate, but to the League of Nations and above all to Italy. News of the sending of units of the Home Fleet to Gibraltar greatly enhanced the impact of the speech. They arrived there on 17 September: two battle-cruisers (*Hood* and *Renown*), accompanied by three six-inch cruisers and six destroyers. Fearing that Britain was in earnest, the Italian Foreign Ministry – who were told by Grandi that Hoare would not hesitate if necessary to use the fleet – tried hard to make Mussolini compromise.[23]

The effect of the speech within the Assembly was electric. Paul Hymans, the Belgian delegate, declared: 'The British have decided to stop Mussolini even if it means using force.' Eden later contended that this was the only conclusion which could be drawn from the speech.[24] Of the subsequent speeches at the Assembly in support of the Covenant, those which had the greatest impact came, paradoxically, from delegates representing the two most racially conscious governments of the world: White South Africa and Black Haiti. Speaking on behalf of the former, Charles te Water declared: 'The long memory of black Africa never forgets and never forgives an injury or an injustice.' His own countrymen genuinely feared that Italy, once in control of Ethiopia, would raise a black army to be deployed elsewhere. General Alfred Nemours from Haiti, speaking as a 'man of colour representing the only black republic in the immense continent of America', distinguished himself by his oratory. In a later speech he gave, in prophetic words, articulate expression to what members from many smaller states dreaded most: 'Great or small,' he exclaimed, 'strong or weak, near or far, white or coloured, let us never forget that one day we may be somebody's Ethiopia.'[25]

The Assembly awaited with great tension Laval's speech. It was delivered on 13 September. Laval chose his words carefully. While he made it abundantly clear that France was 'loyal' to the Covenant, on which her entire security depended, she would act in its support only if the Council's attempts at conciliation were to fail. Taking Hoare's words at their face value he tried to tie him down: 'It was the desire', he pointed out, 'of the United Kingdom to associate herself unreservedly with the system of collective security . . . I rejoice at this and so does my country, which understands the vital necessity of close collaboration with the United Kingdom in defence of peace and for the safeguarding of Europe.' The implication of the last sentence was that Britain had agreed to support France against Germany – which was far from true. Laval had kind words to say about Italy. 'Conscious of the immense value of Franco-Italian friendship', he described the Rome Agreements of 7 January as being not only in the 'interests of France and Italy' but also of the 'peace of Europe'. As a hint of France's future attitude, he concluded: 'I have left nothing undone to prevent any blow to the new policy happily established between France and Italy.'[26]

Joseph Avenol, who had worked behind the scenes against Ethiopia, feared that Hoare, by placing responsibility for upholding collective security on each individual member of the League, had made the task of reaching a compromise 'difficult and even impossible'. But, according to Barros, he was henceforward less willing to lend Italy unconditional support.[27] On 12 September Aloisi, together with Enrico Cerulli, a representative at Geneva from the Italian Colonial Ministry, agreed that in the negotiations of the Committee of Five (which Avenol attended in an unofficial capacity) a distinction should be drawn between the Amharic-speaking core of Ethiopia and those outlying areas conquered by Menelik II. Reversing his previous approach, Avenol observed that, since the peripheral areas were conquered before Ethiopia was admitted to the League, they could not be detached from the rest of the country. Since Ethiopia's sovereignty had to be respected, Italy should concentrate on the issues of slavery and the maltreatment of the minorities. Thereby she could exercise greater control in the internal affairs of Ethiopia than provided for her by Britain and France in the August plan.

Laval, speaking to Aloisi on the same day, was much more generous to Italy. He said that in the course of the negotiations of the Committee of Five he and Eden were considering proposals which in general terms corresponded with Italy's aims. In effect, noted Aloisi, while Italy's right for expansion was recognised, the disarmament of Ethiopia would be subject to international control. In principle Aloisi agreed with these proposals. But he needed to prepare the ground at home for their final acceptance, and he immediately telegraphed Rome.[28] Guariglia was no less keen that the proposals, the details of which he had received in advance, should be accepted as a basis for negotiation. In a memorandum dated 7 September and sent to Mussolini, he maintained that even if the Emperor himself accepted the proposals they would be rejected by those *rases* who had everything to lose if their territory came under Italian rule. With Ethiopia jockeyed into a position in which it seemed that she was in the wrong, Italy would subsequently find a legitimate pretext to go to war. In a second memorandum to Mussolini dated 14 September, Guariglia pointed out that a categorical rejection of the Committee of Five's proposals could have two possible results: either the League would distrust Italy and retaliate with sanctions; or, if the League refused to act, Britain, in defence of her imperial interests, would leave the League and fight Italy single-handed. If, on the other hand, Italy could prove that Ethiopia had given her provocation for going to war, the League would probably condemn Italy morally and impose sanctions of a relatively harmless kind, and Britain herself would have a valid excuse for taking no action against Italy.[29]

The Committee of Five tried its utmost to meet the objections to Ethiopia's behaviour itemised in the Italian memorandum of 4 September. The committee's proposals were similar to those which Aloisi and Guariglia had expected, and they need not be discussed here.[30] On 19 September they were submitted to Addis Ababa and Rome. Mussolini's civilian advisers, including Grandi in London and officials in the Colonial Ministry, were unanimous: the proposals should be accepted as they stood, as a basis for negotiation; categorical rejection would probably result in war with Britain. If the proposals did not meet all expectations immediately, they had, in the opinion of the Italian experts, certain positive merits. They reconciled two apparently contradictory needs: Britain's for imperial defence; Italy's, for expansion. Had the Committee of Five gone further and allowed Italy actual control over the Ethiopian army, British objections would have been well justified, for it was feared in London that Italy would use her new army for operations against the Sudan. Respect also had to be paid to Britain's anxiety lest nationalist opinion within her own Empire be enraged by the spectacle of an independent African state's being stripped of all its sovereignty.

But cautious diplomats, however shrewd in their assessments, were not to be allowed by Mussolini to deter him from his great colonial *impresa*. It has been suggested that his military intelligence service had monitored signals from British ships in the Mediterranean indicating that they had sufficient ammunition only for approximately fifteen minutes or half an hour of firing-time (which was true), and that consequently Mussolini felt able to go ahead with his plans without undue fear of British intervention.[31] Yet the Italian diplomats were, according to Guariglia, unaware of this British shortage of ammunition and it seems doubtful that Mussolini had any convincing reason to withhold such vital information.[32] Even if at some stage of the crisis he knew about the British shortages he could not base his policy on this factor alone without running dangerous risks. Badoglio would certainly have read any important intelligence reports on the matter, but such reports most certainly did not deter him from doing everything in his power to prevent Mussolini from involving Italy in a general war.

In the middle of September, when the British Home Fleet was on its way to Gibraltar, Badoglio again remonstrated with the Duce. Britain had now, he said, a 'crushing superiority' at sea; 'nor can we cherish the illusion' of fighting a war by ambush (presumably with submarines). This would be possible in a narrow sea, such as the Adriatic, but not in the Mediterranean main where a powerful force of British battleships, escorted by destroyers, would be able to deploy itself and inflict damage where it wished on an undefended coast. The 200,000 Italian troops in East Africa were a hostage to the overwhelmingly large naval force which, according to Badoglio, the British could also deploy in the Red Sea. Italy could expect only platonic love from France. Badoglio once again besought Mussolini not to expose Italy to a disaster which would reduce her to the level of a Balkan state.[33]

Mussolini took no heed of Badoglio's warning. As a riposte to the arrival of the Home Fleet at Gibraltar, he announced that the forces sent to Libya early in September had raised Italy's strength there from 20,000 to 56,000 men. Reinforcements were also sent to southern Italy and to the Dodecanese islands. The movement of troops to Libya was logistically sound. They could either be used as a threat against Egypt or else held in readiness to be sent to East Africa when the congestion at Massawa and Mogadishu had eased. Rochat, therefore, draws the correct conclusion that the despatch of the Home Fleet forced Mussolini to mobilise faster than he might otherwise have done. Thus, far from weakening, it strengthened his resolve to attack Ethiopia.[34] Moreover, because of weakness in British imperial defence, especially the shortage of ammunition, there was much shrewdness in the announcement of troop reinforcements in Libya. On account of local unrest, in part stirred up by Italy, the British could no longer draw fully on their forces in India, and could raise the number of troops in Egypt from 11,000 to only 15,000 men.

The balance of naval forces in the Mediterranean favoured Britain in regard to the bigger categories of warship, but Italy had the advantage in lighter craft. In the second half of September, when Badoglio believed that the game was up, the British Empire deployed either at Gibraltar or Alexandria, or on their way to these bases, five battleships, two battle-cruisers, two aircraft-carriers, five heavy cruisers and ten light cruisers. The Italian strength in large warships was: battleships, two; battle-cruisers, none; aircraft-carriers, none; heavy cruisers, seven; light cruisers, ten. In smaller warships the respective dispositions were: destroyers, Italy sixty-five, Britain fifty-four; submarines, Italy sixty-two, Britain eleven; flotilla leaders, Italy eighteen, Britain none. The Italian superiority in submarines (vessels which had proved so effective in the First World War) was especially marked.[35] For air warfare in the

Mediterranean theatre, the advantages certainly lay with Italy. Although her air crews lacked adequate training, the most modern Italian bomber, the S81, based in Libya, had a range of 900 miles and could therefore attack targets in Egypt, where there was an acute shortage of anti-aircraft guns and searchlights. The antiquated R.A.F. bombers were unable to reach targets in Libya. The British were well aware that Italy might gain control of the seaway between Sicily and North Africa, thus forcing them to send troops and supplies round by the Cape of Good Hope. This would strain their communications almost to breaking-point. In any weighing of the pros and cons of war, prime consideration had to be given by Britain to the feasibility of keeping the Mediterranean open to her shipping.[36]

In the Red Sea area Britain's position was especially vulnerable, as the Italians realised. The Haifa—Atbara oil-pipeline was not to be constructed until 1940, and British ships passing through the Mediterranean to the Far East were largely dependent on Aden for refuelling. Late in September 1935 the Italians deployed in the Red Sea theatre two light cruisers, three destroyers, four submarines, two flotilla leaders, two sloops and a transport ship for aircraft (the *Miraglia*). By the end of October her naval strength was increased to three light cruisers, five destroyers and eight submarines. Since these warships could take cover in the islands off Massawa, and were provided with ample air protection, they were a serious threat to British shipping. To meet this emergency the Admiralty moved to this theatre three cruisers, five destroyers and five sloops, mainly from the Fourth Squadron in the Far East. The greater part of the Italian air force, moreover, based in Eritrea and Somaliland could at a moment's notice be diverted from operations in Ethiopia to attack either Aden itself or British shipping. The Italians were also causing trouble for the British among the tribesmen in the Yemen.[37]

Moving ships from the Far East made Britain dangerously exposed in that area, and she now sought an accommodation with Japan. Instead of seeking to maintain peace in the Mediterranean in order to improve their position vis-à-vis Japan, the British were constrained, for a time at least, to weaken their position in the Far East in order to confront Italy.

If war with Britain broke out, the Italians would have no choice but to suspend operations in Ethiopia and, with De Bono's forces in Eritrea, attack the Sudan, while Graziani's forces in Somaliland attacked Kenya. Although an attack on Egypt by Balbo's forces in Libya was under consideration, it entailed too many risks. With an overextended line of communications, the Italians could not expect to reach the Suez Canal before it was closed to their ships. There were also political implications to be weighed. Italian propaganda was extremely active in support of the 80,000 Italians living in Egypt, mainly at Alexandria, some of whom were organised into units of the Fascist militia. It was also directed to the Egyptian nationalists. Since the balance of trade with Italy favoured Egypt, the Italians later could blame the British for forcing Egypt into imposing sanctions at a financial loss. In general, however, opinion in Egypt remained anti-Italian and pro-Ethiopian, largely because of the massacre of the Senussi in Cyrenaica, and there was no danger of an uprising sufficient in scale to facilitate an Italian invasion.[38] The Egyptians merely used the crisis to obtain better terms with Britain leading to virtual independence by a treaty to be signed in August 1936.

It has been seen that, whereas Mussolini's aim in Egypt was to disrupt Britain's authority to win concessions favourable to Italy, he had marked out Palestine as an Italian political sphere of influence. He simultaneously supported both the Jews and the Arabs, evidently believing that both could live in separate autonomous communities. The troubles in Palestine, which were deliberately stirred up by the Italians, were to break out shortly after the attack on Ethiopia. Since the British at that time were converting Haifa into an alternative base to Alexandria, the political disturbances imposed on them an additional military commitment which was to last until the outbreak of the Second World War. The over-all effect of Mussolini's propaganda was to impair Britain's entire defence system in the eastern Mediterranean.[39]

The Italians were also active in the western Mediterranean. Their official representatives on the International Committee for the administration of Tangier might not have had spectacular success in subverting Britain's position in Gibraltar, the harbour of which was exposed to attack from the mainland. Their propaganda, however was more successful in preparing the way for the Italian occupation of Majorca in August 1936 where, unknown to the British, the inhabitants were either indifferent, or hostile, to the sudden political fluctuations taking place on the Spanish mainland. It was learned a year later in London that the inhabitants of Majorca would have welcomed liberation from the Comintern by a foreign power, namely Italy. Although Majorca and Minorca were highly valuable, as an air base and a naval base respectively, Britain in 1935, if called upon to defend these islands, lacked the anti-aircraft guns to do so. For the same reason the British rejected a French request to ask the Spaniards to allow them to use one of the large ports on the mainland, such as Barcelona or Valencia. The Republican government, therefore, during the crisis adopted a waiting attitude in the full knowledge that the Italians and Germans were plotting against them.[40]

Political developments, rather than Britain's unreadiness for war, worked in Mussolini's favour. On 20 September he was told by Drummond that the build-up of forces in the Mediterranean was not intended to imply an 'aggressive intention' towards Italy but was a natural consequence of the violent Anglophobe tone of the Italian press and of Italian propaganda in support of Arab nationalism. Hoare was even more outspoken in favour of his old friend Mussolini. Free from fear of a British attack and ignoring the advice of his diplomats, the Duce could now instruct De Bono to get ready for operations. Only after initial victories would Italy be prepared to negotiate. She would then demand all the peripheral areas, including Tigré, with its Coptic Tigrinyan-speaking population. He immediately found fault with the proposals of the Committee of Five and described them as 'contrary to the interests of Italy in that they mean that the League would take possession of Ethiopia to the exclusion in practice of Italy'. Moreover, the foreign advisers to the Ethiopian government could be appointed only with the consent of the Emperor himself, who was still allowed command of the army. On 22 September, Aloisi (who was later reprimanded by the Duce for favouring acceptance of the proposals) presented Mussolini's refusal — which he described as 'courteous but complete' — to the chairman of the committee, Salvador de Madariaga of Spain. But Aloisi remained optimistic: 'the door' for fresh negotiations, he claimed, 'was shut but not bolted'. Since Ethiopia, but not Italy, had accepted the proposals, no country could go to war with Ethiopia without violating the Covenant.[41]

After Mussolini rejected the proposals of the Committee of Five, the British regarded an invasion of Ethiopia as inevitable. Serious consideration had now to be given to sanctions. According to Drummond, they could be imposed without fear of war with Italy only if France joined the sanctionist states. Since the British were not prepared to give France a firm guarantee in Europe, Laval continued to hedge. The British and French therefore had failed to define their attitude before the war broke out. It has been seen how Laval tricked Aloisi into thinking that Britain had agreed to stand by France in Europe and had thus a free hand to deal with Italy. It is not surprising that at this stage Aloisi described the crisis as 'extremely acute'. Pope Pius XI was equally pessimistic. 'Italy', he declared, 'has put herself in a position' from which 'she can neither advance nor retreat'. On 1 October, in a 'heated' altercation with Aloisi, Mussolini brushed aside all warnings and offered him another post. Later during the meeting Mussolini's anger cooled, and Aloisi was surprised to hear him 'admit that if large vassal regions were given' to Italy, a solution might be found. That same evening, Cerruti, having learned that Mussolini was angling for a compromise, telephoned from Paris to say that Laval was in general agreement with Mussolini's ideas and that he would contact Eden. The next day Mussolini made a direct approach to Hoare, suggesting that there should be a simultaneous withdrawal of British warships and Italian troops from the Mediterranean and Libya. Drummond was told that not only agreement between Italy and Britain was possible, but that a solution could be found, favourable to Italy, in the dispute over Ethiopia. With the way open for a compromise, Mussolini had now less fear of a hostile British reaction to an invasion of Ethiopia.[42]

Mussolini had finally to take into account the most unpredictable of all the European powers: Germany. In no way had he changed his attitude towards Austria, whose armaments factory at Hirtenberg produced invaluable material for the Italian war effort. In an article published on 2 September 1935 in the Paris newspaper Le Soir, De Bono described Germany as 'poised like a cat, ready to pounce on its victim, Austria'. Officials in the Wilhelmstrasse drew the conclusion from this, or from similar comments, that Italy was deliberately trying to fabricate a crisis between Germany and Austria to deflect world attention from Ethiopia.[43] Hitler could not ignore the strong pro-Ethiopian leanings of the Austrian Nazis who, after war broke out, were to distribute thousands of leaflets condemning Italian aggression.[44] But he had also to think in more general political terms. Funke is correct in contending that Hitler used the quarrel between Britain and Italy in order to force the former to co-operate with Germany.[45] Nevertheless, he also had reason to fear that if a European war broke out Germany might become involved before her rearmament was complete. Hitler had thus to walk the tightrope between London and Rome. At the Nuremberg party rally on 15 September he dropped a hint that Germany might not take part in sanctions. The angry response from London to this declaration caused the German government to have misgivings.[46] It knew that the

British lacked ammunition sufficient to ward off an attack by Italian bombers, and it even went so far as to propose, through unofficial channels, selling shells, aircraft and ships to Britain.[47]

But a gradual shift in emphasis in German policy becomes discernible by the second half of September. Hitler no longer feared that Ethiopia would not fight: overwhelming support for her from the League seemed inevitable. He therefore gave orders that there were to be no further shipments of arms, other than those already en route, to Ethiopia, and he rejected a proposal from Steffen for a definitive treaty between Germany and Haile Selassie's government. A new ugly possibility had emerged in his thinking. From Hassell and other sources Hitler learned that Italy could not simultaneously fight Ethiopia and resist sanctions. Despite the reputed effectiveness of her air force, the defeat of Italy now seemed a real possibility, especially if her troops contracted malaria. Defeat might well be followed by the collapse of the Fascist regime, whereupon Communism would gain power in Italy. At all costs measures to prevent the infection's spreading to Germany had to be adopted. With the sharp deterioration in Italy's relations with Russia, Rome and Berlin now had an enemy in common and should concert their policy. Such was the new calculation of probabilities by Germany.[48]

Hence, on 14–15 September, at Gardone near Verona, Admiral Canaris (head of the Reich's Armed Forces Intelligence Service) on orders from Hitler met Roatta, his Italian equivalent. They discussed ways and means of reducing friction between the two countries, the exchange of information on shipping in the Far East, and – most important of all – co-operation between the secret police of Germany and Italy in their 'struggle against the Communist threat'. Although an agreement between the two secret police services was not signed until the end of March 1936, the Canaris–Roatta meeting can be seen as a turning-point.[49] Hitler was to claim in September 1937 that the origins of the Axis could be traced back to the September of 1935. Perhaps he was right.[50] When, later in September 1935, Mussolini rejected a compromise, Hitler, fearing an Italian defeat, allowed the export of coal to Italy to be stepped up; and in February 1936 the Germans sold ten submarines to the Italian government.[51] But in September 1935 Hitler's principal aim had become that of preventing his brother-dictator from embarking on war, not of helping him to win it. On 3 October Hassell told Mussolini that, in Hitler's view, the time was not yet ripe for the great confrontation between the 'dynamic' and the 'static' states. But the German démarche came too late.[52]

On 2 October, at a time when the roll of drums could be heard in Ethiopia summoning its feudal hosts to prepare for war, the pealing of church bells in Italy called on the people to take part in mass rallies organised by the Fascist Party. In his appeal made that day Mussolini declared that the League of Nations 'instead of recognising the just rights of Italy . . . dares to speak of sanctions'. He continued: 'Until there is proof to the contrary I refuse to believe that the free people of Great Britain want to spill blood and push Europe on the road to catastrophe in order to defend an African country, universally stamped as unworthy of taking its place among civilised peoples.' He ended on a defiant note: 'To military sanctions we will respond with military measures, to acts of war we will respond with acts of war. Let no one think he can deflect us without first having had a hard fight.'[53] On 3 October – two days earlier than originally intended – Italian forces, without a declaration of war and on the pretext of continued aggression by Ethiopia, crossed from the Eritrean side of the Mareb river boundary. The invasion of Ethiopia had begun.

15 The Sequel

THE events and ramifications consequent on Italy's invasion of Ethiopia cannot be fully dealt with here. But certain questions can be posed, even though the answers to many of them, for lack of evidence, can only be tentative.

The most vital question of all is whether Mussolini really intended to go to war with Britain if, through the League, that country extended sanctions to include oil, or if she took the even more serious step of closing the Suez Canal to Italian shipping. At a meeting of the Fascist Grand Council, held on 16 November 1935, Mussolini categorically declared that Italy should anticipate sanctions by going to war with Britain. Whether in the event he could have persuaded the Italian service chiefs and diplomats, not to speak of the King, that Italy must take such extreme action, is a matter for speculation.[1]

The British service chiefs, aware of Mussolini's attitude, were fully apprised of the deplorable state of their defences in the Mediterranean in the event of a 'mad-dog' act. So much so that late in November 1935, and supported by Vansittart, they pressed the cabinet for a compromise Ethiopia's expense. Even so, Vansittart realised that, however desirable it was to achieve a settlement, Italy must yet be put under pressure. Thus, while the British government sought to restore friendly relations with Italy, it simultaneously invited Yugoslavia, Romania and Turkey, in association with Greece, to exchange pledges with it for military co-operation. Early in December the states concerned accepted the invitation; but, because of their internal weaknesses and problems not related to Ethiopia (which the Italians were aware of), the military aid expected was negligible.[2]

Although Laval, under pressure from London, agreed on 18 October to staff talks with the British about Mediterranean military problems, he made it clear that France would not go to war against Italy if oil sanctions were imposed. He also assured Italy that he regarded the Franco-Italian military agreements of the summer as being still in force.

Since Laval's parliamentary position was still secure, neither the British nor the Italians could ignore his standpoint.[3]

In these circumstances Vansittart and Grandi worked out terms for a 'redistribution' of Ethiopian territory in Italy's favour. Although Mussolini's first reaction to these dealings early in December was reported to be 'favourable', the resulting Hoare – Laval Plan of 6 – 7 December was unacceptable to him. He was under very strong pressure from the Fascist Grand Council, which met again on 18 December, to accept the terms. But instead of rejecting or accepting them he chose to wait until the following day before taking a firm decision. He evidently hoped that the counter-proposals drawn up by his diplomats on the 15th, which awarded Italy even more territory than proposed under the Hoare – Laval Plan, would be accepted. His delaying tactics brought rich dividends. On the very day of the Grand Council meeting the House of Commons rejected the Hoare – Laval Plan. Mussolini's victory was such as to inspire Aloisi to praise him for his superior intuition.[4]

It has been contended by such a distinguished scholar as A. J. P. Taylor that the 'real death of the League was in December 1935, not in 1939 or 1945'[5] – i.e., as a result of the Hoare – Laval Plan. For one reason alone this statement requires qualification. On 15 December, the day the Italians were drawing up their alternative proposals, the Ethiopians launched their Christmas offensive. Contrary to the expectations of both Hoare and Laval, not to mention Mussolini himself, this proved remarkably successful. The Hoare – Laval Plan was thus made to look ridiculous. For a time it was even believed in London that, as a result of this Ethiopian success, there would for the League be a 'victory without sanctions'. The pro-League lobby in France was also given a new lease of life. On 10 January 1936 the Popular Front formulated its programme.[6] It did so at a time when Italian – French relations took a sudden turn for the worse.

Late in December and early in January 1936 the Italians decided that the Djibuti – Addis Ababa railway and the town of Harar should be bombed. Léger, speaking on behalf of his government, declared that if this plan were put into effect France would regard the Rome Agreements as null and void. He was given no satisfactory assurances, and this no doubt contributed to the fall of Laval.[7] Late in January Mussolini, despite opposition from his diplomats, came to the conclusion that the Anglo-French staff talks on military co-operation in the Mediterranean had destroyed the delicate balance of the treaty of

Locarno and the Stresa agreement.[8]

But, again, political decisions were reached because of a change in the fortunes of war. In mid-January Graziani won a limited success on the southern front. While the British General Staff still believed, as late as 24 February, that Italy could not win the war, the qestion of oil sanctions came up once more for serious consideration. On 26 February, after long deliberations, the British cabinet agreed that oil sanctions must now be imposed. Baldwin personally was won over to this view by the realisation that if Britain, through the League, let Ethiopia down a second time, it would be impossible for the National Government (even more predominantly Conservative in complexion since the 1935 elections) to win over the trade unions and the Labour movement as a whole to the cause of rearmament and industrial conscription.[9]

Before the British decision could be put into effect, the centre of interest switched to Berlin. As late as 17 January Hitler still feared that Italy might lose the war and that the Fascist regime would collapse. New Italian feelers for better relations with Germany were put out early in January. But Austria remained a great stumbling – block. After the miscarrying of the Hoare – Laval Plan and the withdrawal of troops from the South Tyrol, Schuschnigg's government no longer believed that Italy was capable of, or even interested in, defending Austria's independence. His government, moreover, had made itself thoroughly unpopular with the League states because it had not voted in favour of sanctions. To escape total isolation Schuschnigg attempted early in 1936 to come to terms with the Czechs.[10] Mussolini now sought to offer the Germans something which he did not himself have: the control of Austria. On 6 January he informed Hitler through Hassell that Italy would have no objection if Austria, while in the formal sense remaining independent, were to become virtually a satellite of Germany. The Wilhelmstrasse drew the conclusion from Mussolini's change of course (but not of heart) that he wished to embroil Germany in a quarrel with Britain and France over Austria, and so deflect their attention from sanctions. Besides, even after 6 January Mussolini continued to support Schuschnigg.

Hitler was far more interested in the Duce's growing antipathy to Locarno, which became a public issue later in January. On 11 February, at a time of serious tension in the Mediterranean, Hitler decided that Germany should reoccupy the Rhineland. On 14 February he told

Hassell, who was summoned to Germany, that Mussolini should be persuaded to be in the first to repudiate Locarno; Germany would immediately follow suit with the reoccupation of the Rhineland. To mollify Italy he promised to revive the idea of the Four Power Pact, limited in scope to Western Europe.[11]

No sooner had Hassell returned to Rome to sound out Mussolini on Hitler's plan than there was again a dramatic change on the Ethiopian battlefield. Badoglio launched a major offensive on 11 February, and by the 19th the back of Ethiopian resistance in the north was almost broken. This convinced Mussolini that he could win his war even if sanctions were imposed, and he was now in no mood to discuss any more compromise proposals. He wanted, so he said, 'nothing less than the whole of Abyssinia'. On that very same day (19 February) Hitler, with remarkable prescience, told Hassell (who was again in Germany) that Mussolini, after the Italian successes, would now demand 'everything'. Yet for the same reason Mussolini's attitude towards a German reoccupation of the Rhineland was more than ever unpredictable. Italy was now less in need of Germany's support, and could once again act as protector of Austria.

The balancing of the varying factors in Mussolini's thinking was determined by developments at Geneva. On 2 March it was un-expectedly learned in Rome that Eden had declared to the League that Britain favoured the imposition of oil sanctions. The next day Hitler was told that Mussolini would no longer uphold Locarno. In fact, the Duce's anger could scarcely be contained. He decided on 6 March that Italy would answer this British démarche by withdrawing from the League and by a rapprochement with Germany.[12]

But Hitler acted first. On 7 March he announced that German troops were already reoccupying the Rhineland. This news pleased Mussolini. But to his intense annoyance he also learned that Hitler – evidently to make his move less unpalatable to the British – had declared that Germany would rejoin the League, provided that the new status quo was accepted. No mention was now made by him of reviving the Four Power Pact. On 11 March the Italian diplomats, deliberating on the new situation, were at one in thinking that, on their return to Geneva, the Germans would go so far as to join Britain in voting for the imposition of oil sanctions against Italy. Mussolini's advisers main-tained that the only course open to Italy was to take concerted action with France against Germany. But they were overruled by Mussolini who decided that no action should be taken other than sending Grandi to act as an observer in the deliberations of the other Locarno powers.[13]

Elizabeth Wiskemann rightly maintained that there was no collusion between the two dictators at the time of the Rhineland crisis: indeed, they were at cross-purposes.[14] Yet so great was Hitler's esteem for the prowess of Fascist Italy after the victories in Ethiopia that he looked forward to the day when the two countries would be linked by that common destiny which he had foreseen as being in the logic of history. Mussolini, for his part, approached fraternity with Germany more with resignation than with enthusiasm. He realised after the fall of Starhemberg on 18 May that Italy would have to accept an *Anschluss*.[15] Instead of manoeuvring among the powers on the principle of 'equidistance', Italy would in future have to choose one partner alone, Germany, and—whether or not Mussolini fully appreciated the fact—would become subservient to her.

As it was, German and Italy were already, in 1936, co-operating on a number of questions. In February the Germans, based on Haifa, had joined the Italians in stirring up trouble among the Arabs in Palestine. The upshot was a strike in that country in April, and later the despatch of British troops. Germany had also, early in February, sold Italy ten submarines.[16] Above all, the two powers were flexing their muscles for confrontation with those countries (the first of which was Spain) which were to be governed by Popular Fronts. Late in March Himmler and Bocchini concluded in Berlin an agreement for co-operation between the Italian and the German secret police. At Mussolini's insistence, Jews were not to be included among those groups whose actions were to be jointly surveilled.[17]

At the risk of oversimplification, it can be said that, by championing the cause of the Arabs against the British in Palestine, Mussolini made himself sponsor of modern Arab nationalism. Hitler, through his anti-semitism, unwittingly became foster-father of Zionist nationalism.

On 5 May 1936 the Ethiopians were totally defeated. Within a few days Victor Emmanuel III was proclaimed Emperor. Yet Mussolini's was a pyrrhic victory. In internal Italian terms, Badoglio had become a national hero, potentially a man capable of ousting the Duce in a time of national crisis. At the international level Mussolini had to take account of a more immediate enemy. Instead of accepting honourable retirement, Haile Selassie refused to vacate his throne. To do so would have wholly undermined his position within Ethiopia, where it was indeed expected of him that he should stay. Even in exile he remained a standing threat to the Italians, a figure of admonition and admiration to the increasing numbers of people in the democracies who were becoming committed to the idea of resisting Fascism in its various forms. Haile Selassie's eventual restoration in 1941 was to be owed in part to internal risings against the Italians (especially in Gojjam), and in part to Commonwealth forces – especially the King's African Rifles, who proved that they could fight every bit as well as European troops.[18]

The Ethiopian crisis was not only a perilous slide down the slope leading to the Second World War; it also had a radical influence on the way in which belligerent operations in the Mediterranean were later to be conducted. By the time Italy became Germany's co-combatant in June 1940, Britain had made good some of the major deficiencies exposed in 1935. Following the Ethiopian crisis, British officers and men gained invaluable experience of active-service conditions in the desert; and the Royal Navy had a much clearer appreciation of the types of ships required in the Mediterranean for modern warfare. Many lessons were learned in analysing the logistical problems of the frequent movement of men and materials to, and from, Palestine and Egypt.[19]

But the Ethiopian war had an even more significant result. Failing to acquire possessions in the Mediterranean for the Italian empire, Mussolini chose to subvert the authority of Italy's main rivals, Britain and France, throughout the region and the Middle East. Similarly, by conquering Ethiopia he gave a powerful impetus to resentment against European rule in Africa. Italy's subsequent defeat, no less than that of France, in the Second World War was to have a profound influence on the form that decolonisation was to take in Africa. Italy's Ethiopian *impresa* certainly has to be seen in its African as well as its European context.[20] It may be argued that, while Mussolini's success as an empire-builder was shortlived, he contributed – through propaganda, subversion and terrorism, and through his conquests and eventual defeat – to bring about the fall of other empires than his own.

Chronological Table

1890		Italian colony of Eritrea established
1896	1 March	B. of Adowa: Italians defeated by Menelik II's army
1913	13 December	Death of Menelik II confirms Lig Yasu's previous hold on crown
1916	27 October	B. of Sagale: Lig Yasu defeated and exiled, succeeded by Empress Zauditu with Ras Tafari (later Haile Selassie) as Regent
1918		Djibuti–Addis Ababa railway completed
1919	14 February	League of Nations Covenant approved
	23 March	Promulgation of *Fasci di combattimenti* programme
	28 June	Versailles Treaty signed
	10 September	Treaty of St-Germain-en-Laye with Austria
	12 September	D'Annunzio seizes Fiume
1920	10 January	Versailles Treaty comes into force; subsidiary treaties with Hungary and Turkey later in year
	14 August	Czech–Yugoslav alliance
	12 November	Italo–Yugoslav Treaty of Rapallo
1921	27 March	Habsburg coup in Austria fails
	5 June	Czech–Romanian alliance
	7 June	Yugoslav–Romanian alliance
	21–25 October	Habsburg coup in Hungary fails
	6 November	Formal founding of Partito Nazionale Fascista
1922	6 February	Five Power Treaty on Naval Limitations: Italy allowed naval parity with France
	16 April	Russo-German Treaty of Rapallo
	27–30 October	'March on Rome': Victor Emmanuel III appoints Mussolini prime minister

1923		In this year Italy supports Ethiopian admission to the League
	August	Corfu incident: Italian naval action against Greeks
	17 September	Italy formally annexes Fiume
1924	25 January	Franco-Czech alliance
	27 January	Italo-Yugoslav Treaty of Rome
	February	During this month Britain and Italy separately recognise Soviet regime; French and other European recognitions follow during year
	2 October	Geneva Protocol for Pacific Settlement of International Disputes
1925		During this year Italy and Britain exchange notes on future of Ethiopia; British cede Kismayu to Italy
	1 December	Treaties negotiated at Locarno formally signed in London
1926	24 April	Russo-German Treaty of Berlin
	10 June	Franco-Romanian Friendship Treaty
	17 August	Greco-Yugoslav Friendship Treaty
	10 September	Germany joins the League
	16 September	Italo-Romanian Friendship Treaty
	27 November	Italo-Albanian Treaty of Tirana
1927	5 April	Italo-Hungarian Friendship Treaty
	23 May	World Economic Conference, Geneva
	20 June–	
	2 August	Geneva Naval Conference
	11 November	Franco-Yugoslav Treaty of Understanding
1928		During this year Ras Tafari becomes Negus. Italo-Ethiopian Treaty of Friendship and Arbitration signed. Italian control extended over northern Somalia. In Eritrea, Italian railway from Asmara continued to Agordat. Italy admitted to international administration of Tangier
	January	Italian arms, smuggled en route to Hungary, discovered at Szent Gottard in Austria
	27 August	Kellogg–Briand Pact for Renunciation of War

1929	6 January	King Alexander of Yugoslavia proclaims royal dictatorship; Croat terrorist groups (*Ustaši*) flee to Hungary and Italy
		Subsequent Italo-Hungarian military conventions, with Croat extremists as consulting parties; deals arranged for transit of Italian arms to Hungary via Austria
	20 February	Lateran Agreements between Italy and the Vatican
1930	22 April	London Naval Agreements: Italy and France refuse to ratify
	17 May	Briand plan for United States of Europe
	30 June	France completes evacuation of Rhineland
	14 September	Nazi gains in Reichstag elections
	November	Ras Tafari crowned as Emperor Haile Selassie following death of Empress Zauditu. Ethiopia allowed to import arms by Italy, France and Britain
1931		Renewed Church–State conflict in Italy this year.
		During year Haile Selassie promulgates a constitution for Ethiopia
	21 March	Austro-German customs union announced (abortive by September)
	11 May	Kreditanstalt collapses in Austria
	19 May	German pocket-battleship *Deutschland* launched
	July	Italo-French discussions on Ethiopia begin (continued into 1932)
	11 August	London Protocol on Hoover Moratorium on war debts and reparations
	24 August	National Government formed in Britain
1932	2 February	Geneva Disarmament Conference opens
	11 February	Mussolini's audience with Pope: end of Church–State quarrel in Italy
	9 March	Japan sets up puppet-state of Manchukuo in defiance of League
	22 March	De Bono suggests preventive war against Ethiopia
	8 April	Fascist Grand Council discusses Ethiopia

May	Revolt in Gojjam province in support of Lig Yasu
16 June– 20 August	Lausanne Reparations Conference
late July	Mussolini takes over Foreign Ministry from Grandi, who moves to London embassy
August	All matters pertaining to Ethiopia transferred from Palazzo Chigi to Colonial Ministry
September	Lika revolt in Dalmatia: Italian involvement causes crisis with Yugoslavia. King of Italy visits Eritrea
4 October	Gömbös becomes Hungarian Premier
22 October	Mussolini's Turin speech, advocating Four Power Concert of Europe
28 October	Franco-Yugoslav Treaty renewed. Mussolini's retaliatory proposal for Italo-Albanian customs union fails
29 November	De Bono submits first plan for invasion of Ethiopia. Russo-French non-aggression pact signed
2 December	'Lions of Trau' incident: Italo-Yugoslav crisis worsens
15 December	Mussolini accepts De Bono's plan: attack on Ethiopia envisaged for September 1935
1933 January	In this month Italo-Japanese relations deteriorate over Ethiopian royal marriage project
3 January	Mussolini reveals Ethiopian-war plan for first time to his senior diplomats
8 January	Socialist press in Vienna reveals details of Italian arms shipment to Hirtenberg in Austria: major crisis ensues
30 January	Hitler becomes Reich Chancellor
31 January	Renzetti presents Mussolini's congratulations to Hitler
6 February	Italo-Hungarian proposal to Germany for concerting policy; Hitler rejects this plan
16 February	Little Entente powers agree on defensive measures against Germany

1933	March	Early in this month reports reach Rome of a Franco-Yugoslav preventive war against Italy planned for April
	4 March	Mussolini drafts Four Power Pact plan
	5 March	Reichstag elections: Nazis and Nationalists gain a majority
	7 March	Dollfuss suspends parliamentary government in Austria
	9–10 March	Fascist Grand Council agrees on abandoning pro-German policy
	14 March	Mussolini's Four Power Pact plan submitted to Germany, France and Britain
	16 March	Ramsay MacDonald presents a Disarmament Plan
	27 March	Japan leaves the League
	11–12 April	Göring and Papen visit Rome
	17 April	Dollfuss meets Mussolini in Rome
	19–20 April	Mussolini–Hassell 'gentlemen's agreement' on Italo-German consultation over non-European and colonial problems
	7 June	Four Power Pact initialled
	12 June– 27 July	World Economic Conference in London
	July	In this month Mussolini takes over War Ministry
	15 July	Four Power Pact signed (but not subsequently ratified)
	20 July	Concordat between Germany and the Vatican
	late July	Italo-Hungarian agreement for co-operation against an *Anschluss*
	19–20 August	Mussolini–Dollfuss meeting at Riccione: Austria promised Italian economic and military aid
	2 September	Russo-Italian Non-Aggression Pact
	10 September	Dollfuss expels liberal members from his cabinet
	14 October	Germany leaves Disarmament Conference and the League
	November	In this month Mussolini becomes both Air

and Navy Minister

6 November	Göring brings to Rome Hitler's personal letter to Mussolini
14 November	Mussolini's speech attacking the League
December	Late in this month Italian government organises Congress in Rome for students from Middle East countries
5 December	Mussolini presents at Fascist Grand Council his plan for 'reforming' the League
1934	During this year German pilots train in Italy (arrangement terminated in the autumn)
26 January	German – Polish Treaty of Friendship
8 February	Mussolini discusses Ethiopian-war plan with military and political advisers. Russo-Italian Commercial Treaty
12 – 16 February	Civil war in Vienna
17 February	Declaration by Britain, France and Italy supporting Austrian independence
21 February	German – Hungarian commercial treaty renewed
16 March	Hitler orders Austrian Nazis to stop terrorist activities
17 March	Rome Protocols signed by Italy, Hungary and Austria
18 March	Mussolini's 'Second Quinquennial' speech, declaring Italy's main interests to lie in Asia and Africa
21 March	Britain raises with Ethiopia a revival of the Zeila Plan
29 March	Proposal mooted for Mussolini – Hitler meeting
April	In this month funds for first time made available from Rome for preparing Eritrea as a war base
17 April	France rejects British and German proposals for a Disarmament compromise
1 May	Dollfuss declares Austria a corporative state
7 May	Mussolini at meeting of experts decides to send one army corps to Eritrea
12 May	Badoglio urges three-year delay in imple-

		menting war plan against Ethiopia
1934	25 May	Mussolini and advisers decide that an incident in Eritrea, as pretext for war against Ethiopia, is to be staged only after Italy is militarily prepared
	28 May	Mussolini's bellicose article in *Il Popolo d'Italia*
	29 May	Disarmament Conference ends. Mussolini tells Hassell he regards Austria as a 'German' state
	14–15 June	Mussolini and Hitler meet at Venice
	23 June	Italian naval demonstration at Durazzo, Albania: international protests
	25 June	Austrian Nazis at Zürich meeting plan *Putsch* against Dollfuss
	30 June	Röhm and his adherents shot
	July	Mussolini–Dollfuss meeting at Riccione was to have taken place at end of this month
	10 July	Dollfuss sets up emergency cabinet, with himself taking over Ministry of Security
	16 July	Austrian Nazis at Munich finalise plans for *Putsch*
	25 July	Dollfuss murdered, but *Putsch* fails. Start of Italian press campaign against Germany; reinforcements sent to Italy's frontier with Austria
	August	During this month Council of the League decides on Saar plebiscite, to be held in January 1935
	1 August	Yugoslavia declares an Italian invasion of Austria would be a casus belli
	10 August	Mussolini issues directive to counter rumours that Italy intends war with Ethiopia. Italo-Yugoslav tension deepens
	21 August	Mussolini–Schuschnigg meeting at Florence
	September	During this month Italy raises the Canton legation to embassy status, worsening relations with Japan

1934	9 September	Balbo's provocative speech at Zara on Italo-Yugoslav affairs
	18 September	Russia joins the League
	27 September	Italy, France and Britain reaffirm the 17 February declaration on Austria
	30 September	Italo-Ethiopian Treaty of 1928 renewed
	October	During this month King of Italy visits Eritrea and Italian Somalia. Plans made for visit of Barthou to Rome
	3 October	Italo-Yugoslav press warfare intensifies
	6 October	Mussolini's Milan speech takes less hostile line towards Yugoslavia
	9 October	Assassination at Marseilles of King Alexander of Yugoslavia and Louis Barthou, French premier
	28 October	Haile Selassie seeks arms from Germany
	22 November	Yugoslavia accuses Hungary at Geneva of complicity in the Marseilles murders. Italy supports Hungary
	December	During this month plans are finalised for Franco-Italian negotiations in January
	5 December	Mussolini protests to Germany over reports of preparations in Bavaria for air attacks on Italy
	5–6 December	Wal Wal incident in disputed area between Ethiopia and Italian Somalia. Italian reinforcements sent to Somalia
	8 December	Italy demands apology and compensation from Ethiopia over Wal Wal incident
	9 December	Ethiopia invokes article v of 1928 treaty with Italy. Yugoslavia threatens to resume 'freedom of action' regarding Hungary
	10 December	Italian and British efforts avert extreme outcome of Yugoslav–Hungarian crisis
	14 December	Mussolini rejects negotiation under 1928 treaty with Ethiopia; the latter reports Wal Wal incident to the League
	20 December	Mussolini drafts directive for invasion of Ethiopia
	26 December	Haile Selassie receives letter from Hitler

	dated 27 November; Steffen leaves for Ethiopia to discuss German military aid
28 December	Mussolini decides to drop Hungary and reach agrement on South-East Europe with France and Yugoslavia
30 December	Mussolini's military directive for Ethiopian war presented to service chiefs
1935 3 January	Ethiopia invokes article xi of Covenant
4 January	Laval arrives in Rome
7 January	Franco-Italian Rome Agreements signed (with secret clauses on Ethiopia and on military co-operation)
13 January	Saar plebiscite overwhelmingly endorses union with Germany
14 January	Britain renews protest at Italian harassment of British-protected nomads in Wal Wal area
16 January	De Bono reaches Massawa; Mussolini becomes Minister for Colonies
19 January	Italy agrees to negotiate with Ethiopia on basis of 1928 treaty
23 January	Mussolini orders implementation of war preparations against Ethiopia
28 January	Italy fails to win German support for proposal for a European Convention on Non-Intervention
29 January	Vitetti in London informs Simon of a Franco-Italian economic agreement over Ethiopia, and hints at a similar agreement with Britain
4 February	Anglo-French communiqué on Austrian independence also proposes a European air pact
10 February	Army corps prepared in Italy for service in East Africa; international press outcry
20 February	Agreed in London that Simon visit Berlin on 8 March (visit-date later postponed)
27 February	British cabinet discusses Ethiopian issue for first time; Maffey Committee set up to report on British interests in East Africa

1935	1 March	Saar reverts to Germany
	5 March	*Luftwaffe* officially established
	16 March	Germany reintroduces conscription
	17 March	Ethiopia invokes articles x and xv of Covenant
	25–26 March	Simon and Eden meet Hitler in Berlin
	26 March	Hassell denies rumour of intended German invasion of Austria and Italy
	28 March	Germany denies Italian accusations of arms deal with Ethiopia
		In late March De Bono suspects Ethiopia of intending to attack Eritrea; Italian military preparations accelerated
	April	During this month Rome strengthens complaints against anti-Italian press campaign in Germany
	4 April	Guariglia appointed head of new Ethiopian Affairs Department
	8 April	British cabinet discusses its standpoint for Stresa Conference with Italy and France
	10 April	Mussolini finally agrees to arbitration with Ethiopia
	11–14 April	Stresa Conference confirms Locarno obligations; Italian and British officials privately discuss Ethiopia
	15–17 April	Council of the League meets; Simon demands that Italy and Ethiopia nominate conciliators before next Council meeting on 20 May
	24 April	Rome learns of proposed Anglo-German naval negotiations
	2 May	Russo-French Mutual Assistance Treaty signed. Military directive issued in Germany for a possible invasion of Czechoslovakia
	3 May	Grandi asks if Britain will give Italy same free hand in Ethiopia as France has given
	7 May	Italy calls up more age-groups
	13 May	Franco-Italian Air Agreements signed
	14 May	Mussolini's Senate speech affirms Italy's

		willingness to maintain active role in European security-seeking
1935	16 May	Russo-Czech Mutual Assistance Treaty; France and Russia agree on Czech problem
	19 May	Mussolini nominates Italian members of Commission of Conciliation and Arbitration
	20 May	Council of League reconvenes
	21 May	Hitler's Reichstag speech disclaims Germany's intending an *Anschluss*
	25 May	Compromise agreement over Ethiopia at Geneva: quarrel to come before League Council only if C. and A. Commission fails. Mussolini's Chamber speech stresses world-scope of his policies. Germany orders press-truce on Italian policies
		In late May Mussolini contemplates staging a new incident as better pretext than Wal Wal for immediate invasion of Ethiopia. His diplomats and generals veto the proposal. More troops called up
	June	In this month reports reach London of Italian troopships en route to Red Sea
	7 June	British cabinet reshuffle: Baldwin becomes P.M., with Hoare as Foreign Secretary
	18 June	Anglo-German Naval Agreement signed. Maffery Report – draft completed
	19 June	Cabinet accepts Zeila Plan in new form
	20 June	Eden meets Laval in Paris
	24–25 June	Eden meets Mussolini in Rome
	27 June	Peace Ballot results declared
	28 June	Franco-Italian military agreement concluded
	July	Early in this month Italy begins naval mobilisation in Mediterranean and Red Sea. Admiralty takes precautionary measures
		Later in month anti-Italian feeling in Japan

runs strong

1935	3 July	Eden reports to cabinet his conviction that Italy intends to invade Ethiopia
	5 July	Commission of Conciliation and Arbitration reaches deadlock
	17 July	Ethiopia renews approach to Berlin for German arms. *Santa Maria* subsequently conveys them to East Africa
	24 July	Ethiopia urges special meeting of Council of League
	25 July	Archbishops' Appeal for upholding the League
	31 July – 3 August	Council of the League meets
	August	Early in this month Maffey Report is submitted to cabinet
	3 August	Hassell informs Mussolini of Germany's neutrality in Ethiopian crisis
	6 August	Mussolini advises Victor Emmanuel III of possibility of war with Britain
	14 August	Badoglio protests to Mussolini of Italy's unpreparedness for war with Britain.
	15–18 August	Anglo-French-Italian talks in Paris. Mussolini rejects Anglo-French compromise. He tries, but fails, to advance date for invasion
	17 August	Further Italian reinforcements leave for East Africa. Plans implemented for increasing Italian naval strength in Red Sea
	22–24 August	Emergency meetings of British cabinet: decisions taken on new naval dispositions
	23 August	Italian army manoeuvres start in Brenner area: strong protests from Germany and Austria
	29 August	British Mediterranean Fleet leaves Malta for Alexandria
	31 August	Neutrality Act signed by Roosevelt
	September	Early in this month Italy sends reinforcements to Libya. Badoglio again urges Mussolini to avoid war with Britain

1935   3 September   Conciliation and Arbitration Commission,
                           under Politis, gives verdict detrimental
                           neither to Italy nor to Ethiopia
        4 September   Italian accusation to League Council of
                           Ethiopian 'barbarism'
        6 September   Council appoints Committee of Five to seek
                           Italo-Ethiopian compromise
        10 September   Hoare and Laval agree on non-military
                           sanctions only against Italy
        11 September   Hoare denounces Italy in Assembly of the
                           League
        13 September   Laval addresses the Assembly
        14–15 September   Canaris and Roatta discuss secret police
                           collaboration
        15 September   Hitler's speech at Nuremberg hints that
                           Germany will not support sanctions;
                           strong British protests ensue
        17 September   Units of the British Home Fleet reach Gib-
                           raltar. Italy strengthens her Red Sea
                           forces
        19 September   Committee of Five proposals submitted to
                           Italy and Ethiopia
        22 September   Italy rejects proposals
        25 September   Ethiopia requests dispatch of impartial ob-
                           servers to her frontiers
        26 September   The League appoints Committee of Thir-
                           teen to seek a new compromise
        29 September   Ethiopia mobilises
                           In late September – early October Germany
                           offers to sell arms to Britain. Mussolini
                           proposes to Hoare simultaneous with-
                           drawal of British warships and Italian
                           troops in Mediterranean theatre. Hoare
                           indicates that a solution favourable to
                           Italy could be found over Ethiopia
        2 October   Mussolini's defiant speech at Rome rally
        3 October   Italian troops invade Ethiopia from Eritrea,
                           without declaration of war
        7 October   League Council condemns Italy as aggressor
        18 October   Anglo-French agreements on co-operation

		in Mediterranean
1935	6 November	Sanctions Committee supports inclusion of oil in embargo list. Mussolini tells Fascist Grand Council that Italy should anticipate sanctions by going to war with Britian
	14 November	British general election; National Government returned with reduced majority
	2–3 December	Mussolini learns of negotiations favourable to Italy between Grandi and Vansittart in London
	6 December	Eastern European states agree, with reservations, to support Britain in war with Italy if League extends sanctions
	6–7 December	Hoare–Laval Plan finalised in Paris
	15 December	Ethiopians launch counter-offensive. Italians draft reply to Hoare–Laval Plan
	18 December	Mussolini resists Fascist Grand Council pressure to accept Hoare–Laval Plan. The same day, House of Commons rejects Plan and Hoare resigns
1936	5 January	French protest against Italian intention to bomb Djibuti–Addis Ababa railway
	6 January	Hassell in Rome informs Hitler of Italy's withdrawing objections to Austria's becoming a German satellite
	12 January	Graziani launches offensive from the south
	16 January	Popular Front gains in Spanish elections
	17 January	Hitler informs Hassell of his concern lest Italian defeat lead to collapse of Fascism
	19 January	Badoglio's abortive offensive in the north
	22 January	Resignation of Laval
	11 February	Hitler decides to occupy Rhineland. Badoglio launches new offensive on northern front
	14 February	Hitler confers with Hassell
	19 February	Badoglio's offensive successful; Mussolini now seeks to acquire all of Ethiopia. Further Hitler–Hassell discussions
	26 February	British cabinet decides to include oil in

		sanctions
1936	2 March	Eden informs Flandin of oil decision
	3 March	Mussolini hints to Hassell of Italy's not opposing German occupation of Rhineland
	6 March	Mussolini decides on Italy's withdrawal from League and adoption of pro-German policy
	7 March	German troops enter Rhineland. Hitler's simultaneous affirmation of willingness to rejoin League astounds Mussolini
	11 March	Italian Foreign Minister favours support for France under Locarno Treaty, but Mussolini sticks out for neutrality
	30 March	Bocchini – Himmler agreements signed in Rome for co-operation between Italian and German secret Police.

Bibliography

This Bibliography is divided into four sections: 1 Documents and Archives; 2 Memoirs and Diaries; 3 General Works in book-form; 4 Articles, Essays and Theses

1. DOCUMENTS AND ARCHIVES

France: *Documents Diplomatiques Français, 1932–1934 (D.D.F.)*, series 1 and 2, Ministère des Affaires Etrangères (Paris: Imprimerie Nationale, 1963–7)

Germany: *Documents on German Foreign Policy (D.G.F.P.)*, series C (Washington D.C.: Government Printing Office, 1957–)

Italy: Archivio Storico del Ministero degli Affari Esteri (ASMAE), Rome
——: St Antony's Collection (SAC): miscellaneous Italian records at St Antony's College, Oxford, catalogued by F. W. Deakin

League of Nations: *Official Journal* (Geneva)

United Kingdom: *Documents on British Foreign Policy (D.B.F.P.)*, series 2 (London: H.M.S.O., 1950–7); further volumes are in preparation
——: Public Record Office (P.R.O.), London: Foreign Office (F.O.), Cabinet Office (CAB) and other departmental material
——: Royal Institute of International Affairs (R.I.I.A.), London: *Documents* and *Surveys*, 1930–5

2. MEMOIRS AND DIARIES

P. ALOISI, *Journal, 25 juillet 1932–14 juin 1936*, trans. M. Vaussard (Paris, 1957)

LORD AVON (ANTHONY EDEN), *The Memoirs of Anthony Eden: Facing the Dictators* (London, 1962)

W. S. CHURCHILL, *The Second World War*, vol. 1: *The Gathering Storm* (London, 1948)

G. Ciano, *Ciano's Diplomatic Papers, 12 June 1936–30 April 1942*, ed. M. Muggeridge (London, 1948)

E. De Bono, *Anno XIII: The Conquest of an Empire* (London, 1937)
——, 'Diario': quoted in Rochat (see section 3)

Sir Anthony Eden, *see* Lord Avon, *above*

Pierre Etienne Flandin, *Politique française, 1919–1940* (Paris, 1947)

General M. Gamelin, *Servir: Le Prologue du drame, 1930–*août 1939, 2 vols (Paris, 1947)

General R. Graziani, 'Papers': quoted in Rochat (see section 3)

R. Guariglia, *Ricordi, 1922–1946* (Naples, 1950)

U. von Hassell, *Diaries* (London, 1948)

E. Herriot, *Jadis*, ii: *D'une guerre à l'autre, 1914–1936* (Paris, 1952)

Adolf Hitler, *see* Baynes (section 3)

Samuel Hoare, *see* Templewood, *below*

I. Kirkpatrick, *Memoris: The Inner Circle* (London, 1959)

H. de Lagardelle, *Mission à Rome* (Paris, 1955)

A. Lessona, *Memoire* (Florence, 1958)

Benito Mussolini, *see* section 3

A. Rosenberg, *Das Politische Tagebuch Alfred Rosenbergs, aus den Jahren 1934–1935 und 1939–1940*, ed. H.-G. Seraphim (Munich 1964)

E. R. Prince Starhemberg, *Between Hitler and Mussolini* (London, 1942)

Viscount Templewood (Samuel Hoare), *Nine Troubled Years* (London, 1954)

Lord Vansittart, *The Mist Procession: The Autobiography of Lord Vansittart* (London, 1958)

3. GENERAL WORKS

A. Adamthwaite, (ed.), *The Coming of the Second World War*, in 'Historical Problems: Studies and Documents' series' (London, 1977)

G. W. Baer, *The Coming of the Italian–Ethiopian War* (Cambridge, Mass., 1967)

G. St J. Barclay, *The Rise and Fall of the New Roman Empire: Italy's Bid for World Power, 1890–1943* (London, 1973)

A. J. Barker, *The Civilising Mission: The Italo-Ethiopian War, 1935–1936* (London, 1968)

J. Barros, *The Corfu Incident of 1923: Mussolini and the League of Nations* (Princeton, N.J., 1965)

——, *Betrayal from Within: Joseph Avenol, Secretary-General of the League of Nations, 1933–1940* (New Haven, Conn., 1969)

J. Bastin, *L'Affaire d'Ethiopie et les diplomates* (Paris, 1937)

N. Baynes, *Hitler's Speeches* (London, 1942)

K. Bourne and D. C. Watt, *Studies in International History* (London, 1960)

G. Brook Shepherd, *Dollfuss* (London, 1961)

G. Carocci, *La Politica estera dell' Italia fascista, 1925–1928* (Bari, 1969)

A. Cassels, *Mussolini's Early Diplomacy* (Princeton, N.J., 1970)

F. Chabod, *A History of Italian Fascism*, trans. M. Grindrod (London, 1963)

F. Charles-Roux, *Huit ans au Vatican, 1932–1940* (Paris, 1947)

E. Chiavarelli, *L'Opera della marina italiana durante la guerra italo-etiopica* (Milan, 1969)

I. Colvin, *Vansittart in Office* (London, 1965)

G. A. Craig and F. Gilbert, (eds), *The Diplomats, 1919–1939* (Princeton, N.J., 1953)

F. D'Amoja, *Declino e prima crisi dell'Europa di Versailles: Studio sulla diplomazia italiana ed europea, 1931–1933* (Milan, 1967)

R. De Felice, *I Rapporti tra fascismo e nazionalsocialismo fino all'andata al potere di Hitler, 1922–1933: Appunti e documenti* (Naples, 1971)

——, *Storia degli Ebrei italiani sotto il fascismo* (Turin, 1972)

——, *Mussolini il Duce: Gli Anni del consenso, 1922–1936* (Turin, 1974)

F. W. Deakin, *The Brutal Friendship: Mussolini, Hitler and the Fall of Fascism* (London, 1962; paperback 1966)

A. Del Boca, *The Ethiopian War, 1935–1941*, trans P. D. Cumins (Chicato and London, 1961)

R. Divine, *The Illusion of Neutrality* (Chicago, 1962)

J. D. Fage, *An Atlas of African History* (London, 1958)

Ladislas Farago, *Abyssinia on the Eve* (London, 1935)

M. Funke, *Sanktionen und Kanonen: Hitler, Mussolini und der internationale Abessinienkonflikt* (Dusseldorf, 1970)

G. M. Gathorne-Hardy, *A Short History of International Affairs, 1920–1939* (Oxford, 1950)

J. Gehl, *Austria, Germany and the Anschluss, 1931–1938* (London, 1963)

P. Gilkes, *The Dying Lion: Feudalism and Modernisation in Ethiopia* (London, 1975)

R. Greenfield, *Ethiopia: A New Political History* (London and New York, 1965)

W. K. HANCOCK, *Survey of British Commonwealth Affairs*, 1: *Problems of Nationality* (London, 1937)

F. HARDIE, *The Abyssinian Crisis* (London, 1974)

R. HATTON AND M. S. ANDERSON, (eds), *Studies in Diplomatic History* (London, 1970)

R. L. HESS, *Italian Colonialism in Somalia* (Chicago and London, 1966)

K. HILDEBRAND, *Deutsche Aussenpolitik, 1933–1945: Kalkül oder Dogma?* (Stuttgart, 1971)

L. HORY AND M. BROSZAT, *Der kroatische Ustascha-Staat, 1941–1945* (Stuttgart, 1964)

D. IRVING, *The Rise and Fall of the Luftwaffe: The Life of Luftwaffe Marschal Erhard Milch* (London, 1973)

H.-A. JACOBSON, *Nazionalsozialistische Aussenpolitik, 1933–1938* (Frankfurt, 1968)

K. H. JARAUSCH, *The Four Power Pact, 1933* (Madison, Wisc., 1965)

L. JEDLICKA, *Ein Heer im Schatten der Parteien: Die Militär-politische Lage Österreichs, 1918–1938* (Graz, 1955)

A. H. M. JONES AND E. MONROE, *A History of Abyssinia* (London, 1935; rev. ed. 1960)

L. KEREKES, *Abenddämmerung einer Demokratie: Mussolini, Gömbös und die Heimwehr* (Vienna, 1966)

I. KIRKPATRICK, *Mussolini: Study of a Demagogue* (London and New York, 1964)

C. F. LATOUR, *Südtirol und die Achse Berlin–Rom, 1938–1945* (Stuttgart, 1962)

F. D. LAURENS, *France and the Italo-Ethiopian Crisis, 1935–1936* (The Hague, 1967)

I. M. LEWIS, *The Modern History of Somaliland* (London, 1965)

C. J. LOWE AND F. MARZARI, *Italian Foreign Policy, 1870–1940* (London, 1975). The author unfortunately has not been able to make use of this splendid work.

C. A. MACARTNEY, *October Fifteenth: A History of Modern Hungary, 1929–1945*, 2 vols (Edinburgh, 1961)

—— AND A. W. PALMER, *Independent Eastern Europe* (London, 1966)

M. H. MACARTNEY AND P. CREMONA, *Italy's Foreign and Colonial Policy, 1914–1937* (London, 1938)

J. MARLOWE, *Anglo-Egyptian Relations* (London, 1969)

W. N. MEDLICOTT, *Contemporary England* (London, 1967)

K. MIDDLEMAS AND J. B. BARNES, *Baldwin: A Biography* (London, 1969)

E. MONROE, *The Mediterranean in Politics* (London, 1938)

J. W. Morley, (ed.), *Dilemmas of Growth in Pre-War Japan* (Berkeley, Cal., 1973)

B. Mussolini, *Omnia Opera di Benito Mussolini*, ed. E. and D. Susmel, 36 vols (Florence, 1954–63)

N. Ørvik, *The Decline of Neutrality, 1914–1941* (Oslo, 1953)

Jens Petersen, *Hitler – Mussolini: Die Entstehung der Achse Berlin – Rom, 1933–1936* (Tübingen, 1973)

P. Pieri and G. Rochat, *Badoglio* (Turin, 1974). The author has not been able to consult this work.

I. S. O. Playfair, *History of the Second World War: The Mediterranean and the Middle East* (London, 1956)

S. H. Roberts, *The History of French Colonial Policy, 1870–1939* (London, 1963)

E. M. Robertson, *Hitler's Pre-War Policy and Military Plans* (London, 1963)

—— (ed.), *The Origins of the Second World War: Historical Interpretations* (London and New York, 1971)

G. Rochat, *Militari e politici nella preparazione della campagna d'Etiopia: Studio e documenti, 1932–1936* (Milan, 1971)

S. W. Roskill, *Naval Policy Between the Wars*, vol. I (London, 1968); vol. II (in preparation)

D. Ross, *Dollfuss und Hitler: Die deutsche Österreich-Politik, 1933–1934* (Hamburg, 1966)

E. Rossi, *Il Manganello e l'aspersorio* (Bari, 1968)

G. Rossini, (ed.), *L'Europa fra le due guerre* (Turin, 1966)

G. Rumi, *Alle Origini della politica estera fascista, 1918–1923* (Bari, 1968)

G. Salvemini, *Prelude to World War II* (London, 1953)

A. O. Sarkissian (ed.), *Studies in Diplomatic History and Historiography in Honour of G. P. Gooch* (London and New York, 1961)

W. E. Scott, *Alliance Against Hitler: The Origins of the Franco-Soviet Pact* (Durham, N.C., 1962)

C. Seton-Watson, *Italy from Liberalism to Fascism, 1870–1925* (London, 1967)

F. Siebert, *Italiens Weg in den Zweiten Weltkrieg* (Bonn, 1962)

D. Mack Smith, *Mussolini's Roman Empire* (London and New York, 1976). The author has not been able to consult this work.

B. Sundkler, *Nathan Söderblom: His Life and Work* (London, 1968)

A. J. P. Taylor, *The Origins of the Second World War* (London, 1964 ed.)

——, *English History, 1914–1945* (London, 1965)

H. THOMPSON, *The Anti-Appeasers: Conservative Opposition to Appeasement in the 1930s* (Oxford, 1971)

C. THORNE, *The Limits of Foreign Policy: The West, the League and the Far Eastern Crisis of 1933–1933* (London, 1972; paperback edn, London and Basingstoke, 1973)

M. TOSCANO, *The History of Treaties and International Politics* (Baltimore, Md, 1966)

GENERAL P. E. TOURNOUX, *Défense des frontières: Haut Commandment – Gouvernement, 1919–1939* (Paris, 1960)

L. VILLARI, *Storia diplomatica del conflitto italo-etiopico* (Bologna, 1943)

——, *Italian Foreign Policy* (London, 1959)

D. WALEY, *British Public Opinion and the Abyssinian War, 1935–1936* (London, 1976). The author has not been able to consult this recent work.

F. P. WALTERS, *A History of the League of Nations*, 2 vols (London, 1952)

G. WARNER, *Pierre Laval and the Eclipse of France* (London, 1968)

D. C. WATT, *Personalities and Politics: Studies in the Formulation of British Foreign Policy in the Twentieth Century* (London, 1965)

——, *see also under* BOURNE in this section

G. L. WEINBERG, *The Foreign Policy of Hitler's Germany: Diplomatic Revolution in Europe, 1933–1936* (Chicago, 1970)

E. WISKEMANN, *The Rome – Berlin Axis* (London, 1966 ed.)

——, *Europe of the Dictators, 1919–1945* (London, 1966)

——, *Fascism in Italy: Its Development and Influence* (London, 1968)

C. ZAGHI, *L'Africa della coscienza europea e l'imperialismo italiano* (Naples, 1973)

4. ARTICLES, ESSAYS AND THESES

A. AQUARONE, 'Italy: The Crisis and Corporative Economy in the Great Depression', *J. Contemporary History*, IV 4 (1969)

W. C. ASKEW, 'Italian intervention in Spain: The Agreements of 31 March 1934 with the Spanish Monarchist Parties', *J. Modern History*, XXIV (June 1952)

——, 'The Secret Agreement between France and Italy on Ethiopia, January 1935', *J. Modern History*, XXV (March 1953)

H. BRADDICK, 'A New Look at American Policy during the Italo-Ethiopian Crisis, 1935–1936', *J. Modern History*, XXXIV (Mar 1962)

P. V. CANNISTRARO AND E. D. WYNOT (Jr), 'On the Dynamics of Anti-

Communism as a Function of Fascist Foreign Policy, 1933–1943', *Il Politico*, XXXVIII (1973)

G. CAROCCI, 'Salvemini e la politica estera del fascismo', *Studi Storici*, X (1968)

V. CERRUTI, 'Perchè Hitler aiutò il Negus', *Il Tempo*, XX (Apr 1959)

G. CRAIG, 'Totalitarian Approaches to Diplomatic Negotiation', in Sarkissian, ed. (1961): *see* section 3

R. DE DAMPIERRE 'Dix années de politique française à Rome', *Revue des Deux Mondes* (15 Sep 1953; 1 Nov 1953)

——, 'Une Entente Italo-Yougoslave', *Revue des Deux Mondes* (1 Sep 1955)

R. DE FELICE, 'Alle Origine del patto d'acciaio: L'Incontro e gli accordi tra Bocchini e Hitler nel marzo – aprile 1936', *Cultura*, I (1963)

——, 'Le Relazioni del Maggiore Giuseppe Renzetti: Una Pagina ignota dei rapporti Mussolini – Hitler prima dell 'ascesa nazista', *Corriere della Sera* (19 Feb 1968)

A. J. DE GRAND, 'Curzio Malaparte: The Illusion of the Fascist Revolution', *J. Contemporary History*, VII (1972)

P. G. EDWARDS, 'The Austen Chamberlain – Mussolini Meetings', *Historical J.*, XIV 1 (1971)

——, 'Britain, Fascist Italy and Ethiopia, 1925–1928', *European Studies Review*, IV (Oct 1974)

A. L. GOLDMAN, 'Sir Robert Vansittart's Search for Italian Co-operation against Hitler, 1933–1936', *J. Contemporary History*, IX (1974)

R. L. HESS, 'Italy and Africa: Colonial Ambitions in the First World War', *J. African History*, IV (1963)

H. S. HUGHES, 'The Early Diplomacy of Italian Fascism, 1922–1932', in Craig and Gilbert, eds (1953): *see* section 3

A. IADAROLA, 'Co-operation and Conflict: Anglo-Italian Relations towards Ethiopia, 1919–1934' (doctoral thesis, Georgetown University, Washington D. C., 1975)

——, 'Ethiopian Admission into the League of Nations: An Assessment of Motives', *J. African Studies*, VIII 4 (1975)

L. JEDLICKA, 'Neue Forschungsergebnisse zum 12.2.1934', in *Österreich, 1918–1938* (Vienna, 1970)

P. KENT, 'The Repercussions of the Lateran Agreements on Mussolini's Policy' (doctoral thesis, New Brunswick University: in preparation)

L. KEREKES, 'Neuer Aktenfund zu den Bezichungen zwischen Hitler und Dollfuss im Jahre 1933, *Acta Historica*, XVIII (1972)

C. A. MACDONALD, 'Radio Bari and Italian Propaganda in the Middle East and British Counter Measures', *Middle East Studies* (for publication during 1977)

M. MAGISTRATI, 'La Germania e l'impresa italiana di Ethiopia: Ricordi di Berlino', *Rivista di Studi Politici Internazionali*, XVII (Dec 1950)

A. MARDER, 'The Royal Navy and the Ethiopian Crisis of 1935—1936', *American Historical Review*, LXXV (1970)

M. MARTELLI-CHANTARD, 'L'Expansion japonaise en Afrique', *L'Afrique Française*, XLIV (1934)

W. N. MEDLICOTT, 'Britain and Germany: The Search for Agreement, 1930—1937', The Creighton Lecture (London, 1970); published in pamphlet form

R. A. C., PARKER, 'Great Britain, France and the Ethiopian Crisis of 1935—1936', *English Historical Review* , LXXXIX (1974)

K. J. PASSMORE, 'The Failure of France and Italy to Conclude a Military Alliance' (London University M.A. dissertation, 1972)

J., PETERSEN, 'Deutschland und Italien im Sommer 1935: Der Wechsel des italienischen Botschafters in Berlin', *Geschichte in Wissenschaft und Unterricht*, XX 6 (1969)

——, 'Konflikt oder Koalition zwischen Christlich Sozialen und Sozialdemokraten, 1933—1934?: Ein Brief Ernst Karl Winters', *Österreich in Geschichte und Literatur*, 16 (1972)

——, 'La Politica estera del fascismo come problema storiografico' *Storia Contemporanea*, III (1972)

——, 'Gesellschaftssystem, Ideologie und Interesse in der Aussenpolitik des Faschistischen Italien', *Quellen und Forschungen aus italienischen Archiven und Bibliotheken*, LIV (Tübingen, 1974)

M. POULAIN, 'Aussenpolitik zwischen Machtpolitik und Dogma: Die deutsch—italienischen Beziehungen von der Jahreswende 1932—1933 bis zur Stresa Konferenz' (Frankfurt University doctoral thesis 1971)

R. QUARTARARO, 'La Crisi mediterranea del 1935—1936', *Storia Contemporanea*, (Dec 1975)

——, 'Imperial Defence in the Mediterranean on the Eve of the Ethiopian Crisis: July—October 1935', *Historical J.* (for publication during 1977)

——, 'Le Relazione Anglo-Italiane fra Europa e Mediterraneo, 1933—1938' (Rome University doctoral thesis 1976)

C. J. ROBERTSON, 'The Hoare – Laval Plan', *J. Contemporary History*, x 3 (1975)

E. M. ROBERTSON, 'Zur Wiederbesetzung des Rheinlandes, 1936', *Vierteljahrshefte für Zeitgeschichte*, x 2 (1962)

——, 'L'Europa e l'avvento di Hitler', in Rossini, ed. (1966): *see* section 3

——, 'Mussolini and Ethiopia: The Pre-History of the Rome Agreements of January 1935', in Hatton and Anderson, eds (1970): *see* section 3

——, 'Hitler and Sanctions: Mussolini and the Rhineland', *European Studies Review* (for publication during 1977)

M. ROOKE, 'Britain and Eastern Europe, 1933 – 1939' (L.S.E. doctoral thesis: in preparation)

R. ROTUNDA 'The Rome Embassy of Sir Eric Drummond, 6th Earl of Perth' (L.S.E. doctoral thesis 1972)

G. RUMI, ' "Revisionismo" fascista ed espansione coloniale, 1925 – 1935', *Il Movimento di Liberazione in Italia*, XVII 85 (1965)

F. G. STAMBROOK, 'The German-Austrian Customs Unions Project of 1931: A Study of German Methods and Motives', *J. Central European Affairs*, XXI (1961)

M. TOSCANO, 'Eden's Mission to Rome on the Eve of the Italian – Ethiopian Conflict', in Sarkissian, ed. (1961): *see* section 3

D. C. WATT, 'The Anglo-German Naval Agreement of 1935: An Interim Judgement', *J. Modern History*, XXVIII (1956)

——, 'South African Attempts to Mediate between Britain and Germany', in Bourne and Watt, eds (1960): *see* section 3

——, 'The Secret Laval – Mussolini Agreement of 1935 on Ethiopia', *Middle East J.*, XV (1961); reprinted in Robertson (ed.), *Origins of the Second World War*: *see* section 3

R. H. WHEALEY, 'Mussolini's Ideological Diplomacy: An Unpublished Document', *J. Modern History*, XXXIX (1967)

P. WRIGHT, 'Italy's African Dream: Fatal Victory', *History Today* (Mar, Apr, May 1973)

Notes and References

ALL works cited are given fuller listing in the Bibliography. A work cited in the Notes and References more than once is in its subsequent occurrences introduced with a 'short title' at the first reference to it in each ensuing chapter-section. Thereafter, within each section, the 'short title' is maintained in the case of an author who has more than one work cited in the book; in all other cases a work is referred to by author's name only, after its first citation in each chapter-section.

ABBREVIATIONS

ASMAE	Archivio Storico del Ministero degli Affari Esteri, Rome
CAB	Cabinet Office, London
D.B.F.P.	*Documents on British Foreign Policy*
D.D.F.	*Documents Diplomatiques Français*
D.G.F.P.	*Documents on German Foreign Policy*
F.O.	Foreign Office, London
P.R.O.	Public Record Office, London
R.I.I.A.	Royal Institute of International Affairs, London
SAC	St Antony's Collection, Oxford
W.O.	War Office, London

INTRODUCTION

1. See I. Kirkpatrick, *Mussolini: Study of a Demagogue* (1964) pp. 84–8.
2. Grandi described the demographic problem in his Italian Senate address of 3 June 1932: see D'Amoja, *Declino e prima crisi dell'Europa di Versailles* (1967) pp. 71–2. See also F. Chabod, *A History of Italian Fascism* (1963) pp. 76–7.
3. Enrico Corradini's criticism against the liberals: see Christopher Seton-Watson, *Italy from Liberalism to Fascism, 1870–1925* (1967) p. 351.
4. Professor Jens Petersen has kindly allowed me to read his 'Gesellschaftssystem, Ideologie und Interesse in der Aussenpolitik des Faschistischen Italien' (1974) where the ideological aspects of Mussolini's policy are discussed. These are also described, in regard to foreign policy, by P. V. Cannistraro and E. D. Wynot, 'On the Dynamics of Anti-Communism as a Function of Fascist Foreign Policy, 1933–1943' (1973).
5. For a good account of the role of émigrés and ideological considerations in Mussolini's policy, see A. Cassels, *Mussolini's Early Diplomacy* (1970) pp. 365–76, and 9.
6. G. Salvemini, *Prelude to World War II* (1953) esp. pp. 119–20. For a detailed discussion of modern Italian historiography, see J. Petersen, 'La Politica estera del fascismo come problema storiografico' (1972).
7. Salvemini, ch. 59.

8. G. Carocci, 'Salvemini e la politica estera del fascismo' (1968) pp. 218–24.

9. Quoted from Petersen, 'Politica estera', p. 665.

10. Seton-Watson; and Cassels. See also H. S. Hughes, 'The Early Diplomacy of Italian Fascism, 1922–1932', in G. A. Craig and F. Gilbert, eds (1953).

11. G. Rumi, ' "Revisionismo" fascista ed espansione coloniale, 1925–1935' (1965); Petersen, 'Politica estera', p. 672.

12. Petersen, p. 674.

13. For summary of Mussolini's speech of 1 Nov 1936 describing Italy as an island, see *Ciano's Diplomatic Papers* (1948) pp. 60–1.

14. F. W. Deakin, *The Brutal Friendship: Mussolini, Hitler and the Fall of Fascism* (1962) pp. 19–22. For Mussolini's long-term aims in the Mediterranean, see G. Rumi, *Alle Origini della politica estera fascista, 1918–1923* (1968).

15. D'Amoja, p. 132.

16. G. Carocci, *La Politica estera dell' Italia fascista, 1925–1928* (1969) pp. 18–31

17. R. De Felice, *Mussolini il Duce: Gli Anni del consenso, 1922–1936* (1974) pp. 367–70, describes the changes emerging after Grandi's appointment as Foreign Minister.

18. Carocci, loc. cit.

19. I am much indebted to Frau Ilse von Hassell, widow of Ulrich von Hassell, for suggesting this view.

20. Kirkpatrick, p. 273. For the text, see SAC, Job 1/3.

21. See R. L. Hess, *Italian Colonialism in Somalia* (1966) ch. 7.

1. THE RESUFFLE OF JULY–AUGUST 1932

1. For the text of the 1906 Agreement, see A. J. Barker, *The Civilising Mission* (1968) appendix 1, pp. 303–7.

2. R. Greenfield, *Ethiopia: A New Political History* (1965) pp. 134–9.

3. R. L. Hess, 'Italy and Africa: Colonial Ambitions in the First World War' (1963).

4. G. W. Baer, *The Coming of the Italian – Ethiopian War* (1967) p. 14; Seton-Watson, *Italy . . . 1870–1925*, pp. 683–4.

5. F. Hardie, *The Abyssinian Crisis* (1974) pp. 17–19; Cassels, *Mussolini's Early Diplomacy*, pp. 297–300; P. G. Edwards, 'Britain, Fascist Italy and Ethiopia, 1925–1928' (1974) and 'The Austen Chamberlain – Mussolini Meetings' (1971). Edwards disputes the view that Britain needed Italian support to put pressure on Turkey to achieve the incorporation into Iraq of Mosul province. Dr Antoinette Iadarola, in 'Co-operation and Conflict: Anglo-Italian Relations towards Ethiopia, 1919–1934' (1975) discusses Ethiopia's admission to the League (ch. 2) and the Anglo-Italian agreements of 1925 (ch. 3). Basing her account partly on the documents of the Committee of Imperial Defence, she maintains that Britain needed the co-operation of other powers, possibly including Italy, against Turkey in 1924–5. (I am grateful for her allowing me to refer to her work.)

6. F. P. Walters, *A History of the League of Nations* (1952) pp. 397–8.

7. *Documents Diplomatiques Fraṇais(D.D.F.)*, series 1 vol. 11, 182, annexes; Iadarola, ch. 3.

8. See M. Toscano's Introduction to P. Aloisi, *Journal 25 Juin – 14 Juillet, 1936* (1957).

9. Hardie, pp. 20–2.

10. See J. Petersen, *Hitler – Mussolini: Die Entstehung der Achse Berlin – Rom, 1933–1936* (1973) p. 381.

11. Baer, p. 19; G. Rochat, *Militari e politici nella preparazione della campagna d'Etiopia: Studio e documenti, 1932–1936* (1971) p. 23.

12. *D.D.F.* (1) 11, 182, annexe 7.

13. R. Guariglia, *Ricordi, 1922–1946* (1950) pp. 127ff.

14. See G. Warner, *Pierre Laval and the Eclipse of France* (1968) pp. 42–4.

15. Archivio storico del Ministero degli Affari Esteri (ASMAE), fasciolo 3, sotto fascicolo 2: Grandi to Mussolini, 25 July 1932.

16. E. De Bono, *Anno XIII: The Conquest of an Empire* (1937) p. 3; Rochat, pp. 26–9.

17. St Antony's Collection (SAC), Job 263 (1).

18. D'Amoja, *Declino, pp. 72–3.*

19. Guariglia, pp. 164, 180 and appendix A, pp. 763–73.

20. Ibid.

21. *D.D.F.* (1) II, 182, annexes.

22. Cassels, pp. 364–5; S. H. Roberts, *The History of French Colonial Policy, 1870–1939* (1963) pp. 285–93. See also *D.D.F.* (1) II, 41: dispatch from Rome, 28 Nov 1932.

23. *D.D.F.* (1) II, 182; Cassels, pp. 361–4. Mussolini also supported a movement for autonomy in Corsica, an important French air-base for possible attacks on the industrial areas of northern Italy: see Cassels, pp. 87–8; Seton-Watson, p. 692; and note 49 below.

24. *D.D.F.* (1) I, 105, 110; II, 182. See also Guariglia, pp. 184ff.

25. *D.D.F.* (1) I, 179; Cassels, pp. 362–5. For a general account of the Italian settlements in the Mediterranean, See Elizabeth Monroe, *The Mediterranean in Politics* (1938) pp. 125–9, 172, 196.

26. Guariglia, pp. 184, 198–9, 773–89. See also D'Amoja, p. 107.

27. *D.D.F.* (1) I, 105, 110, 260. See also *Documents on British Foreign Policy (D.B.F.P.)*, series 2, vol. VI, 357 n. 1.

28. Seton-Watson, p. 697–8.

29. *D.D.F.* (1) II, 182, annexes.

30. Ibid. 174, 182, 197; IV, 17; V, 486.

31. Guariglia, p. 450: and *D.D.F.* (1) I, 317; II, 182, annexes.

32. Guariglia, pp. 139ff.

33. *D.D.F.* (1) II, 182.

34. Ibid. I, 214; II, 182.

35. Guariglia, pp. 139–40.

36. Ibid., p. 144. Berthelot preferred to conduct these negotiations with Theodoli rather than with the Italian ambassador in Paris.

37. Ibid., pp. 144–64.

38. Ibid., pp. 175–6. For an account of the émigré problem, see Cassels, pp. 365ff.

39. *D.D.F.* (1) I, 214; II, 183.

40. Guariglia did not think that the difficulties encountered were sufficient to deter Italy from continuing with the *politica periferica*: see Guariglia, appendix A.

41. ASMAE, Grandi Papers, fascicolo 3, sotto fascicolo 2*, 309: text of a conversation of June or July 1932 between Grandi and Paganon, an associate of Herriot.

42. *D.D.F.* (1) I, 260, 266, 772, 273. For the attitude of the French army, see I, 244, 250, 260, 277; II, 203; IV, 168. De Felice, *Mussolini*, pp. 363, 384–5 discusses Italian–French naval and colonial rivalry.

43. *D.D.F.* (2) I, 329.

44. *D.D.F.* (1) I, 266, annexe to note of 21 Oct 1932.

45. Seton-Watson, pp. 692–3.

46. *D.D.F.* (2) I, 82, 83.

47. *D.D.F.* (1) I, 203. It is of interest that General Weygand strongly criticised the view that French military planning should be based on the assumption that a future war would be purely defensive.

48. Ibid. I, 266.

49. Aloisi, 14 Jan 1933. The French remained concerned about Italian aims in Corsica in Sep 1933: *D.D.F.* (1) IV, 188.

50. See Cassels, pp. 85–7.

51. For a full account, see G. Barros, *The Corfu Incident of 1923* (1965) pp. 42–57. See also Walters, pp. 245–55; Cassels, pp. 86–7.

52. British naval policy after 1930 will be discussed in S. W. Roskill, *Naval Policy between the Wars*, vol. II (in prep.). For British policy in the Far East, see C. Thorne, *The Limits of Foreign Policy* (1972; paperback 1973).

53. I am most obliged to Professor Peter Kent, New Brunswick University, for permission to quote from his chapter on Malta in his doctoral thesis 'The Repercussions of the Lateran Agreements on Mussolini's Policy' (in prep.). See also W. K. Hancock, *Survey of British Commonwealth Affairs*, vol. I: *Problems of Nationality* (1937).

54. For an illuminating account of pressure groups seeking to formulate Italian foreign policy, see Carocci, *Politica estera*, ch. 2, pp. 18–31.

55. P.R.O. F.O.–C1742/24/22, 1 Mar 1929. There were other causes for Vatican complaint; Strickland had refused to allow the Church authorities to expel for disciplinary reasons a certain wayward priest: P.R.O. F.O.–C1535/24/22, 25 Feb 1929.

56. Ibid., F.O.–800/281, Arthur Henderson's Papers: letter from Graham to Henderson, 6 May 1930.

57. Ibid., F.O.–C2670/3/22, 20 Apr 1931.

58. Ibid., F.O.–C1474/1027/22, 22 Feb 1932.

59. Ibid., F.O.–C8719/491/22, 14 Oct 1932.

60. Ibid., F.O.–C7428/7/22, 21 Aug 1933; ibid., C7821/7/22, 5 Sep 1933; Aloisi, 6 Nov 1933. See also *D.B.F.P.* (2) VI, 164.

61. Guariglia, pp. 144–64.

62. Ibid., p. 434.

63. D'Amoja, pp. 74, 106.

64. Ibid., pp. 82–3; Aloisi, 26 July 1932, n. 2.

65. Aloisi, 26 July 1932; D'Amoja, pp. 73, 109–10.

66. D'Amoja, pp. 88, 133ff.

67. Ibid., pp. 95ff., 99.

2. EUROPE AND AFRICA, 1932–33

1. Aloisi, *Journal*, 28 July 1932. The extent of the reshuffle is exaggerated by G. Craig, 'Totalitarian Approaches to Diplomatic Negotiation', in A. O. Sarkissian, ed. (1961) pp. 107–25.

2. Aloisi, 26 July, 13 Sep, 4, 28 Oct 1932.

3. Petersen, *Hitler – Mussolini*, p. 142, n.37.

4. Mussolini, *Omnia Opera di Benito Mussolini*, E. and D. Susmel, eds, (1954–63) vol. XXV, pp. 141–4. See also D'Amoja, *Declino*, pp. 132–5.

5. Aloisi, 27 Oct, 6 Nov 1932; *D.D.F. (1)* I, 271. See also D'Amoja, pp. 132–5.

6. Aloisi, 3, 4, 25 Dec 1935.

7. Ibid., 28 Nov 1932.

8. Ibid., 6, 8, 10 Nov 1932; *D.D.F.* (1) I, 317.

9. *D.D.F.* (1) II, 182: see also III, 415. The text of this conversation has not been reproduced in the French documents; Aloisi describes it under 14 Jan 1933.

10. For a detailed account, see D'Amoja, pp. 146–57; L. Hory and M. Broszat, *Der kroatische Ustascha-Staat* (1964) ch. 1.

11. C. A. Macartney and A. W. Palmer, *Independent Eastern Europe* (1962) pp. 268–77.

12. D'Amoja, pp. 153–4; *D.D.F.* (2) III, 304.

13. Macartney and Palmer, pp. 224–6. See also Royal Institute of International Affairs (R.I.I.A.), *Survey 1934*, pp. 540–54.

14. For Mussolini's treatment of the Germans in South Tyrol, see C. F. Latour, *Südtirol und die Achse Berlin–Rom, 1932–1945* (1962) ch. 2. See also Seton-Watson, *Italy 1870–1925*, pp. 679, 689; Cassels, *Early Diplomacy*, pp. 338–48.

15. Aloisi, 15 Dec 1932.

16. D'Amoja, pp. 146–55. See also *Documents on German Foreign Policy* (*D.G.F.P.*), series c, vol. i, 99, for a summary of 19 Mar 1933 of Italian – Yugoslav relations; and Macartney and Palmer, pp. 294–5.

17. Aloisi, 5 Dec 1932.

18. *D.G.F.P.* (c) i, 99; see also D'Amoja, p. 148.

19. D'Amoja, pp. 137–9. The author has used the unpublished German memoirs of Starhemberg held in Vienna (cf. fo. 137, n. 47) as well as the published version.

20. Aloisi, 28, 30 Nov, 30 Dec 1932. See also Petersen, *Hitler – Mussolini* pp. 81–4.

21. D'Amoja, pp. 159ff.; R.I.I.A., *Survey 1934*, p. 555.

22. ASMAE, B3/FX: note of 14 Dec 1932, signed by the Duce.

23. *D.D.F.* (i) ii, 54, 110, 120, 129; and especially 142: report from Rome, 28 Dec 1932. See also ibid., 419: French Foreign Ministry summary of Italian – Yugoslav relations, 16 Mar 1933.

24. Aloisi, 25 Dec 1932.

25. Ibid., 15 Dec 1932.

26. E. De Bono, *Anno XIIII*, ch. 1; Rochat, *Militari e politici*, pp. 26–33 and document 1.

27. Rochat, pp. 25–6; Barker, *Civilising Mission*, pp. 136–9.

28. Hess, *Somalia*, pp. 153–4; Rochat, 78–9.

29. Greenfield, *Ethiopia*, pp. 100–1; Hess, *Somalia*, p. 146; Rochat, p. 159.

30. Hess, *Somalia*, pp. 153–4.

31. Ibid., pp. 9–10, 99ff., 185.

32. For a recent account of the social structure of Ethiopia, see P. Gilkes, *The Dying Lion: Feudalism and Modernisation in Ethiopia* (1975) chs 1 and 2.

33. For an account of the Ethiopian church, see A. H. M. Jones and E. Monroe, *A History of Abyssinia* (1935) pp. 35–43, 105–18.

34. Greenfield, pp. 15, 53–7; Gilkes, ch. 7.

35. Rochat, pp. 29–32, and documents 1 and 2.

36. Ibid.

37. Ibid.; Aloisi, 15 Dec 1932.

38. Aloisi, 3 Jan 1933.

39. See Toscano's Introduction to Aloisi; Baer, *Italian – Ethiopian War*, pp. 23–4.

40. E. R. Prince Starhemberg, *Between Hitler and Mussolini* (1942) p. 107.

41. Aloisi, 7 Jan 1933.

42. Ibid., 8 Jan 1933. For a fuller account of the Hirtenberg affair, see L. Kerekes, *Abenddämmerung einer Demokratie* (1966) p. 125; Petersen, *Hitler – Mussolini*, pp. 95–7.

43. Aloisi, 8, 9 Jan 1933. See also *D.D.F.* (i) ii, 196.

44. *D.D.F.* (i) ii, 202, 259, Aloisi, 12 Feb 1933. For the German account, see *D.G.F.P.* (c), i, 81.

45. D'Amoja, p. 187ff.; Petersen, *Hitler – Mussolini*, pp. 98–9. See also Aloisi, 18 Mar 1933.

46. Staff talks among service chiefs of the Little Entente were first held on 1 Dec 1932: *D.D.F.* (i) ii, 54. See also ibid., 120, 124, 194, 204, 209, 302; and Macartney and Palmer, pp. 329, n. 2.

47. Aloisi, 14 Jan 1933. See also Petersen, *Hitler – Mussolini*, pp. 88ff.

48. SAC, Job 20, Renzetti's report to Mussolini, 23 Jan 1933. See also Petersen, *Hitler – Mussolini*, pp. 111ff.; De Felice, *Mussolini*, p. 442.

49. SAC, loc. cit., Renzetti report, 31 Jan 1933; Aloisi, 13 Feb 1933.

50. SAC, loc. cit.

51. R. De Felice, *I Rapporti tra fascismo e nazionalsocialismo fino all'andata al potere di Hitler, 1922–1933: Appunti e documenti* (1971) p. 207; and Petersen, *Hitler – Mussolini*, p. 113.

52. Aloisi, 21 May 1933.

53. Petersen, *Hitler – Mussolini*, pp. 164–5.

54. Aloisi, 4 Feb 1933; Hassell's dispatches: *D.G.F.P.* (c) I, 12, 15, 29. M. Poulain, 'Aussenpolitik zwischen Machtpolitik und Dogma' (1972) fos 41ff., describes Hassel's character and aims.

55. For Gömbös's démarche of 6 Feb 1933, see *D.G.F.P.* (c) I, 15; Macartney and Palmer, p. 299. See also D. Ross, *Dollfuss und Hitler: Die deutsche Österreich-Politik, 1933–1934* (1966) p. 15.

56. *D.D.F.* (1), II, 282.

57. Aloisi, 13, 16 Jan 1933; *D.D.F.* (1) II, 194.

58. Aloisi, 16, 17 Feb 1933. Starhemberg in his memoirs (ch. 7) may have exaggerated the anti-Nazi and not the anti-Socialist role he was playing at this time.

59. Aloisi, 18 Feb 1933. For French financial policy in Austria, see L. Kerekes (ed.), 'Neuer Aktenfund zu den Beziehungen zwischen Hitler und Dollfuss in Jahre 1933' (1972).

60. *D.G.F.P.*, (c) I, 51, 64: Hassell's dispatches, 6, 8 Mar 1933.

61. See E. M. Robertson, *Hitler's Pre-War Policy and Military Plans* (1963) pp. 4–7.

62. Described in a dispatch, 10 Feb 1933, by François-Poncet, French ambassador in Berlin: *D.D.F.* (1) II, 282, 319. See also memorandum by Bülow, 18 Feb 1933: *D.G.F.P.* (c) II, 24 and n. 3.

63. *D.D.F.* (1), II, 332, 424: dispatches 22 Feb, 17 Mar 1933; and ibid. III, 150: report by Jouvenel to Paul Boncour and François-Poncet, 20 Apr 1933. See also Petersen, *Hitler–Mussolini*, pp. 123ff.

64. *D.G.F.P.* (c) I, 206: Köpke's instructions to Rieth in Vienna, 23 Mar 1933; ibid. 112: memorandum to Director of Department II, 23 Mar 1933. For a very clear discussion of the entangled question of Austria, see Ross, pp. 23–7.

65. Ross. pp. 19ff.; J. Gehl, *Austria, Germany and the Anschluss, 1931–1938* (1963) ch. 3.

66. On 4 Mar 1933, Aloisi was told by Suvich that Parazzoli, a close friend of Mussolini and Paris correspondent of the *Popolo d' Italia*, had sent an 'important report' to the Duce claiming that General Weygand intended to launch a preventive war in April: Aloisi, 4, 5 Mar 1933. See also *D.D.F.* (1) II, 136.

67. De Felice, *Mussolini*, p. 446, quotes an interesting document from the Lancellotti Papers relating to Mussolini's attitude to Germany and France in April 1933.

68. *D.D.F.* (1) II, 360: dispatch of de Feurin, French ambassador in London, 1 Mar 1933 describes Grandi's opposition to an *Anschluss*.

69. *D.B.F.P.* (2) V, 38: Simon to Graham, 8 Mar 1933. See also Aloisi, 10, 11 Mar 1933.

70. De Felice, *Mussolini*, p. 444; *D.D.F.* (1) II, 421. Peterson, *Hitler–Mussolini*, p. 145, dismisses the widely held view that the Duce, in proposing a Four Power directorate, either followed Britain's initiative, or concerted his action with Britain's.

71. *D.G.F.P.* (c) I, 83, 84, 95, 98.

72. K. H. Jarausch, *The Four Power Pact of 1933* (1965).

73. Aloisi, 13 Apr 1933, n. 1; 17 Apr 1933.

74. R. De Felice, *Storia degli Ebrei italiani sotto il fascismo* (1972) pp. 147–51; Petersen, *Hitler–Mussolini*, pp. 156–61. See also *D.G.F.P.* (c) I, 119, 122.

75. De Felice, *Ebrei italiani*, p. 155. See also Mussolini's comments to Jouvenel on Hitler's anti-semitism: Aloisi, 30 Mar 1933.

3. STRAINED RELATIONS WITH GERMANY AND AUSTRIA, 1933

1. Ross, *Dollfuss und Hitler*, pp. 26ff.

2. Aloisi, *Journal*, 18 Mar 1933; *D.D.F.* (1) II, 142.

3. *D.G.F.P.* (c) I, 107: instructions of 22 Mar 1933 from Köpke to Rieth, German

minister in Vienna. See ibid., 112 for Frank's activities; also ibid., 128 for Neurath's dispatch to Hassell, 27 Mar 1933.

4. Aloisi, 18 26 Mar 1933.

5. Ibid., 11, 12 Apr 1933; see also Petersen, *Hitler–Mussolini*, pp. 164–8.

6. Aloisi, 17 Apr 1933; *D.G.F.P.* (c) I, 173, for Hassell's dispatch, 20 Apr 1933. Also Poulain, 'Aussenpolitik', fos 66–8; Petersen, *Hitler–Mussolini*, p. 188.

7. Petersen, *Hitler–Mussolini*, pp. 189–90. See Ross, pp. 19ff. for an account of general events in Austria early in 1933.

8. *D.D.F.* (1) II, 379.

9. Ross, pp. 33–8.

10. *D.G.F.P.* (c) I, 219, 234, 249, 256.

11. Ibid., 262.

12. Ibid., 267: *Note verbale* from Austrian government, 27 May 1933.

13. Ross, pp. 50–6.

14. *D.G.F.P.* (c) I, 298, 305, 306, 307; Petersen, *Hitler–Mussolini*, pp. 190–1, 215–16.

15. Robertson, *Hitler's Pre-War Policy* pp. 15–16.

•16. *D.B.F.P.* (2) v, p. 246.

17. Aloisi, 19 June 1933. See Petersen, *Hitler–Mussolini*, p. 195 for an account of the Duce—Dollfuss meeting in early June 1933.

18. Simon stated this view to Graham, British ambassador in Rome, 12 July 1933: *D.B.F.P.* (2) v, 249. See ibid., 257 for Vansittart's attitude on Germany policy in Austria in dispatch to Rome, 18 July 1933; and ibid., 274 for Graham's reply, 26 July. For Vansittart's general attitude to the League, see I. Colvin, *Vansittart in Office* (1965) ch. 3. See also A. L. Goldman, 'Sir Robert Vansittart's Search for Italian Co-operation Against Hitler, 1933–1936' (1974).

19. *D.G.F.P.* (c) I, 83, 164, 171.

20. On 19 Apr 1933 Hassell proposed that a 'gentlemen's agreement' for general consultation with Italy should be reached: Aloisi, 19 Apr 1933; and *D.G.F.P.* (c) I, 164. See also Petersen, *Hitler–Mussolini*, pp. 171ff.

21. *D.D.F.* (1) III, 7, 35, 37.

22. See *D.G.F.P.* (c) I, 451–5 for extracts from the text. See also ibid., 239 for unsigned German Foreign Ministry memorandum on disarmament, 15 May 1933.

23. Ibid., 269, 272, 274, 276, 282, 290.

24. Ibid., 324, 330; Aloisi, 7, 27 July 1933.

25. *D.G.F.P.* (c) I, 365.

26. Graham to Simon, 11 July 1933: *D.B.F.P.* (2) v, enclosure to 233, minute 4; and ibid., 246. See also Gehl, *Anschluss*, pp. 62ff.

27. *D.B.F.P.* (2) v, 270: Vansittart to Harvey and Graham; see also ibid., 271, 376, 385, 390, 391.

28. *D.G.F.P.* (c) I, 389: Bülow's memorandum, 31 July 1933.

29. Ibid., 397: Hassell's dispatch, 8 Aug 1933; and ibid., 398: Neurath's letter to Hitler, 9 Aug 1933. See also ibid., 401, 402, 407.

30. See Aloisi, 25 July 1933 for Italian–Hungarian Agreement. See also Ross, pp. 78–80; Petersen, *Hitler–Mussolini*, p. 205.

31. *D.B.F.P.* (2) v, 338, 343, 345, 353, 356. See also Ross, 79–80.

32. *D.G.F.P.* (c) I, 408, 411, 416: dispatch from Rome, 21 Aug 1933.

33. Ibid., 427, 485; Ross, pp. 85, 89.

4. MUSSOLINI AND DISARMAMENT, 1933

1. *D.G.F.P.* (c) I, 251; Petersen, *Hitler–Mussolini*, pp. 233ff.

2. *D.D.F.* (1) III, 372, 400, 415; *D.G.F.P.* (c) I, 322.

3. Aloisi, *Journal*, 2 Sep 1933.
4. *D.B.F.P.* (2) v, 269; *D.G.F.P.* (C) I, 370, 374.
5. *D.G.F.P.* ibid., 396.
6. Ibid., 413.
7. Ibid., 426.
8. Ibid., 431.
9. *D.D.F.* (1) IV, 241, 242, 243, 246; see also *D.B.F.P.* (2) v, 406, 407; Aloisi, 23 Sep 1933.
10. *D.D.F.* (1) IV, 241, 242, 243, 296.
11. *D.G.F.P.* (c) I, 441, 442, 445, 446, 475.
12. Ibid., 478, 479.
13. *D.B.F.P.* (2) v, 444.
14. *D.G.F.P.* (c) I, 194, 448, 502; Aloisi, 13 Oct 1933.
15. *D.G.F.P.* (c) I, 489.

5. DISENCHANTMENT IN EUROPE, OCTOBER 1933–MARCH 1934

1. *D.G.F.P.* (c) II, 2, 4, 10, See also ibid. IV, 61 for Hassell's description (in undated memorandum, evidently of April 1935) of Mussolini's reaction to Hitler's decision.
2. *D.B.F.P.* (2) v, 457, 476; *D.D.F.* (1) IV, 346.
3. Aloisi, *Journal*, 14 Oct 1933.
4. *D.G.F.P.* (c) II, 28, 67, 104; IV, 61.
5. *D.D.F.* (1) IV, 280.
6. *D.G.F.P.* (c) II, 28, for Neurath's marginal note on Hassell's dispatch of 25 Oct 1933.
7. Ibid. II, 499. See N. Baynes, *Hitler's Speeches* (1942) vol II, p. 1147, for Hitler's interview with Fernard de Brinon in Nov 1933. For Hitler's general policy towards France in 1933, see G. L. Weinberg, *The Foreign Policy of Hitler's Germany* (1970) pp. 169–74.
8. Aloisi, 28 Oct 1933; *D.G.F.P.* (c) II, 32.
9. *D.D.F.* (1) IV, 277, 293.
10. Ibid. IV, 281. See also R.I.I.A *Survey 1934*, p. 495–6.
11. *D.D.F.* (1) IV, 294, 313, 333, 382.
12. Ross, *Dolfuss and Hitler*, pp. 94ff.
13. *D.G.F.P.* (c) II, 50: Hassell memorandum, 8 Nov 1933. See also ibid. IV, 61 for Hassell's description of visit in summary of German–Italian negotiations evidently written in April 1935. Aloisi described visit under 3, 6, 7 Nov 1933.
14. *D.D.F.* (1) IV, 404; Aliosi, 6 Nov 1933.
15. *D.G.F.P.* (c) II, 45, unsigned memorandum evidently of 3 Nov 1933. See also Aloisi, 18 Nov 1933. In 1934 Cerruti claimed that important Italian documents fell into Hassell's hands, which might explain why Göring asked for Cerruti's dismissal: see Aloisi, 4 Feb 1934.
16. *D.G.F.P.*(c) II, 104.
17. Aloisi, 21 July, 27 Aug, 20 Nov 1933. See also Petersen, *Hitler–Mussolini*, p. 182.
18. Peterson, pp. 182–3, describes the most important articles, Four and Five.
19. Aloisi, 2 Sep, 3, 4 Dec 1933.
20. *D.G.F.P.* (c) II, 130, from Hassell, 15 Dec 1933. See Aloisi, 3, 4, 5 Dec 1933 fpr references to Litvinov's visit.
21. *D.G.F.P.* (c) II, 120, 126, 145, 219, 224; Aloisi, 8 Feb 1934.
22. *D.G.F.P.* (c) II, 32. See also Petersen, *Hitler–Mussolini*, pp. 268ff.
23. Aloisi, 16, 18 Nov, 3, 6, 7 December 1933: for Mussolini's talk with Drummond, 12 Dec 1933, see *D.B.F.P.* (2) VI, 290. See also *D.G.F.P.* (c) II, 208, 266.

24. *D.B.F.P.* (2) I, 71; Walters, *League of Nations*, p. 711.

25. *D.G.F.P.* (C) II, 160, 166, 167, 179, 184, 188.

26. Ross, pp. 163–9.

27. *D.G.F.P.* (C) II, 213, and editor's note, pp. 442–3. On the role of the League and Austria, see Gehl, *Anschluss*, pp. 78–81.

28. L. Jedlicka, 'Neue Forschungsergebnisse zum 12.2.1934', in *Österreich 1918–1934* (1970) pp. 73–93; *D.B.F.P.* (2) VI, 275.

29. *D.G.F.P.* (C) II, 254; Ross, pp. 175–7; Gehl, pp. 81ff.

30. Petersen, *Hitler – Mussolini*, p. 311.

31. Aloisi, 12 Dec 1933.

32. Rochat, *Militari e politici*, p. 39.

33. For the text, see *D.B.F.P.* (2) V, 331, Drummond to Simon, 17 Feb 1934.

34. Aloisi, 27 Jan, 4 Feb 1934. See Petersen, *Hitler – Mussolini*, pp. 225–31, for a full account of Italian policy in South-East Europe.

35. *D.G.F.P.* (C) III, 246 and n.2 describe political constellation in the Balkans.

36. Hory and Broszat, *Der kroatische Ustascha-Staat*, p. 24.

37. R.I.I.A., *Survey 1934*, pp. 503, 548–50.

38. *D.G.F.P.* (C) II, 72, 91, 92.

39. Ibid., 192, 309, 316, 318; ibid. III, 13. See also Petersen, *Hitler – Mussolini*, pp. 308–10; Macartney and Palmer, *Eastern Europe*, pp. 315–17.

40. For a conversation between Mussolini and Cerruti, see Aloisi, 5 Feb 1934.

41. Aloisi, 27 Feb, 7, 12–17 Mar 1934. For summary of text of Rome Protocols, see R.I.I.A., *Survey 1934*, pp. 499–500; Petersen, *Hitler – Mussolini*, pp. 314–24. See *D.G.F.P.* (C) II, 332 for Hassell's description of negotiations leading to Rome Protocols.

42. For Austrian Nazis and Yugoslavia, see Jedlicka, 'Neue Forschungsergebnisse . . .'.

43. This agreement is described in W. C. Askew 'Italian Intervention in Spain' (1952).

44. Mussolini, *Omnia Opera*, vol. XXVI, pp. 185–93. For summary of the speech see R.I.I.A., *Survey 1934*, pp. 314–24. See also *D.D.F.* IV, 23 n.1; *D.B.F.P.* (2) VI, 361.

45. For Yugoslav reactions to the speech, see *D.G.F.P.* (C) III, 381; for Turkish reactions, see R.I.I.A., *Survey 1936*, p. 330, n. 2.

46. Rochat, pp. 40, 97.

6. THE ASSASSINATION OF DOLLFUSS

1. *D.G.F.P.* (C) II, 328; IV, 61. See also Petersen, *Hitler – Mussolini*, pp. 328, 330.

2. *D.G.F.P.* (C) II, 368, 393; Petersen, pp. 332–6.

3. *D.G.F.P.* (C) II, 389, 393.

4. Ross, *Dolfuss und Hitler*, p. 198.

5. *D.G.F.P.* (C) II, 409; Ross, pp. 200–1.

6. For the Vatican view, see Petersen, *Hitler – Mussolini*, p. 351. For events in Austria, see Ross, pp. 208ff.

7. *D.G.F.P.* (C) II, 459, 462.

8. SAC, Job 20, Renzetti's report, 15 June 1934.

9. *D.G.F.P.* (C) II, 461, 462, 479, 492, 501; ibid. III, 3, 17. See also Petersen, pp. 342–3; Ross, p. 217.

10. *D.G.F.P.* (C) II, 449; Aloisi, *Journal*, 9 May 1934; Petersen, pp. 325–7, 351.

11. *D.D.F.* (I) VI, 97, 142, 165.

12. *D.G.F.P.* (C) II, 472.

13. Ibid., 449.

14. Ibid., 472, also see 432, 449, 472. For an account of the different views held on

Hitler's Austrian policy, see Petersen, *Hitler – Mussolini*, pp. 336–8, esp. n. 34.

15. See Weinberg, *Foreign Policy*, pp. 172ff. for a general study of the disarmament issue in April and May.

16. Rosenberg, *Das Politische Tagebuch Alfred Rosenbergs*, ed. H. G. Seraphim (1964) p. 39.

17. Ross pp. 208–9; Petersen pp. 342–4.

18. Ross p. 21; Jedlicka, 'Neue Forschungsergebnisse . . .'.

19. E. Wiskemann, *The Rome – Berlin Axis*, 2nd ed. (1966) pp. 53–5. For a full account, see Petersen, pp. 344ff.

20. Aloisi, 14 June 1934; Rosenberg, pp. 39ff.

21. *D.G.F.P.* (c) III, 5, 7, 10.

22. Aloisi, 14, 15 June 1934.

23. Rosenberg, pp. 39–40.

24. *D.G.F.P.* (c) III, 26.

25. Ibid., 56, 62, n. 3.

26. Petersen, pp. 357–9; Ross, pp. 218–21.

27. Ross, p. 225.

28. Rosenberg, p. 39.

29. Ross, pp. 228–30.

30. Ibid., pp. 231–2.

31. *D.G.F.P.* (c) III, 56, 100.

32. SAC, Job 20, Renzetti's report, 14 July 1934.

33. *D.G.F.P.* (c) III, 100, 112.

34. Ross, p. 233.

35. *D.G.F.P.* (c) III, 89, 100.

36. Ross, pp. 235–5. The French ambassador in Berlin, François-Poncet, expected on 24 July that a rising would take place next day: *D.D.F.* (1) VI, 497. The British took a similar view: *D.B.F.P.* (2) VI, 326.

37. Petersen, pp. 360–6; Ross, 236–43. See also *D.B.F.P.* (2) VI, 522, 524, 528.

38. *D.G.F.P.* (c) III, 115, 123.

39. Ibid., 135, 141.

40. SAC, Job 20, Renzetti's reports, 4, 21 August 1934.

41. Aloisi, 27 Apr 1934; *D.B.F.P.* (2) VI, 380. See also P.R.O. F.O. 371/19577 R 1910: Henderson to Simon, 16 Mar 1935.

42. R.I.I.A., *Survey 1934*, p. 536 and section D (1) p. 556; Aloisi, 23 June 1934; *D.D.F.* (1) VI, 397, 422.

43. Macartney and Palmer, *Eastern Europe*, pp. 319–20.

44. *D.G.F.P.* (c) III, 23, 27. For a general account of Yugoslav policy in June 1934, see *D.D.F.* (1) VI, 318.

45. Jedlicka, 'Das Jahr 1934', pp. 73–93.

46. Macartney and Palmer, p. 326.

47. For the speech at Bari, 6 Sep 1934, see Mussolini, *Omnia Opera*, vol. XXVI, pp. 318–20.

48. Macartney and Palmer, p. 326; Aloisi, 26 July 1934.

49. Aloisi, 30 July 1934.

50. *D.G.F.P.* (c) III, 134.

51. Aloisi, 27 July 1934.

52. *D.G.F.P.* (c) II, 122, 127, 134.

53. Aloisi, 1 Aug 1934.

54. Ibid., 21 Aug 1934. See also *D.D.F.* (1) VI, 509, 511.

55. Aloisi, 21 Aug 1934.

56. Ibid., 30 Aug 1934.

57. See *D.B.F.P.* (2) XII, 124.

58. Rochat, *militari e politici*, pp. 76–7 and document 21. This directive is published in A. Adamthwaite (ed.), *The Coming of the Second World War* (1977).

7. THE MARSEILLES ASSASSINATIONS AND THEIR AFTERMATH

1. Aloisi, *Journal*, 27 Aug 1934. For description of the Italian – Yugoslav quarrel, see *D.B.F.P.* (2) XII, 15.
2. Aloisi, 19 Aug 1934.
3. Ibid., 1 Sep 1934.
4. R.I.I.A., *Survey 1934*, p. 557; *D.B.F.P.* (2) XII, 15.
5. *D.D.F.* (1) VI, 246, 332, 336, 340, 371; *D.B.F.P.* (2) XII, 9, 14.
6. Aloisi, 1 Sep 1934.
7. This speech is discussed in R.I.I.A., *Survey 1934*, pp. 330, 558. For Alexander's pro-German leanings, see *D.B.F.P.* (2) XII, 112.
8. Aloisi, 9, 14 Oct 1934. According to Aloisi (13 Oct), the assassin's pseudonym was Kadeder but his real name was Kortoff. He was a member of the Ustaši who left Arezzo on 25 Sep 1934; Bocchini, head of the Italian police, recognised him from a photograph. According to the editor's note in *D.G.F.P.* (C) III, 468, the assassin's name was Vlado Georgiejev.
9. Aloisi, 20 Oct 1934. See also Macartney and Palmer, *Eastern Europe*, p. 327.
10. *D.G.F.P.* (C) III, 263: dispatch, 22 Oct 1934, from German minister in Yugoslavia. See also ibid. III, 264, 269, 273; *D.B.F.P.* (2) XII, 112, 133.
11. *D.G.F.P.* (C) III, 284, 305, 335.
12. SAC, Job 20: memorandum signed by Renzetti dated 10 Oct 1934.
13. Aloisi, 16, 20 Oct 1934.
14. SAC, Job 321–3, 'Francia'.
15. Aloisi, 14 Oct 1934. According to dispatch of 17 Oct from Hoesch, German ambassador in London, Laval's appointment was an 'improvement' on that of Barthou: *D.G.F.P.* (C) III, 254. See also Warner, *Laval*, p. 58.
16. *D.G.F.P.* (C) III, 230, 231, 235, 337 n.7, 347, 362, 398. See also *D.G.F.P.* (2) XII, 139, 182, 195.
17. *D.G.F.P.* (C) III, 241, 266, 291, 292, 310 n4.
18. SAC, Job 20, 'Renzetti' file, 30 July 1934.
19. *D.G.F.P.* (C) III, 352. According to Aloisi, 21 July 1935, Mussolini claimed that a coup d'état by the Reichswehr could be expected at any moment; Cerruti was therefore to remain at his post. The British also suspected there might be a *Putsch*: *D.B.F.P.* (2) XII, 120.
20. Aloisi, 16 Oct 1934.
21. D. Irving, *The Rise and Fall of the Luftwaffe* (1973) p. 31; *D.G.F.P.* (C) III, 381.
22. *D.G.F.P.* (C) III, 363, 406; Petersen, *Hitler – Mussolini*, pp. 271, 377.
23. *D.G.F.P.* (C) III, 352.
24. Ibid., 406.
25. Ibid., 376.
26. Ibid., 388: Bülow's memorandum, 10 Dec 1934.
27. Ibid., 266: Hassell's conversation with Mussolini, 23 Oct 1934, in which the German ambassador regretted certain 'derisory and extremely hostile comments' in the German press made after the murder of Alexander.
28. Ibid., 381: the book was published by a certain Adolf Klein in Leipzig. See also ibid., 383, for conversation of 7 Dec 1934 between Cerruti and Neurath.
29. Ibid., 376.
30. Irving, pp. 42–3.
31. Petersen, *Hitler – Mussolini*, p. 376 n.33.
32. Ibid., p. 377.

33. *D.G.F.P.* (c) III, 381, 385; see ibid., 406 n.6, for Mussolini's remark of 1 Jan 1935 to *Fliegerkapitän* Hoffmann von Waldau that the role of the armed forces must be determined by political considerations.

34. Ibid., 293 for meeting of German military attachés in Europe.

35. *D.B.F.P.* (2) XII, 250; Aloisi, 23, 24 Nov, 1, 2, 3 Dec 1934. For an account of German policy on the Saar plebiscite, see Weinberg, *Foreign Policy*, pp. 173–4, 203–4. For French policy, see Warner, pp. 60–3, and Lord Avon (Anthony Eden), *The Eden Memoirs: Facing the Dictators* (1962) pp. 102–6.

36. *D.B.F.P.* (2) XII, 174, 529, 662; see also *D.G.F.P.* (c) III, 370 n. 3.Warner (p. 71) maintains that, after the plebiscite, Laval believed the way would be open for an agreement between France and Germany.

37. *D.G.F.P.* (c) III, 373.

38. Aloisi, 16 Nov 1934.

39. R.I.I.A., *Survey 1934*, pp. 574–7.

40. Aloisi, 9 Dec 1934; Avon, pp. 100, 104–5.

41. Aloisi, 10, 14 Dec 1934.

42. Rochat, *militarie politici*, pp. 87–8 and table p. 89.

43. E.g., Baer throughout his *Italian – Ethiopian War* perhaps lays too much stress on the central control Mussolini gave to Italian foreign policy, as well as on his success in isolating Ethiopia step by step.

8. MUSSOLINI DECIDES ON WAR

1. *D.D.F.* (1) II, 197: report, 14 Jan 1933.

2. Aloisi, *Journal*, 17, 21, 22 Dec 1933.

3. I am here indebted to Dr Rosaria Quartararo for allowing me to consult her thesis on Anglo-Italian relations (1976) and to Dr Callum A. MacDonald for a similar kindness in regard to a monograph, 'Radio Bari: Italian Propaganda in the Middle East and British Counter Measures' (1977).

4. De Felice, *Ebrei italiani*, *passim*, deals with this subject in detail.

5 Wiskemann, *Rome – Berlin Axis*, pp. 47–8; Aloisi, 17 Mar 1934.

6. Mussolini, *Omnia Opera*, vol XXVI, pp. 190–2, 18 Mar 1934; Baer, *Italian – Ethiopian War*, pp. 29–30.

7. R.I.I.A., *Survey 1934*, vol. II, pp. 40–2. Particularly serious raids in British Somaliland occurred on 23 Feb and 2, 6 Mar. Sir Sidney Barton, British minister to Ethiopia, and the Colonial Office were greatly preoccupied by them during the early months of 1934.

8. See Patricia Wright, 'Italy's Imperial Dream' (1973).

9. Mussolini, vol. XXVI, pp. 224–6; Baer, p. 28.

10. Rochat, *Militari e politici*, pp. 33–4.

11. For Badoglio's attitude in 1934, see P. Pieri and G. Rochat, *Badoglio* (1974) p. 194.

12. Letter to Baistrocchi, quoted in Rochat, *Militari e politici*, p. 35.

13. Ibid., pp. 43–5.

14. Ibid., p. 45. On 22 Mar 1934 Baistrocchi took up Banzani's ideas.

15. Ibid., p. 37.

16. Ibid., pp. 39–40.

17. Ibid., p. 47.

18. Ibid., p. 55.

19. Ibid., p. 56–63.

20. Ibid., pp. 65–9.

21. This meeting is not discussed in Rochat. For a summary of what took place see Hess, *Somalia*, pp. 172–3.

226   MUSSOLINI AS EMPIRE-BUILDER

22. Rochat, pp. 73–5.
23. Aloisi, 30 June 1934.
24. Ibid., 29 June 1934. For a short account of the Eastern Pact, see G. M. Gathorne-Hardy, *A Short History of International Affairs, 1920–*1939 (1950) pp. 371–2.
25. Aloisi, 12 July 1934.
26. Ibid., 20 July 1934; Jones and Monroe, *Abyssinia*, 1st ed. (1935) p. 172.
27. Rochat, pp. 76–7; Adamthwaite (ed.), *Second World War*.
28. Aloisi, 9 Oct 1934.
29. SAC, Job 321–3, 'Francia'. Although rumours of a Franco-Italian understanding were denied in Rome on 26 Sep 1934, Barton reported Count Vinci's confirming to the Ethiopian Foreign Minister that Rome and Paris had reached agreement: P.R.O. F.O. 371/18022, J 2468/15/1. This document is due to be published in D.B.F.P. (2) XIV (in prep.).
30. R.I.I.A., *Survey 1935*, vol. II, pp. 27–8. An admirable account of the gossip in Rome, can be found in Ronald Rotunda's thesis, 'The Rome Embassy of Sir Eric Drummond' (1972). On 19 Sep 1934, John Murray (Rome) discussed these rumours with Suvich, who was highly embarrassed by them, but said it was necessary for Italy to improve the military establishment in her colonies because of Ethiopian rearmament: Murray to Simon, 21 Sep 1934, P.R.O. F.O. 371/18032, J2247/2082/1.
31. Aloisi, 2 Oct 1934; Petersen, *Hitler – Mussolini*, p. 387.
32. Aloisi, 28 Sep 1934. Se also *D.G.F.P.* (C) III, 239; Bülow's memorandum, 10 Oct 1934.
33. Aloisi, 28 Sep 1934; Rosenberg, *Tagebuch*, p. 165: memorandum, 12 May 1934; R.I.I.A., *Survey 1935*, vol. II, pp. 28, 164 n.2; M. Martelli-Chantard, 'L'Expansion japonaise en Afrique' (1934).
34. *D.G.F.P.* (C) III, 280. See also Petersen, *Hitler – Mussolini*, pp. 386–7, 389.
35. See *D.G.F.P.* (C) III, 402 for Haile Selassie's appeal to Germany; and Petersen, p. 388.
36. Manfred Funke, *Sanktionen und Kanonen: Hitler, Mussolini und der Internationale Abessinien Konflikt, 1934–*1936 (1970) p. 31.
37. *D.D.F.* (1) I, 383, 486; IV, 301.
38. Greenfield, *Ethiopia*, pp. 165–86; Gilkes, *Dying Lion*, ch. 7; Jones and Monroe, p. 171.
39. These problems are due to be discussed in *D.B.F.P.* (2) XIV: Aug 1934–3 Oct 1935 (in prep.).
40. Greenfield, pp. 100–1; Hess, pp. 185–6.
41. Baer, pp. 45–6.
42. Hess, p. 154.
43. Baer, pp. 50–65.
44. R.I.I.A., *Survey 1935*, vol. II, pp. 40–1; see also Jones and Monroe, p. 172.
45. P.R.O. F.O. 371/18022 J26468/15/1: Wallinger's memorandum, 15 Oct 1934.
46. Baer, pp. 49, 51–2.
47. Rotunda, 'Drummond'; *D.D.F.* (1) V, 338: report, 6 Feb 1934.
48. See *D.D.F.* (1) V, 338 for French attitude: report, 6 Feb 1934 by De Reffy, minister in Addis Ababa. *D.B.F.P.* (2) XIV (in prep.) will deal with Anglo-Italian relations and the 'Red Line' as the Zeila proposal was called.
49. Baer, pp. 56–7; Rotunda, op. cit. See also Wallinger's memorandum, 15 Oct 1934, cited Note 45 above.
50. Rochat, p. 88.
51. For Vinci's visit, see Aloisi, 25 Dec 1934.
52. Rotunda, op. cit.
53. Hardie, *Abyssinian Crisis*, pp. 85–6.
54. A. Lessona, *Memorie* (1958) pp. 165–71. See also Baer, p. 58.
55. Rochat, p. 101, n. 1 and 2.

56. Aloisi, 24 Dec 1934.

57. Ibid., 25 Dec 1934.

58. Ibid., 14, 29, 30 Dec 1934.

59. Walters, *League of Nations*, pp. 229–30.

60. *D.G.F.P.* (c) III, 402, 403; Petersen, *Hitler – Mussolini*, p. 389.

61. Fragments of a report signed by Steffen and submitted to the Party Office for Foreign Affairs. It was 'exclusively for secret and internal use'. Hess and Göring apparently knew of Steffen's plan; a minute of a conversation between Hess and Rosenberg of 18 Dec 1935 suggests that this subject was under discussion. See Funke, pp. 36–7.

62. Funke; Petersen, *Hitler – Mussolini*, pp. 390–2, n. 112.

63. M. Magistrati, 'La Germania e l'impresa italiana di Etiopia: Ricordi di Berlino' (1950) 585.

64. V. Cerruti, 'Perchè Hitler aiutò il Negus', *Il Tempo*, 20 Apr 1959. I am grateful for knowledge of this document to K. J. Passmore, 'The Failure of France and Italy to conclude a Military Alliance' (1972).

65. The full text is discussed and reproduced in Rochat, pp. 102–4 and document 92. For English translation, see Adamthwaite (ed.).

66. Rochat, pp. 105, 108.

9. THE MOBILISATION OF ITALIAN TROOPS

1. Aloisi, *Journal*, 2, 3, 4 Jan 1935.

2. Warner, *Laval*, pp. 66–71. See SAC, Job 321–3, 'Francia', 62 for summary of the text of the Agreements, extracts from which are given in W. C. Askew, 'The Secret Agreements between France and Italy on Ethiopia, January 1935' (1953) 47–8. For a thorough analysis of them, see D. C. Watt 'The Secret Laval – Mussolini agreements of 1935 on Ethiopia', (1961) 19–20, republished in E. M. Robertson (ed.), *The Origins of the Second World War* (1971).

3. *D.G.F.P.* (c) III, 459, 646. For Hungary's reaction, see Aloisi, 9 Jan 1935.

4. P.R.O. F.O. 371/19577 R 1910. Weinberg, *Foreign Policy*, pp. 321–3.

5. See *D.B.F.P.* (2) XII, 285 for Italian fears of German action after Saar plebiscite.

6. R. A. C. Parker, 'Great Britain, France and the Ethiopian Crisis of 1935–1936' (1974) 295.

7. Baer, *Italian – Ethiopian War*, p. 84.

8. M. Gamelin, *Servir: Le prologue du drame, 1930–Août 1939* (1946) vol. II pp. 166 ff.

9. *D.D.F.* (2) I, 99 and n., 180.

10. De Felice, *Mussolini*, p. 220; the letter has been found in the Lancellotti papers, ASMAE collection.

11. See *D.B.F.P.* (2) VI, 357 and n., for Weygand's description of the final French operations in Morocco to the British military attaché. See also Baer, p. 84.

12. Wiskemann, *Rome – Berlin Axis*, pp. 61–2; J. Bastin, *L'Affaire d'Ethiopie et les diplomates* (1937) p. 90, quoted in Baer, p. 84.

13. E. Rossi *Il Manganello e l'aspersorio* (1968) pp. 230–1. See also *D.G.F.P.* (c) III, 361: 29 Nov 1934; III, 459: 27 Jan 1935.

14. Barker, *Civilising Mission*, p. 59; and 'Ethiopian Church', in F. L. Cross (ed.), *Oxford Dictionary of the Christian Church* (Oxford, 1963).

15. See R.I.I.A., *Survey 1935*, vol. II, pp. 57–9, 64–5 for the attitude of the non-Roman Catholic Churches. B. Sundkler, *Nathan Söderblom: His Life and Work* (1968) p. 385, describes how a Swedish churchman, J. Kolmodin, had acted as adviser to Haile Selassie. Professor D. P. Waley discusses this problem in *British Public Opinion and the Abyssinian War, 1935–1936* (1976).

16. J. Barros, *Betrayal from Within: Joseph Avenol 1933*–1940, pp. 54–61.
17. P.R.O. F.O. 371/18027 J179/18; and 371/18027 J3181/18: 27 Dec 1934.
18. Guariglia, *Ricordi*, p. 215.
19. Aloisi, 14 Jan 1935; P.R.O. F.O. 371/19101 J165/1: Drummond's dispatch, 15 Jan 1935.
20. Aloisi, 23 Jan, 1 Feb 1935. See also Baer, p. 200.
21. Rochat, *Militari e politici*, pp. 127 ff.; Aloisi, 15 Feb, 1 Mar 1935.
22. P.R.O. F.O., 371/20931 J47/47/1:30 Dec 1936, referring to Grandi–Simon conversation of 29 Jan 1935. See also Guariglia, pp. 214–15; and, for new evidence, De Felice, *Mussolini*, p. 648.
23. See Rochat, p. 146 for military preparations in late Feb and Mar. See also Aloisi, 6, 10, 12 Feb 1935 for political preparations.
24. K. Middlemas and J. B. Barnes, *Baldwin: A Biography* (1969) p. 830.
25. Guariglia, pp. 216–17.
26. Colvin, *Vansittart*, p. 122. See Goldman, 'Vansittart's Search' (1974) for highly valuable evidence on Vansittart's attitude, which was not so anti-German as is usually supposed.
27. *D.B.F.P.* (2) XII, 285, 495.
28. Guariglia, pp. 216–17.
29. Rochat, p. 114
30. Ibid. pp. 117 ff.
31. Ibid., p. 108. For Graziani's character and appointment, ibid., p. 111, pp. 168 ff.
32. For a detailed account of the controversies of Italian historians on the primacy of foreign over domestic policy, and vice versa, see Petersen, 'Politica estera' (1972).
33. See Alberto Aquarone, 'Italy: The Crisis and Corporative Economy in the Great Depression' (1969).
34. Rochat, pp. 146–7.
35. Ibid., pp. 143, 148.
36. Ibid., p. 153 n. 48 ff.

10. THE STRESA INTERLUDE

1. Aloisi, *Journal*, 1, 2 Mar 1935.
2. For the Anglo-French communiqué, see: *D.B.F.P.* (2) XII, 397, 348, 400; *D.G.F.P.* (C) III, 501–3; Weinberg, *Foreign Policy*, pp. 203–5.
3. SAC, Job 54, 'Grandi Papers'; *D.B.F.P.* (2) XII, 519.
4. W. N. Medlicott shows how far the British cabinet was prepared to go in giving Germany satisfaction in Europe and overseas; see his 'Britain and Germany: the Search for Agreement' (1970).
5. *D.B.F.P.* (2) XII, 642.
6. Weinberg, pp. 204–6.
7. Aloisi, 24 Mar 1935; *D.B.F.P.* (2) XII, 584, 610.
8. Baer, *Italian–Ethiopian War*, pp. 114 ff.
9. Aloisi, 20, 25 Mar 1935; see also *D.B.F.P.* (2) XII, 579, 584.
10. Aloisi, 27 Mar 1935; *D.B.F.P.* (2) XII, 651.
11. *D.G.F.P.* (C) III, 555, 564.
12. Funke, *Sanktionen und Kanonen*, pp. 37–8.
13. Guariglia, *Ricordi*, p. 233.
14. *D.G.F.P.* (C) III, 557: Bülow's instructions to Hassell, 26 Mar 1935; ibid. III, 558: Hassell's dispatch of same date.
15. This was the opinion of D. Hall, one of Haile Selassie's advisers who was half-German: see Funke, p. 38/n.6.

16. *D.G.F.P.* (c) III, 557; SAC, Job 320, 'Germania', pp. 9–10, and job 20, 'Renzetti'.
17. *D.G.F.P.* (c) III, 457.
18. Ibid., 559, 563.
19. Ibid., 568; D. C. Watt, 'The Anglo-German Naval Agreement of 1935: An Interim Judgement' (1956).
20. Baer, pp. 111–12.
21. Ibid., p. 116; Barros, *Betrayal*, pp. 63–7; Hardie, *Abyssinian Crisis*, p. 87.
22. Baer (p. 116) tends to take this view.
23. Aloisi, 4 Apr 1935; Guariglia, pp. 212 ff.
24. Guariglia, p. 213 n.1. See Aloisi, 15 Mar 1935, for Cardinal Dolci's bitter complaint about Ciano; P.R.O. F.O. 371/19103 J775/1/1: Drummond's dispatch, 19 Feb 1935. Rotunda ('Drummond', fo. 198) points out that, although Drummond stressed that war was unpopular, this did not mean that it would not take place.
25. Guariglia, pp. 226–8.
26. De Felice, *Mussolini*, pp. 661–2.
27. *D.B.F.P.* (2) XII, 696: Simon's memorandum on Stresa, dated 4 Apr 1935. See Parker, 'Britain, France and Ethiopian Crisis' (1974) p. 295 for the cabinet meeting of 8 Apr 1935.
28. Avon, *Facing the Dictators*, p. 175; Guariglia, 226–8.
29. *D.B.F.P.* (2) XII, 717 n. 28, 722 n. 43. See also Rotunda, fos 219–27, 234–6.
30. Lord Vansittart, *The Mist Procession* (1958) p. 520. Hardie, p. 117, accepts Vansittart's account. It is quite untrue that the question of Ethiopia was not raised at Stresa.

11. TOWARDS A DETENTE WITH GERMANY

1. Walters, *League of Nations*, pp. 609–14.
2. Aloisi, *Journal*, 17 Apr 1935.
3. *D.G.F.P.* (c) IV, 36 and n. 2: Cerruti–Bülow conversation, 17 Apr 1935. See also ibid., 65 for editor's note; and Aloisi, 20 Apr 1935.
4. Aloisi, 24, 30 Apr 1935; and 13 May 1935 re. Air Convention signed by General Valle, Italian Deputy Minister of Air, and General Bergeret.
5. For a comprehensive summary of Hassell's action, see his memorandum (evidently drawn up in April 1935) in *D.G.F.P.* (c) IV, 61.
6. *D.G.F.P.* (c) IV, 5: Hassell's dispatch, 1 Apr 1935; ibid., 9: Neurath's reply, 4 Apr 1935. See also Aloisi, 19 Apr 1935.
7. Aloisi, 30 Apr, 5 May 1935; *D.B.F.P.* (2) VI, 380. A new Italian ambassador had been sent to Belgrade in March 1934. On 24 June 1935 Stoyadinović replaced the anti-Italian B. Jeftić as Yugoslav premier and foreign minister: Macartney and Palmer, *Eastern Europe*, p. 338.
8. Warner, *Laval*, 72–6, 81–2; Warner has used Russian documents on these negotiations. See W. E. Scott, *Alliance Against Hitler* (1962) for a detailed account.
9. Robertson, *Hitler's Pre-War Policy*, pp. 89–92.
10. *D.G.F.P.* (c) IV, 245: Hassell's dispatch, 3 Aug 1935.
11. SAC, Job 320, 'Germania', *passim*.
12. *D.G.F.P.* (c) IV, 83.
13. See Avon, *Dictators*, pp. 246–7 for Portuguese anxieties. For South African attitude, see D. C. Watt, 'South African attempts to mediate between Britain and Germany', in Bourne and Watt, eds (1960).
14. Funke, *Sanktionen und Kanonen*, pp. 45–7.
15. League of Nations, *Official Journal 1935*, pp. 577, 749. See also Baer, *Italian–Ethiopian War*, pp. 131–2.

16. Hardie, *Abyssinian Crisis*, pp. 86–7; Baer, pp. 133–4; Barros, *Betrayal*, pp. 69–70.
17. Guariglia, *Ricordi*, pp. 229–33.
18. Ibid., pp. 235–7.
19. Hardie, pp. 119, 126.
20. Rochat, *Militari e politici*, pp. 155ff; for Italian mobilisation in May, see Lessona, *Memorie*, p. 177.
21. Mussolini, *Omnia Opera*, vol. xvii, pp. 72–4. See also Baer, pp. 141–3.
22. Guariglia, pp. 236–8; Avon, pp. 204–6.
23. For text see *D.G.F.P.* (c) iv, 171–9; see also Aloisi, 21, 22 May 1935.
24. *D.G.F.P.* (c) iv, 120, 124; Funke, p. 46.
25. Aloisi, 24 May 1935.
26. Baer, p. 154.
27. Guariglia, pp. 238–9.
28. Aloisi, 22 May 1935; Barros, p. 70.
29. For these proceedings, see Baer, p. 156; Walters, pp. 633–5; Avon, pp. 204–9.
30. Mussolini, vol. xxviii, pp. 76–80; Baer, p. 162.
31. Aloisi, 20, 27, 28 May 1935.
32. Rochat, pp. 158ff; Aloisi, 30 May 1935.
33. See Aloisi 18 Jan 1933.
34. Guariglia, p. 139.
35. Watt, 'Anglo-German Naval Agreement' (1956). For a full account of the cabinet changes, see Middlemas and Barnes, *Baldwin*, pp. 821–3.
36. *D.B.F.P.* (2) xii, 419. See also Middlemas and Barnes, pp. 826–8; and Barros, pp. 88–9. See N. Orvik, *The Decline of Neutrality* (1953) ch. 1 for a general account of the Scandinavian states and the Ethiopian crisis.
37. sac, Job 20, 'Renzetti'. See also De Felice, *Mussolini*, p. 491–2.
38. Aloisi, 21 July 1935.
39. Ibid., 19 Feb 1936.
40. *D.G.F.P.* (c) iv, 164, 166.

12. THE CONFRONTATION WITH BRITAIN, JUNE – JULY 1935

1. Middlemas and Barnes, *Baldwin*, pp. 845–6.
2. P.R.O. F.O. 371/19113 J 2435/1: extracts from cabinet meeting 33 (35). See also Goldman, 'Vansittart's Search', p. 115 and n. 76; and Hardie, *Abyssinian Crisis*, p. 124.
3. This is discussed in Rosaria Quartararo, 'Imperial Defence in the Mediterranean on the Eve of the Ethiopian Crisis' (1977). She cites P.R.O. F.O. 371/19124 J 365/1/1: Campbell's memorandum, 9 Aug 1935; and Baer, *Italian – Ethiopian War*, pp. 188–9. The full text of the Maffey report is in P.R.O. F.O. 371/19184/97/1. It is to be published in *D.B.F.P.* (2) xiv (in prep.). See also Baer, p. 277.
4. See E. Chiavarelli, *L'Opera della marine italiana durante la guerra italo-etiopica* (1969) pp. 24–44 for an account of the logistic role of the Italian navy. For Italian naval construction between 1934 and 1936, see Quartararo, 'La Crisi mediterranea del 1935–36' (1975).
5. See M. Toscano, *The History of Treaties and International Politics* (1966) p. 29, where it is claimed that Mussolini used the Maffey report (which reached him through Italian Military Intelligence) as proof that Britain would not fight. But the report evidently reached him in the autumn of 1935.
6. Funke, *Sankitionen und Kanonen*, pp. 54–5, 157–8. F. Chabod, in *Italian Fascism*, pp. 76–8, takes the view that the Italians as a whole were at first apathetic to the forthcoming Ethiopian venture until British opposition was encountered in Summer 1935.
7. Baer, pp. 206–7.

8. According to Middlemas and Barnes, p. 834, three distinct groups in the cabinet emerged: 1. Chamberlain, Eden and Eustace Percy (Baldwin's choice as ambassador to Washington) favoured action through the League against Italy; 2. MacDonald (now President of the Council) favoured Stresa; 3. Runciman (President of the Board of Trade) and B. M. Eyres Monsell (First Lord of the Admiralty) favoured Vansittart's 'realism'. Eyres Monsell was most concerned about sea communications through the Mediterranean, and hence opposed sanctions.

9. Lord Templewood (Samuel Hoare), *Nine Troubled Years* (1954) pp. 153–4; Baer, p. 191; Hardie, pp. 124–6.

10. Barros, *Betrayal*, pp. 71–3. For conditions at Massawa, see Barker, *Civilising Mission*, pp. 137–8; and Rochat, *Militari e politici*, pp. 162–3.

11. Barros, pp. 77–80; Guariglia, *Ricordi*, pp. 241–3.

12. Baer, p. 193.

13. For Eden's account, see Avon, *Dictators*, pp. 221–2. For an account from Italian documents, see M. Toscano, 'Eden's Mission to Rome on the Eve of the Italo-Ethiopian Conflict', in A. O. Sarkissian, ed. (1961).

14. Guariglia, p. 245.

15. Aloisi, 25, 26 June 1935.

16. See Walters, *League of Nations*, pp. 531–3 for an account of the Chaco affair.

17. Middlemas and Barnes, pp. 839–40; Parker, 'Britain, France and Ethiopian Crisis', p. 301.

18. The Italians were encouraged by the Persians to make trouble for the British in Egypt, but they were told that the real issue should be Malta, not Ethiopia: Aloisi, 8 July 1935. For Italian propaganda in Egypt, see J. Marlowe, *Anglo-Egyptian Relations* (1969) p. 306.

19. P. E. Tournoux, *Défense des frontières* (1960) p. 337.

20. Gamelin, *Servir*, vol. II, pp. 167–9. See also De Felice, *Mussolini*, p. 615 n. 2.

21. Middlemas and Barnes, p. 846.

22. For internal problems in France, see Warner, *Laval*, pp. 85–9.

23. *D.G.F.P.* (c) IV, 373: memorandum of 21 Oct 1935 (signed by M. Lorenz, an official of Department II of the Foreign Ministry responsible for Italy and South-East Europe) summarising Intelligence reports drawn up early in July 1935 and later.

24. Gamelin, vol. II, p. 175.

25. Baer, pp. 208–9; Aloisi, 5, 10, 21 July 1935.

26. Middlemas and Barnes, p. 846; Baer, pp. 217–18; Aloisi, 10, 11 July 1935.

27. Baer, p. 220.

28. Ibid., pp. 220–1.

29. *D.G.F.P.* (c) IV, 212; Funke, pp. 43–5.

30. D.G.F.P. (c) IV, 246.

31. Aloisi, 23 July 1935, for Italian complaint about Britain's allowing arms exports through her territory. See also P. Wright, 'Italy's African Dream' (1973).

32. *D.G.F.P.* (c) IV, 246, 261.

33. Aloisi, 22 July 1935. Sir Arnold Toynbee, in R.I.I.A., *Survey 1935*, vol. II, p. 28, even claimed that Japan was Italy's enemy nember one in the Italian press until July 1935, Britain becoming so only after July.

34. See Angelo Del Boca, *The Ethiopian War, 1935–1941* (1969) p. 25, where he cites the *Sunday Times* of 20 Sep 1935. For the proposal to finance Japanese volunteers for Ethiopia, see J. W. Morley, ed., *Dilemmas of Growth in Pre-War Japan* (1973) p. 298.

35. See E. M. Robertson, 'Hitler and Sanctions: Mussolini and The Rhineland' (1977), for discussion of this subject; also Funke, pp. 43–50, 84–121, 181–6.

13. THE ANGLO-FRENCH COMPROMISE OF AUGUST 1935

1. Baer, *Italian–Ethiopian War*, p. 234.
2. Ibid., p. 234.
3. Barros, *Betrayal* , pp. 88–9.
4. Colvin, *Vansittart*, pp. 67–8.
5. P.R.O. F.O. 371/19120 J 3204.
6. Barros, p. 89.
7. Parker, 'Britain, France and Ethiopian Crisis', pp. 298–300.
8. Ibid.
9. See Middlemas and Barnes, *Baldwin*, chs 27, 28 for a general account of British rearmament; J. Marder, 'The Royal Navy and the Ethiopian Crisis of 1935–1936' (1969), pp. 1327–56 for British naval policy in the Mediterranean; and Quartararo, 'Imperial Defence' for a new interpretation of Britain's military prospects arising from the Ethiopian crisis.
10. Middlemas and Barnes, p. 762–3.
11. P.R.O. F.O. 371/19150 J 7493: Drummond's dispatch, 5 Nov 1935, containing the British naval attaché's report of 29 Oct which summarised events in the earlier stages of the crisis.
12. Marder, pp. 1340–3.
13. Baer, p. 470.
14. The British, however, knew of the existence of the Franco-Italian military agreements, which they described as the 'Sandwich Plan': *D.B.F.P.* (2) XII, 197 n. 2.
15. Guariglia, *Ricordi*, pp. 250–2.
16. Avon, *Dictators*, p. 245; Aloisi, *Journal*, 31 July, 1 Aug 1935; Guariglia, pp. 250–1.
17. Walters, *League of Nations*, pp. 647–8.
18. Rochat, *Militari e politici*, p. 225 n. 27.
19. Aloisi, 5, 8, 9 Aug 1935.
20. Rochat, pp. 226–7.
21. Guariglia, p. 259; Baer, pp. 300–2.
22. Aloisi, 8, 11 Aug 1935.
23. Barros, p. 91.
24. Aloisi, 17 Aug 1935; Avon, pp. 249–51. For a recent account see Hardie, *Abyssinian Crisis*, pp. 91ff.
25. Rochat, p. 218.
26. *D.G.F.P.* (C) IV, 265.
27. Guariglia, p. 256.
28. Aloisi, 19 Aug 1925.
29. *D.G.F.P.* (C) IV, 375: evidence from German intelligence reports.
30. *D.B.F.P.* (2) XII, 533: the editors of the British documents evidently referred mistakenly to the mobilisation on the Brenner in 1934, not in 1935.
31. Aloisi, 21 Aug 1935. Mussolini used the threat of withdrawing troops from the Brenner on the eve of Hoare's speech of 11 Sep 1935: see Hardie, p. 136.
32. C. F. Latour, *Südtirol und die Achse Berlin–Rom* (1962) p. 21.
33. De Felice, *Mussolini*, p. 677.
34. E. De Bono, quoted in Hardie, p. 132. For the reference to Vansittart, see Aloisi, 19 Aug 1935.
35. Middlemas and Barnes, pp. 852–4; Hardie, ch. 15. See SAC, Job 320–3, 'Gran Bretagna', 16 for an Italian summary of British policy in 1935, giving 24 Aug as the date of the cabinet meeting.
36. Marder, *passim*.
37. Warner, *Laval*, pp. 102–3.

38. Guariglia, p. 241; Barros, pp. 91–2.
39. Avon, pp. 257–8; Warner p. 103.

14. TOWARDS THE OUTBREAK OF WAR

1. Guariglia, *Ricordi*, p. 261; Aloisi, *Journal*, 5 Aug 1935.
2. Rochat, *Militari e politici*, p. 233.
3. Ibid., pp. 195ff.
4. See ibid., p. 222 for Lessona's memorandum of 19 July 1935; and p. 223 for Suvich's.
5. This subject is dealt with in Robertson, 'Hitler and Sanctions: Mussolini and the Rhineland'.
6. Guariglia, pp. 257–8.
7. Walters, *League of Nations*, p. 641.
8. Baer, *Italian–Ethiopian War*, p. 305; Walters, pp. 306–7.
9. For the American view, see H. Braddick, 'A New Look at American Policy During the Italian–Ethiopian Conflict' (1962) 64–73; and R. Divine, *The Illusion of Neutrality* (1962) pp. 64–73.
10. SAC, Job 321–3, 'Francia', *passim*, shows the great stress laid by the Italians on the anti-British tone in the French press, which lasted after the outbreak of hostilities.
11. R.I.I.A., *Survey 1935*, vol. II, pp. 178–9; Baer, pp. 297–8.
12. Guariglia, pp. 250–4; Aloisi, 3 Sep 1935.
13. For the text, see *League Official Journal; 1935*, pp. 1137, 1595–1601. See also Walters, pp. 642–4; Baer, pp. 311–12.
14. Ladislas Farago, *Abyssinia on the Eve* (1935) p. 45.
15. At a meeting of the Council in May 1934 Eden had condemned Liberia for failing to honour her obligations under article 23 of the Convenant: see Walters, p. 571. He blushed when the subject of Ethiopia's expulsion was raised: see Aloisi, 5 Oct 1935.
16. Walters, p. 645; Aloisi, 7 Sep 1935; Guariglia, p. 258.
17. Walters, p. 645; Baer, pp. 318–19.
18. Aloisi, 6 Sep 1935.
19. Templewood, *Nine Troubled Years*, pp. 167–9; Avon, *Dictators*, pp. 260–3; Baer, p. 322.
20. For Hoare's discussions with Baldwin and Chamberlain, see Middlemas and Barnes, *Baldwin*, pp. 885–6; Avon, pp. 261–2; Baer, p. 332. For the most recent account, see Hardie, *Abyssinian Crisis*, pp. 96–9.
21. Parker, 'Britain, France and Ethiopian Crisis', p. 307. Long extracts from the speech are given in Baer, pp. 338–9.
22. Aloisi, 10, 11 Sep 1935.
23. Guariglia, p. 264.
24. Walters, pp. 650–5.
25. Ibid., pp. 648–9; Avon, p. 262.
26. Baer, pp. 338–9.
27. Barros, *Betrayal*, pp. 94–5.
28. Ibid.; and Aloisi, 12 Sep 1935.
29. Guariglia, pp. 264–9.
30. See R.I.I.A., *Documents*, vol. II, pp. 106–10 for the text of the Committee's proposals. See also Baer, pp. 343–4.
31. P.R.O. F.O. 371/19197 J 3863/G, J/3861/1. For Italian Intelligence, see L. Villari, *Storia diplomatica nel conflitto italo-etiopico* (1943) p. 141. Toscano, *History of Treaties*, p. 29 accepts Vallari's account, but Admiral Denti (Italian commander-in-chief in the Mediterranean) told Aloisi early in 1936 that Britain had absolute supremacy on land, sea

and air; no mention was made by Denti of British shortages in ammunition: Aloisi, 7 Feb 1936.

32. Guariglia, p. 270.

33. Rochat, p. 226—9.

34. Ibid., p. 229; Baer, pp. 360—1.

35. Marder, 'Royal Navy and Ethiopian Crisis', *passim*.

36. These figures, taken from Marder, p. 1338, correspond with those of Chiavarelli, *Marina italiana*, pp. 77—8.

37. See Quartararo, 'Imperial Defence', on the increase of Italian submarines in the Red Sea, and on the *Miraglia*'s duties. For Britain's position in Aden, see P.R.O. Air Staff Note 8/189, 2 Oct 1935. See P.R.O. F.O. 371/20411 R 5839 G, 20 Oct 1936, for Italian anti-British activities in the Mediterranean.

38. P.R.O. F.O. 371/19077 J 6767/110/16 and J 7255/110/16: Lampson's reports of 18, 21 Oct 1935. Aloisi and the new Egyptian ambassador to Rome discussed an insurrection: Aloisi, 19 Nov 1935.

39. My thanks are due to Callum A. MacDonald for pre-publication access to his monograph on 'Radio Bari'.

40. P.R.O. CAB 24/265, CP 335 (36), 'Spain—the Balearic Islands December 1936'. Professor Kent has kindly allowed me to consult his chapter on Spain in the draft of his 'Repercussions of the Lateran agreements'.

41. Aloisi, 18, 19, 24 Sep 1935. See also Baer, pp. 361—2, 370; Middlemas and Barnes, p. 858.

42. The Italians through their Intelligence services had quite an accurate knowledge of what passed between London and Paris: see SAC, Job 320—3, 'Gran Bretagna'; and Job 321—3, 'Francia'.

43. See Funke, *Sanktionen und Kanonen*, pp. 53—4 for extracts from De Bono's letter. According to Barker, *Civilising Mission*, p. 141, there was only one Alpine division operating in Tigré at the end of 1935. Some of the troops deployed near the Brenner reached the Dodecanese in Oct: P.R.O. W.O. 106/284.

44. *Sunday Times*, 6 Oct 1935; quoted from Del Boca, *Ethiopian War*, pp. 25, 85.

45. Funke, p. 60.

46. *D.G.F.P.* (C) IV, editor's note, 632—3; *D.B.F.P.* (2) XIII, 500, 502, 513, 533.

47. P.R.O. F.O. 371/19891 C 1831, with Note by Hankey on conversations between Laube (a German industrialist) and Leo Amery (a Conservative M.P. well-known for his pro-Italian views). This subject is discussed in Quartararo, 'Imperial Defence'.

48. Funke, p. 59 n.70, pp. 68—9.

49. Whealey, 'Mussolini's Ideological Policy' (1967) pp. 432—7.

50. Wiskemann, *Rome—Berlin Axis* (1966) p. 70.

51. P.R.O. F.O. 371/20419 R794/22: Drummond's dispatch, 11 Feb 1936, transmitting a report from the British consul in Trieste.

52. *D.G.F.P.*(C) IV, 322, 323, 325.

53. See Mussolini, *Omnia Opera*, vol. XXVI, pp. 155—60. For a summary, see Baer, pp. 369—70.

15. THE SEQUEL

1. Aloisi, *Journal*, 16, 20 Nov 1935, 26 Jan 1936. *D.B.F.P.* (2) XV (in prep.) is due to cover this period; the relevant material of *D.D.F.* (2) has not been published for this period.

2. Marder, 'Royal Navy and Ethiopian Crisis', pp. 1333 ff. Michael Rooke in 'Britain and Eastern Europe, 1933—1939' (thesis in preparation) describes in detail the attitude and expected military performance of the states of Eastern Europe.

3. Warner, *Laval*, pp. 108–9, 114.

4. Guariglia, *Ricordi*, pp. 289, 292–3; Aloisi, 2 Dec 1935. The most recent account of the Hoare–Laval Plan is by J. C. Robertson (1975).

5. A. J. P. Taylor, *Origins of the Second World War* (1964 ed.) p. 274. Taylor's conclusions have been accepted perhaps too much at their face value by Hardie, *Abyssinian Crisis*, p. 6.

6. Warner, pp. 126–8.

7. Rochat, *Militari e politici*, p. 239. See also Aloisi, 5, 9, 20, 22 Jan 1936.

8. Funke, *Sanktionen und Kanonen*, p. 107 n.120.

9. Hardie, pp. 207–10.

10. This problem is discussed in E. M. Robertson, 'Hitler and Sanctions'.

11. Ibid.

12. Ibid.

13. Aloisi, 11 Mar 1936.

14. Wiskemann, *Europe of the Dictators* (1966) pp. 114–15.

15. Aloisi, 13 May 1936.

16. Robertson, 'Hitler and Sanctions'.

17. De Felice, 'Alle Origini'.

18. Gilkes, *Dying Lion*, chs 6–8.

19. I. S. O. Playfair, *History of the Second World War: The Mediterranean and Middle East*, vol. I, ch. 1.

20. C. Zaghi, *L'Africa nella coscienza europea e l'imperialismo italiano* (1973) discusses this problem at length from a Marxist viewpoint.

Index